IN THE HOUSES OF THE holy

Led Zeppelin
and the
Power of
Rock Music

SUSAN FAST

UNIVERSITY PRESS

2001

OXFORD

UNIVERSITY PRESS

Oxford   New York
Athens   Auckland   Bangkok   Bogotá   Buenos Aires   Cape Town
Chennai   Dar es Salaam   Delhi   Florence   Hong Kong   Istanbul   Karachi
Kolkata   Kuala Lumpur   Madrid   Melbourne   Mexico City   Mumbai   Nairobi
Paris   São Paulo   Shanghai   Singapore   Taipei   Tokyo   Toronto   Warsaw

and associated companies in
Berlin   Ibadan

Library of Congress Cataloging-in-Publication Data
Fast, Susan.
In the houses of the holy : Led Zeppelin and the
power of rock music / Susan Fast.
p.   cm.
Includes bibliographical references and index.
ISBN 0-19-511756-5; ISBN 0-19-514723-5 (pbk.)
1. Led Zeppelin (Musical group).   2. Rock music—History and criticism.
3. Gender identity in music.   4. Subjectivity in music.
5. Sex in music.   I. Title.

ML421.L4 F37   2001
782.42166'092'2—dc21   00-048367

9 8 7 6 5 4 3 2

Printed in the United States of America
on acid-free paper

Contents

Discuss one of the
and reasons critics
cite criticisms
of LZ use
of Eastern
musics.

IN THE HOUSES OF THE HOLY

Acknowledgments

When I began this project about five years ago, I had no intention of conducting a survey of Led Zeppelin fans and incorporating their observations into the book. It was Rob Walser's inclusion of a fan survey in *Running with the Devil* that suggested to me the value of ethnography in the kind of study of the band's music that I wanted to make. Without the fans' voices, this book would be considerably poorer—in fact, several of the points I argue would have been impossible to make without the evidence I gathered from fans—and so I would first like to thank those who responded to my survey for their time and effort in completing it and for their thoughtful comments, many of which are found throughout the book. Their enthusiasm for this project has been heartwarming: I received many offers from them to answer follow-up questions, and several fans offered me bootleg recordings and access to their collections of memorabilia; one fan sent an original watercolor painting of the band on their 1980 tour. Rick Barrett, owner of Merit Adventures in Houston, which specializes in Led Zeppelin memorabilia, sent me a package of magazines and other collectibles. I am very thankful for all of these gestures. I would also like to thank Hugh Jones for running the survey in an issue of his fanzine, *Proximity*, and for putting me in touch with photographer Marty Perez, who generously sent me his precious slides of Led Zeppelin in concert in Chicago in 1977; some of these appear in this book, and I wish to thank Marty for allowing me to use them. Jeremy Mixer graciously offered to post the fan survey on his Web site, zoso.net, and I wish to express my thanks to him for that. Another fan (and professional photographer), Wendy Annibell, offered me her photograph of Robert Plant in concert at Madison Square Garden in 1973 and went to considerable lengths to improve the quality of that photograph so that I could use it here; thank you, Wendy.

Special thanks are due Matt Link, a committed fan of Led Zeppelin's music and a good friend of mine, with whom I spent countless hours discussing the band's music and this project. Matt's knowledge of popular music and his ability to articulate this knowledge without any formal training (he's an amateur guitar player) has taught me a great deal about how deeply many in the fan community think about the sounds of popular music and hence the importance of academic work that addresses sound in a manner that is accessible to these fans.

I am grateful to John Paul Jones for engaging in a lengthy exchange of e-mails with me in order to answer a plethora of questions I had for him; I also owe thanks to his manager, Richard Chadwick, for facilitating the exchange.

Several of my colleagues read and commented on various parts of the manuscript. For their valuable suggestions I wish to thank Bev Diamond, Rob Walser, Teresa Magdanz, Rob Bowman, John Covach, Ellen Koskoff, Richard Leppert, Susie O'Brien, and the anonymous readers for Oxford University Press and for the journal *American Music*, in which a version of chapter 5 appears. I would also like to thank those authors on whose work I draw throughout the book for their insights, especially those who wrote on popular music. Although I sometimes take issue with what they have to say, at a fundamental level I appreciate and value their work, which has allowed me to shape mine.

There are certainly advantages to working in a school of art, drama, and music, where the various arts disciplines are constantly rubbing up against one another, opening up opportunities for collaboration that are bound to make one's work considerably richer. I would like to give special thanks to my colleague in drama, Catherine Graham, for the countless hours she and I spent discussing my work on this project and for her extremely valuable perspective on many difficult issues with which I grappled; if there are some good ideas in this book, they are probably hers. Another colleague of mine in art, Judy Major-Girardin, gave freely of her time and expertise to create the illustrations that accompany this book, making it possible for me to discuss in some detail important images for which photographs are difficult to come by. My thanks to Judy.

Two of my students were especially helpful with this project. Jennifer De Boer had the overwhelming task of sorting through more than four hundred fan surveys, the statistical information of which she carefully tabulated. She also sifted through all of the answers to other questions, grouping together those that were similar, deleting extraneous material, and so forth, which made it easy for me to make use of the information. Simon Wood collected, copied, and organized a great deal of the journalistic literature for me, and out of this work he wrote a paper on Led Zeppelin and the media, from which I borrow ideas in chapter 2. Jen and Simon were both efficient and enthusiastic, and I thank them for their help.

I wish to thank the editors at Oxford University Press for their help with this project: Maribeth Payne, Jonathan Wiener, and Maureen Buja; thanks also to

Bill Johnson and Phil Hanrahan for their enthusiasm and Bob Milks for his careful reading of the manuscript in the final stages of production. I am especially grateful to Soo Mee Kwon, who guided the book proposal through various channels at OUP in a timely fashion and whose enthusiasm for this project was encouraging.

In the spring of 1994, Susan McClary gave a series of lectures at McMaster University, some of which have now been published in her book *Conventional Wisdom: The Content of Musical Form*. At that time, I was, I thought, firmly ensconced in the world of positivistic musicological scholarship, although my interest in the social meanings of music (ill defined in my own mind) fit rather uneasily into the old paradigms. Hearing Susan speak was a revelation to me, and it radically altered what I wanted to accomplish in my own academic work. I want to thank her for opening that door for me and for all her invaluable scholarship over the last decade that has done so much to change the discipline of musicology.

Thanks to my parents, Abe and Frieda, for their unflagging support, and to my sister, Louise, for always listening and for her guidance in every aspect of my life. Thanks also to my brother, Robert. I thank my cats for keeping me company during long hours of writing, and to my friends Karen and Liam for dragging me out to socialize once in a while. To Liam, who has been convinced for the past two years that he has the perfect line with which to begin this book, here it is: "It was a dark and stormy night...."

In the Houses of the Holy

Introduction
Led Zeppelin and the Carnivalesque

I 'm so happy," wrote a thirty-five-year-old male respondent to my Led Zeppelin fan questionnaire, "that after years of being put down for worshipping
such a 'déclassé' band . . . someone like you is giving their oeuvre the deserved
attention of an academic." There has always existed a gap between the millions
of fans who are devoted to Led Zeppelin's music and the rock establishment—
critics and other artists—who found Zeppelin's music bombastic, their offstage
antics unruly even by rock standards, and their business practices ruthless and
suspect. One does not want to exaggerate this gap, however. There have always
been critics and artists who have admired and supported the band—*Melody
Maker*'s Chris Welch and Canadian journalist Ritchie Yorke were wildly enthusiastic about Led Zeppelin from the band's inception—and in recent years the
band has become increasingly well respected in the upper echelons of rock
journalism; a case in point is the laudatory essay on the band's music by veteran
rock critic Robert Palmer, written upon the release of the first boxed set recordings in 1990.[1] Yet the band is still largely relegated to the category of heavy metal
or "proto-metal" in most writings, and the implication remains that such music
is, as the fan puts it, "déclassé."[2] Given the diversity of the band's output, they
might easily be differently categorized, but this rarely occurs. One must wonder
why not.

The band was formed in 1968 by Jimmy Page, who had in 1966 taken over
from Jeff Beck as guitarist for the Yardbirds. Page recruited John Paul Jones, a
veteran session player whom he knew from his own days as a studio musician in
London, as well as singer Robert Plant and drummer John Bonham, who were
active musicians but virtually unknown outside their native Birmingham. Led
Zeppelin's musical tastes were eclectic, and a wealth of influences made their

way into the band's music. These were shaped into a sound louder, more bottom-heavy, arguably more raw, certainly more bodily, more emotionally charged, and in some cases more deliberately unpolished than any other white rock of the time. Yet there are certainly elements of progressive rock in some of their music, and there are a substantial number of acoustically based, folk-inspired songs in their repertory as well. Humor also figured significantly, as in the country and western send-up "Hot Dog" or the reggae-influenced "D'yer Mak'er." The latter was partly intended as a joke on themselves, the lumbering sound of Bonham's characteristically heavy drumming and Plant's 1950s-inspired lyric and crooner-style singing largely undermining what should be an airy reggae groove: it's funny because they sound incompetent. "The Crunge" parodies James Brown's funk style (with a little Otis Redding thrown in by Plant). In this case, the irregular meter makes it sound as though the band does-n't quite understand how to work the groove (and even though this may not have been their intent, in both "D'yer Mak'er" and "The Crunge" the band's assumed rhythmic ineptitude makes fun of their whiteness). Their develop-ment of a sound that would come to characterize heavy metal, however, over-shadowed the stylistic diversity and made it all but impossible for critics to understand the humor.

The band's heavy sound was also mapped onto certain elements of their image that tended to characterize them in a monodimensional way. Led Zep-pelin was managed by Peter Grant, who signed them to Atlantic Records with an advance of $200,000, an enormous sum for the time. This was not only the beginning of their phenomenal commercial success, in both record sales and sold-out concert tours, but also the beginning of suspicions that the band was all hype with little musical substance. Grant "changed the way business was done on the concert circuit, shifting the power—and the money—from the pockets of the promoters to the hands of the artists,"[3] and he ruled with a heavy hand. There are tales of suspected bootleggers at concerts having their equip-ment broken by members of Zeppelin's management. In fact, Grant's method of dealing with bootleggers of any stripe is immortalized in a scene from the docu-mentary film *The Song Remains the Same*, in which he is seen reprimanding those responsible for hawking bootleg photographs at Madison Square Garden during a 1973 concert. There is also the infamous story of Grant, another mem-ber of his management team, and John Bonham being involved in an assault on one of promoter Bill Graham's employees at a 1977 Oakland Coliseum concert, and there are plenty of other examples.[4] The band's reputation for trashing hotel rooms, keeping the company of extremely young groupies, abusing drugs, including alcohol, and indulging in the lewdest of offstage pastimes is well known and has been sensationalized (and probably also exaggerated) in the two best-known, if unofficial, biographies of the band, those by longtime road man-ager Richard Cole (*Stairway to Heaven*) and Stephen Davis (*Hammer of the Gods*). The latter relies heavily on the ruminations of Cole, who may have been largely responsible for most of the bad behavior.[5]

But the "low" status of the band probably rests, ultimately, with their commercial success, their onstage image, and, crucially, their sound. As for the commercial success, Davis summed it up well when he wrote:

The musicians and fans of the late sixties were highly ambivalent about the unprecedented commercial success of rock music; young record company employees were known as 'corporate freaks' and were ideologically suspect as agents of bourgeois capitalism. Any new band that hadn't been through 1967 was suspected of the sin of corporate hype—being foisted upon the rich and gullible public by some big conglomerate without authentic anarcho-hippie credentials.[6]

Rolling Stone critic Jon Landau made the well-worn issue of the difference between commercial success and artistic integrity (the latter, naturally, determined by the rock press) in Led Zeppelin eminently clear:

Zeppelin forced a revival of the distinction between popularity and quality. As long as the bands most admired aesthetically were also the bands most successful commercially (Cream, for instance) the distinction was irrelevant. But Zeppelin's enormous commercial success, in spite of critical opposition, revealed the deep division in what was once thought to be a homogeneous audience. That division has now evolved into a clearly defined mass taste and a clearly defined elitist taste.[7]

If huge commercial success was the band's first sin, the second was surely the sound of the music coupled with the theatricality of the performances. Rolling Stone's Jim Miller refers to Zeppelin's "blunt style of rock" and their "sonic concussion bombs" (he generously acknowledges that these can be "intricately crafted").[8] An early review in Variety condemned the band for their "obsession with power, volume and melodramatic theatrics" and for their forsaking of "musical sense for . . . sheer power."[9] The band's theatricality and volume drew a similar condemnation from Keith Richards, who in 1986 commented: "Now, I don't like Led Zeppelin at all, piss on 'em—sorry chaps, and all, but it just never appealed to me. Lots of banging with lead singers with flying gold locks and the whole bit: never had any use for them."[10]

One way in which Led Zeppelin's exclusion from the elite of rock culture can be theorized is through Mikhail Bakhtin's idea of the carnivalesque:

As opposed to the official feast, one might say that carnival celebrates temporary liberation from the prevailing truth of the established order; it marks the suspension of all hierarchical rank, privileges, norms and prohibitions. Carnival was the true feat of time, the feat of becoming, change and renewal. It was hostile to all that was immortalized and complete.[11]

The appeal of Zeppelin to the "great masses," while the elite of rock culture regularly leveled the sharpest criticism, positions the band in opposition to "the official feast." Their intensely physical music—music that calls attention to, as Bakhtin calls it, the lower bodily stratum—the gut, the sexual organs—and that allowed lengthy, sometimes technically shaky improvisations that truly allowed the process of "becoming" to be heard onstage, was too much for many. The particular brand of theatricality that Led Zeppelin practiced onstage was also disconcerting. While some might find it odd that Keith Richards, whose partner Mick Jagger is, without question, a "theatrical" performer, would condemn Zeppelin for their theatricality, his comment throws the distinction between the kind of carefully considered posturing undertaken by performers such as Jagger, acceptable to Richards and the journalists who applaud it, and the less self-conscious, less emotionally contained performances by Zeppelin. Jagger's personas are clearly artificial, contrived, marked by ironic distance. He obviously retains a distinct and emotionally in-control subjectivity as he acts. The hyperbolic wailing and moaning undertaken by Plant and the extravagant poses made by Page, not to mention a gesture such as the setting on fire of Bonham's gong at the end of a concert, were not marked by such ironic distance. The musical and theatrical hyperbole of Zeppelin is marked by *realism*. These excessive uses of the body, these emotional outpourings, were meant to be taken as unconstructed, as *real*, and this feature of white hard rock music has often been deemed laughable by the critical establishment. The "theatricality" of the performances, their physicality (including the intense depth and volume of the sound), their enormous length, the sometimes meandering improvisations, and even Page's "sloppy" playing—moments during which he is clearly more interested in creating a particular emotional landscape than in getting all the notes right—were all pressed into the service of celebrating an ecstatic loss of control, and all transgress the boundaries of practices acceptable to "high" rock culture. Even though it is more than thirty years since the first Led Zeppelin album was made, one can still easily comprehend their difference from the prevailing sound of rock music at the time by juxtaposing a Beatles, Stones, or Hendrix album with *Led Zeppelin*. The heaviness of the sound, the vast sonic space created, and the unbridled emotional landscape are still overwhelming. In addition, one should really go beyond the studio recordings and listen to live recordings from, especially, 1969, listed in the discography here, in order to appreciate just how far removed those performances were from what else was being heard at the time. The Who might be comparable in terms of theatrics but certainly not in sound; Hendrix comes closest in both sound and the theatricality of his performances, but he was black and therefore sanctioned by the largely white rock press to engage in emotional and sexual hyperbole.[12] Led Zeppelin represents the world of carnivalesque exuberance "of ceaseless overrunning and excess"; they represent the spirit of carnivalesque laughter, with its "vulgar, 'earthy' quality," and its ability to revive.[13]

FEW ACADEMIC STUDIES in popular music have focused on a single artist, paying as much analytical attention to the music as to other factors. The result has been that our knowledge of and assumptions about artists have tended to harden, and the same generalizations, often simply wrong or too broadly drawn, are continually perpetuated without further critical reflection. This is precisely what has occurred with Led Zeppelin in most journalistic and certainly in academic writing about the band. One has to look in magazines devoted to guitar playing, fanzines, and some of the books written by knowledgeable fans in order to move beyond generalizations, and even there the details of the music and their cultural significance are rarely discussed. Two examples of writing about the band, one academic and one journalistic, both typical, might suffice here to indicate a need for a more detailed critical study of Led Zeppelin and also to begin a general discussion about Led Zeppelin's music.

Allan F. Moore's *Rock: The Primary Text*, which appeared in 1993, was one of the first academic books to examine the details of rock *music*, admirably attempting to ascribe cultural significance to the way in which the music is constructed. Moore discusses Led Zeppelin's music together with that of Cream and early Fleetwood Mac, arguing that "the 'inspiration' which some critics suggest the blues supplied [for these bands] is hard to sustain,"[14] concluding that his "extensive discussions" of the music (two and a half pages for Led Zeppelin) "show how little their music relates to the blues."[15] Moore argues that the first five Led Zeppelin albums are marked by stylistic diversity, a "clear style" being achieved with the double sixth album, *Physical Graffiti*, "which the rest of their output further explores and refines," the rest of their output amounting to two albums of new material, *Presence* and *In Through the Out Door*, and an album of outtakes, *Coda*.[16] He takes the piece "Kashmir" as representing "the most typical elements" of this style, pointing to several factors: 1) "its chromatic riff and metrical niceties,"[17] 2) John Bonham's "mature" drumming style, "one of the key features [of which] is the crispness of his tone, resulting from his extremely heavy touch," and 3) a "mature" approach to the construction of an extended piece ("four self-contained stretches of music" as opposed to "inexorable growth towards a great climax," the prototypical example of the latter being "Stairway to Heaven"; Moore also mysteriously cites the blues tune "Since I've Been Loving You" as an example of this technique).[18] Despite his view that there is no unified Led Zeppelin style, at least early on, Moore identifies certain elements "that are clearly Led Zeppelin and nobody else," for example John Bonham's drum sound, occasional metrical and rhythmic irregularities, bass and guitar playing the same lines (which Moore says occurs from *Physical Graffiti* onward), and Robert Plant's voice, which Moore characterizes as having a very high tessitura, adding, "[B]ut the range, rarely reaching down to middle C, is larger than it seems. Tremolos and 'less often' vibrato appear on long notes, with a tendency to lose pitch (as an assumed expression of emotional intensity) toward the end of phrases. His tone is . . . pinched."[19]

It is telling of the state of popular music scholarship that Moore would consider his discussion of Led Zeppelin's music extensive: in fact, in the context of what else has been written about the band's music, two and a half pages *is* fairly extensive, although since Moore's book appeared there have been two academic articles written about Led Zeppelin that do discuss the music, one by Dave Headlam, the other by Steve Waksman (see bibliography). Most of what Moore says about the music can be challenged, and this is, again, not so much Moore's fault as it is the state of popular music scholarship. Moore's task was enormous in that he chose to write about a considerable number of artists on whose music almost no serious scholarship had been undertaken. In other words, in his descriptions of the music he was almost always starting from scratch. I use Moore's comments here as a starting point for a discussion of some general characteristics of the band's music, and I challenge what he has to say concerning Led Zeppelin's music in the spirit of trying to set the record straight—in my privileged position of writing a book-length study on only one band.

Moore's overriding assertion that the blues was not the significant influence on this band that is sometimes claimed is false. It is, surprisingly, echoed by David Hatch and Stephen Millward, in *From Blues to Rock*, in which the authors claim that "[w]ith the band's second LP release (*Led Zeppelin II*, 1969), links with the blues were formally severed."[20] There is, however, essentially a twelve-bar blues on every Led Zeppelin album except *Houses of the Holy*, and this formal reliance on the genre only scratches the surface of the blues and R&B influence in the band's music. Lyrically, Plant leaned very heavily on blues songs, often combining sections from several sources into a single song (for example, "How Many More Times," "The Lemon Song," "Custard Pie," "Nobody's Fault but Mine"). Page's guitar style throughout Led Zeppelin draws extensively on blues licks derived primarily from the Delta blues scale, and even a late song such as "In My Time of Dying" utilizes bottleneck guitar playing derived from the blues. On the last tour the band undertook in 1980, they included the R&B standard "Train Kept A Rollin'"—the first tune the four musicians ever played together—as a show opener.

Physical Graffiti is a strange choice of album to cite as an example of stylistic unity, since the material was written and recorded at various times and places, over a period of more than three years. The elements of stylistic unity that Moore identifies as being present in "Kashmir" are nowhere to be found in pieces like "Down by the Seaside" or "Ten Years Gone," which also appear on this album. These are as stylistically diverse as works on previous albums. *Presence*, the album that followed *Physical Graffiti*, is perhaps the most stylistically unified, but it follows a very different aesthetic from its forerunner (among other things, it contains no acoustic songs, which always constituted an important feature on Led Zeppelin albums).

The way in which Moore addresses some of the other musical technicalities is also troubling. How is the multisectional structure of "Kashmir" more "mature" than that of "Stairway to Heaven"? Extended pieces constructed in several sections (like "Kashmir") can be found on the first Led Zeppelin album ("Dazed and Confused" or "How Many More Times"), so this construction cannot really be linked to a "mature" (as in later) style. Robert Plant's vocal tone may be pinched in some instances ("Achilles Last Stand" is a good late example) but not consistently. It is one of his strengths as a rock vocalist that he is able to mold his voice to suit the character of a particular piece, changing timbre and texture much like a guitarist. The important technical device of bass and guitar (or multiple guitars) doubling each other is used on the first album and every one thereafter. This technical feature, which has come to be a hallmark of hard rock and heavy metal playing, was employed by Cream and the Jimi Hendrix Experience before Led Zeppelin used it.

Journalistic descriptions of the band are equally troublesome—if slightly more colorful. The one that appears in *Rock of Ages: The Rolling Stone History of Rock and Roll* is typical of much journalistic writing on the band:

> Jimmy Page's explosive guitar lines cleared the ground for Robert Plant's voice, and its baleful white blues squawk echoed across a vast sonic plane. The rhythm section of John Bonham and John Paul Jones then marched slowly, ominously, implacably across the landscape, providing a feeling of dread and inevitability to the band's music. There was nothing else like it, nothing so cruel and powerful and overwhelmingly pessimistic on the face of sunny rock and roll. Page, his head full of old English legends, fairy tales, and Aleister Crowley's black magic, composed dense, often impenetrable thickets of lyrics whose meaning could be construed only through Plant's phrasing—that's why "Stairway to Heaven" can be listened to forever: it's an unknowable song, but one that nonetheless exerts a terrible, beautiful allure. At the same time Led Zeppelin was widely perceived as a group of bombastic showboaters with a heavy beat and pseudo/profound lyrics, but it is now clear that the band changed the landscape against which rock and roll is played. And so the basic formula for heavy metal was codified: blues chords plus high-pitched male tenor vocals singing lyrics that ideally combined mysticism, sexism, and hostility.[21]

Most of these assumptions can be challenged with recourse to the music itself (the issue of sexism will be dealt with extensively in chapter 5). There is nothing pessimistic or hostile about Led Zeppelin's music; by and large, Robert Plant's lyrics reflect his allegiance to hippie ideals of peace and love and are generally full of optimism. In "Friends," "The Rover," and "The Song Remains the Same," for example, Plant speaks of the importance of friendship ("The greatest thing you ever can do, is trade a smile with someone who's blue"), pleads for human beings to "just hold hands," and celebrates similarities among various cultures in the global community, respectively. Musical examples can be given that express this same optimism (the joyful ringing guitars in "The Song Remains the Same" might be the best example; the lighthearted folksy romp of "Bron-Y-

Aur Stomp"—which, incidentally, describes the bond between Plant and his dog Strider, hardly the stuff of metal gloom—is another). Robert Plant, not Jimmy Page, wrote all but the earliest of Led Zeppelin's lyrics (and certainly those to "Stairway to Heaven"), and it was Plant, not Page, who studied Celtic history and lore. The writer makes reference to one song only and then in the most general way: *how* might Plant's phrasing create meaning for the lyrics in "Stairway to Heaven" and how does it exert a "terrible, beautiful allure"?

Getting the details of the music right does not have to be an exercise in "wrongheaded formalism," as Neil Nehring would have it; rather, it hinges on whether or not we make accurate and relevant judgments about the cultural and political economies of the music.[22] As Richard Middleton warns,

> If we do not try to grasp the relations between popular music discourses and the material musical practices to which they refer, and at the same time the necessary distinctness of level between these, we are unlikely to break through the structures of power which, as Foucault makes clear, discursive authority erects. And we are likely to abandon the sphere of the concrete to the positivists and that of theory to the essentialists, rather than to theorize the relationship of the two at a higher structural level.[23]

In the chapters that follow, I have devoted a good deal of attention to musical detail. Four of the five chapters make the analysis of a single piece of music a focus; in chapter 4, I examine many different works in somewhat less detail. My interest is not in carrying out musical analysis as an end in itself but in order that we may better understand how the music works as part of "cultural practice," as Lawrence Kramer has put it.[24] While there are those who may think that musical sound is not a primary locus of cultural meaning in popular music or that sound "transcends" culture, it is my belief that the sounds are critically important to the construction of meanings. It is this musical construction of meaning, in conjunction with visual imagery, the use of the body in performance, and the discourse that was created around the band by fans, the rock press, and band members themselves that I explore in the pages that follow.

This book is not intended as a comprehensive survey of Led Zeppelin's music; rather, I have chosen several issues that I think are critically important to consider with respect to the cultural significance of the band. Chapter 1 examines mostly the issues of intertextuality, ritual, and gender through the analysis of "Dazed and Confused," but in fact this chapter serves as a microcosm of the rest of the book, touching on nearly all of the issues that will be elaborated upon (viewed again through a different lens, we could say) in later chapters. Chapter 2 addresses the way in which Led Zeppelin and those who wrote about the band constructed the mythology that surrounds them and of what pivotal importance this mythology is in the lives of fans. I analyze "Stairway to Heaven" in order to discover how the musical discourse taps into mythical and ritualistic constructs that are entrenched in Western culture. In a brief coda to this chapter, I point to the band's little-discussed acoustic music and, particularly, the "acoustic set" that became an important part of many performances in 1970 and after, as an integral part of the band's mythology, the acoustic set as a significant confessional practice. In chapter 3, "Kashmir" serves as the centerpiece for a discussion of cultural appropriation, especially that of "the East." In chapter 4, I theorize the relationship of Led Zeppelin's riff-based music to the body, using, especially, the theory of philosopher Mark Johnson as well as others. That chapter also includes a study of the ways in which band members used their bodies in performance—what Eugenio Barba calls the construction of "fictional bodies"—and how the use of the body on stage helps define power relations within the band. In chapter 5, I challenge the well-established assumptions that concern hard rock/heavy metal and constructions of masculinity, as well as issues of gender and sexuality in general with respect to this music, relying heavily on fan comments, especially those from the many women who responded to a fan survey I distributed (see later), as well as my own gendered experience with the music. (You might already be wondering why a woman would write a book about music that is generally considered to be a male domain; some answers are given in this final chapter.) An analysis of "Whole Lotta Love" serves as an example of how fluid gender performativity is in this music.

I have included a minimum of notated musical examples[25] and have tried to use language that is not overly technical, so that those who do not have formal training in music—especially fans—might not be alienated by the discussion. Some technical description is necessary, however, in order to best elucidate what is happening in the music, and I would hope that those who are not familiar with the terminology would turn to a book on the fundamentals of music to guide them along (it's not difficult, really!). The notated examples are in no way intended to replace the real primary sources—the recordings—and I would urge the reader to have these close at hand. As central as I believe the music to be in discussions of popular music, I have also recognized the enormously important place of visual imagery—the use of the body, costumes, the performance space, and so on—by beginning four of the five chapters with descriptions of significant images from the band's concert performances that serve to problematize the central issue of the essay. As mentioned previously, I also make a discussion of the use of the body in performance a central part of chapter 4 and draw attention to the visual aspect of the band elsewhere in the book. For several of these discussions I have relied on the photographs of the band by Marty Perez and Wendy Annibell, the cover photo by Neal Preston, and the illustrations that supplement these by my colleague Judy Major-Girardin. The photos and illustrations are not intended as window dressing but as an integral part of the discussion. I am especially pleased that the photographs included in this book were taken by avid fans who happen also to be professional photographers; it is one way in which I have tried to include the voices of those who love the music.

I have tried to make this study as dialogic as possible. I am an avid fan of the music as well as a trained musicologist, and my interpretations are colored by my fandom as much as by my academic training. My desire to write a book on Led Zeppelin stemmed initially from my love of the music and my discovery that the music and culture around it had not really been examined in a substantial way. I have drawn on a diverse number of secondary sources, academic and journalistic, as well as the work of such fans as Dave Lewis, Louis Rey, Robert Godwin, Charles R. Cross, and Hugh Jones, among others, who have an encyclopedic knowledge of the band that puts mine to shame. I have also perused some of the hundreds of Led Zeppelin Web sites, where much of the information from the print sources can be found (including discographies, tour dates, audio and video clips of bootlegs, interviews with band members, lyrics, and more).[26] I have included statements made by members of the band, many of these from interviews they have conducted over the years with journalists, but also from my e-mail conversations with John Paul Jones, who was kind enough to answer a long list of questions that I posed to him. Comments that come from our correspondence are dispersed throughout the book and appear without bibliographic references. I extended invitations to Plant and Page to speak with me about the project on two occasions but was told by their management via fax that "[u]nfortunately we cannot accommodate your request as Jimmy Page and Robert Plant do not participate on books of any variety relating to Led Zeppelin." I suspect that part of their reasoning is that they are none too eager to endorse such projects through their participation, which is fair enough; but their silence also serves to preserve the mystique that they have worked so hard to create around the band.[27]

When Jones agreed to answer my questions, he expressed his concern that so much of what gets written about the band focuses on Page and Plant, often to the exclusion of the rhythm section. While this is certainly true in journalistic and academic writing, fans very much acknowledge the importance and unique contributions of all members of the group. I have tried to be inclusive in my discussions, but since part of what I wish to examine in this book is the way in which the band has been received (what has been said about issues of gender and sexuality or representation, for example) and the theatricality of the performances—which was largely the purview of Page and Plant—I, too, have often slipped into making the guitarist and the singer the focal point of my discussions. I therefore want to acknowledge here my understanding that without Bonham's particular combination of power and subtlety the music would have sounded substantially different, would generally have been much less effective, and would have been received in a completely different way. The other members of the group recognized his importance by, in fact, disbanding Led Zeppelin upon his death in 1980. Further, the contribution to the sound of the music made by Jones was pivotal. According to Jones, songwriting credit was largely determined by who brought in the chord progression or riff, that is, the "shell," of the song, as opposed to contributions made to the arrangement, and so Page and Plant often received sole credit (Page for the music, Plant for the lyrics). But Jones contributed substantially to the way in which many songs ended up sounding, including melodic bass lines in many of them (the bass lines created by Jones in a song such as "Ramble On," to give only one example, are of central importance), as well as the organ opening of "Good Times, Bad Times," the harpsichord ending of "Over the Hills and Far Away," and so forth. These elements of the songs are, of course, crucially important to how they have been received and how they are interpreted.

Even though the band ceased to exist in 1980, it continues to enjoy a remarkably large following, evident in record sales,[28] the vitality of Internet discussion lists, fanzines, and the now-annual Zep Fest (a convention for Led Zeppelin fans that meets in a different location every year—in Cleveland at the Rock and Roll Hall of Fame in 1998, in Toronto in 1999, and so forth), not to mention the success of the 1995 and 1998 tours by Jimmy Page and Robert Plant, which featured Zeppelin songs almost exclusively. Because there is such a thriving fan community, I decided to develop a fan survey in order that the voices of those with the greatest investment in the band might be heard throughout the book. I posted the survey on the Internet and in a major U.S. Led Zeppelin fanzine called *Proximity*, run by Hugh Jones out of Seattle; answers were collected between June and November 1998. While the Internet is an immensely important resource for this kind of ethnographic study, offering the possibility of covering a wide geographic region and allowing for the quick turnaround of information and the possibility of further dialogue with fans beyond the limits of the questionnaire, the major drawback is that not all fans own or have access to a computer and so particular segments of the fan community, especially those who are economically disadvantaged, are left out of the discussion. Distributing the survey in *Proximity* was intended as a partial remedy to this problem. The fanzine is not only sent to subscribers but also sold inexpensively in record stores across the United States (it has a circulation of 1,200 copies per issue). The Internet discussion list to which I sent the survey is called "For Badgeholders Only" ("FBO"). It is the main Internet discussion site for Led Zeppelin fans, and many of them are very knowledgeable about the band. *Proximity* readers are generally also hard-core fans. Many of the answers that I received from these two sources amounted to short dissertations, written with enormous passion and commitment. All of the fans of whom I asked follow-up questions responded enthusiastically with further information. I also posted the survey on a Led Zeppelin Web site called zoso.net at the invitation of its owner, Jeremy Mixer, from which I received a more mixed set of responses, including some from casual fans. I received 323 usable responses in all. The respondents range in age from ten through fifty-nine and are in occupations that include professionals (doctors, dentists, lawyers, professors), business owners, artists, managers, laborers, retail sales clerks, computer programers and consultants, and students (the questionnaire and the personal information statistics are reproduced in the appendix). The information that I received from fans turned out to be the best evidence that so much of what has been written about the band is at odds with the impressions of those who listen to the music. Because they had so much to say and often expressed it so eloquently, I have quoted extensively from their answers. I did not think it appropriate simply to summarize—to speak for them in my own voice. Still, the answers I reproduce here are only representative samplings. Answers to some questions, as those who read the survey will discover, were not included at all because the information did not ultimately further enhance the points I wished to make here; that is, I would have had to veer off in several other directions in order to include it and, unfortunately, my space was limited. Beyond collecting statistics about, primarily, sex, occupation, and age, my aim was to map trends in answers, not to be rigorous about numbers. I have, though, done my best not to distort the information I received and to include all the views that were expressed on a particular issue: if a particular point of view is stressed, that is because it appeared repeatedly in the fans' answers.

I do not assume that by asking a few questions of a fairly narrow segment of the Led Zeppelin fan population I have solved all questions of representation and neatly put to rest issues around the ritual use of the music, gender, cultural appropriation, or anything else. Indeed, as James Clifford and others have been observing for some time, ethnographies come with their own set of difficulties, among which must be acknowledged that they are "constructed, artificial . . . cultural accounts," which only seem less mediated than other forms of writing.[29] Still, I hope to have balanced, to some degree, my own voice, the voices of the producers, and those of the fans, although even in this I realize that the interpretative authority still rests squarely with me.[30]

Led Zeppelin's studio recordings tell only a part of the musical story of this band, which is why I have tried in my analyses to take into account video performances and live recordings as well. Unfortunately, there is only one official video, the documentary film *The Song Remains the Same*, and only one official live recording, the double-album soundtrack recording of the film. But there are literally thousands of bootleg recordings and several bootleg video performances available and most avid fans of the band's music have heard some of these or collect them to some extent (I do myself). I wanted to include more analyses of these live recordings, but since they are not readily available to everyone, I limited their use, relying mostly on the video of *The Song Remains the Same* and descriptions of the live recordings that the general reader will, I hope, be able to comprehend.[31]

The chapters that follow are only partly about Led Zeppelin. On the one hand, they are intended to celebrate Zeppelin's music and the profound impact it has had on my life and the lives of other fans. While some might accuse me of writing an apologia for the band, this is by no means my intent. The essays are critical, my aim being to probe the reasons for the music's impact, to uncover the constructions and cultural convergences that make such an impact possible at any given moment, while respecting the craftsmanship, power, and beauty of the music and, especially, the experiences of fans. Ultimately, though, the issues that I examine have to do with more than Led Zeppelin or their music: they apply to rock culture in general and especially to how subjectivities, both those of the producers and those of the consumers, are shaped and reshaped through the medium of music. I have tried to problematize what have become entrenched views on issues such as gender and sexuality, musico-cultural appropriation, and the spiritual significance of hard rock music to listeners in order, I hope, that we might begin to nuance these views, if not, in some cases, significantly alter them.

ONE

Dazed and Confused

Intertextuality, Ritual, Gender

During the performance of "Dazed and Confused" in Led Zeppelin's documentary film, *The Song Remains the Same*, the camera cuts away from concert footage to a film vignette constructed by Jimmy Page in which he is seen climbing a mountain in the dead of night, his way lit by a full moon, bare hands clutching at clumps of weed as he struggles to reach the summit. At the top of the mountain stands a hermit who carries a lamp that has lit Page's way up the mountain. When Page has nearly reached the summit, he struggles to make physical contact with the hermit, his arm, hand, and fingers overextended in an attempt to meet the fingertips of the hermit. When contact is established, the hermit undergoes a process of transformation, his face changing from that of an old man, to that of an increasingly younger man. We come to recognize this man as Page himself. He is taken back into the womb, and then the process is reversed, Page being transformed back into the hermit. The sequence ends with an animated version of the hermit waving a multicolored wand in a semicircle over his head, a gesture that is mimicked by Page when the scene returns to live performance. The music heard during this vignette comes from the improvisatory middle section of the piece. Page is playing his electric guitar using a violin bow, creating fantastic new timbres that are privileged over all other musical elements; the rhythm section has dropped out to give way to these sounds, allowing the full focus of attention to be directed toward them. The only other sound heard is Robert Plant's voice, which weaves sensuously in and out of the texture, engaging in sympathetic dialogue with Page's playing.

This excerpt from the only legitimately released live performance of "Dazed and Confused" encapsulates what makes the piece such a rich text through which to explore a variety of issues in Led Zeppelin's music and image. "Dazed and Confused" was arguably the most important locus for musical experimentation from the group's inception in 1968 through their live appearances in 1979—in other words, for the entire life of the band save the last tour.[1] It became the most malleable and extended piece in the band's repertory, sometimes running to half an hour or more in performance;[2] within this expanse of time, the musicians were free to roam wherever their imaginations took them. It is the nature of these experimentations, as well as the general structure of the song from which they grew, that is the focus of this chapter. In particular, I have chosen to view the piece, including the visual imagery from live performances, from three different perspectives: formal openness and intertextuality, Page's guitar solos in terms of their ritualistic qualities, and the construction of gender in Plant's singing and in his musical relationship with Page. These subjects intersect at various points and are further linked to the cultural economies of the work.

What were these cultural economies? It requires no great leap of the imagination to, at least as a first layer of analysis, locate the aural and visual images of the film vignette from *The Song Remains the Same* generally within the counterculture of the late 1960s and early 1970s.[3] The rejection of the dominant culture's values, perceived as overly rigid and rational, is reflected in Page's filmic "spiritual quest," which suggests a religious epistemology far removed from the Judeo-Christian norm. The open musical structure and the sheer length of the piece made it unsuitable for A.M. radio airplay or, in general, quick and easy consumption; the importance of this lies in the impression that such a song stands apart from capitalist interests, from marketplace values. The experimentation with sound, especially Page's trademark use of the violin bow to play his electric guitar, radically expanded the sonic palette, serving as a metaphor for the expansion of consciousness into unchartered territory, and on this count the piece is a classic example of psychedelia. Sonic experimentation, especially in the context of improvisation, has been viewed as "the musical equivalent of hallucinogenic experience,"[4] with "altered and effected instrumental sounds, reverb, echoes, and tape delays that created a sense of space" as well as other effects pressed into service in order to re-create the hallucinogenic experience.[5] And as Jim DeRogatis explains, the "subculture that developed around the use of psychedelics" was in part defined by the idea that their use "had spiritual and intellectual connotations beyond the usual druggie goal of 'getting wasted.'"[6] Music of this sort was perceived as being part of the experience of an alternative spirituality, one that valued questing for self-knowledge through an intense understanding of personal subjectivity, hence the appropriateness of the film vignette that accompanies it in the documentary.[7] Lengthy improvisations that gave the performer ample opportunity to search out and develop ideas and that took the listener along on the journey played a significant role in this experiential matrix. Page, Plant, and Jones certainly all had previous experience with psychedelia. Page, after all, came to Led Zeppelin fresh from the psychedelic experiments of the late Yardbirds. That band's "Happenings Ten Years Time

Ago," with its bright guitar sounds, prolific use of reverb, and other production values reminiscent of San Francisco bands such as the Jefferson Airplane, is perhaps the best example of this. Its sound-collage middle section comes complete with police sirens, manic laughter, incomprehensible speech, and a Middle Eastern riff and melody. Jones produced Donovan's trippy "Mellow Yellow," and the San Francisco influence was of paramount importance in one incarnation of Plant's Band of Joy, "whose act was to paint their faces and perform in hippie regalia."[8]

But however useful these generalizations may be, they can, as Richard Middleton points out in his discussion of progressive rock and its links with the counterculture, be applied equally well to a host of diverse music produced around this time; none of the characteristics should be analyzed rigidly as being representative of countercultural values.[9] Certainly "Dazed and Confused" is one of the pieces that most closely reflects Led Zeppelin's affinity with the counterculture, and the song's appearance in 1969, at the height of the countercultural movement, locates it there historically.[10] Any analysis of the work must take this connection into account. But the semiotics of this piece are also bound up with other cultural paradigms that were not really in sympathy with the counterculture. One such paradigm was the notion of rock as "art music," the musicians viewing themselves as artists in the tradition of nineteenth-century Western classical music, playing out the same tensions between craft and inspiration in the cultivation of music as classical composers. Both Page and Jones honed their skills as musical craftsmen during their days as studio musicians, in which job they had to become fluid with all current popular styles. Both left that profession in order to exercise their musical creativity more fully in an environment in which they were not enslaved to playing what others expected but could express themselves in what they perceived to be a freer and more honest way. There was an interest not only in experimentation with sound but also in developing instrumental technique in the same way as classical musicians do. In a rare early interview, for example, Page told reporter Chris Welch, "I've been practicing three hours a day. Unfortunately [because of touring] there has been a great lack of practice in the last year or so. I play a long improvised solo to get fluency and then attempt a difficult phrase to see if I can pull it off."[11]

Further, any correlation made between this piece and the counterculture cannot be a static one, for although the piece was born amid that cultural economy, it remained a staple in performance and relevant to both the musicians and a wide audience long after the last vestiges of that movement had receded into the past.

Text/Intertext

Overt intertextuality is a fact of rock music; it owes its very beginnings to the mingling of disparate styles. Therefore, simply to identify "Dazed and Confused" as intertextual is inconsequential: the point, as Mikhail Bakhtin puts it, is not "merely to uncover the multiplicity of languages in a cultural world or the speech diversity within a particular national language—[but to] see through to the heart of the revolution, to all the consequences flowing from it."[12] One of the main points in discussing intertextuality here is that for many of Led Zeppelin's fans, the most important thing about the band is its musical diversity and eclecticism, their openness to all kinds of musical influences, their dialogism, and the consequent difficulty in neatly categorizing them. When asked on the fan survey: "What is it you like about the band's MUSIC (as opposed to the lyrics, images, etc.)?" the overwhelming majority of people commented on the group's musical diversity:

> I think more than anything, I like the diversity in the style of the band. . . . A lot of bands play only hard music, or soft music, or in between. Zeppelin can do it all.

> I like the variety, for one thing. They could do rock, blues, acoustic, whatever. And they were ahead of their time musically. They were pre-everything.

Some also commented on the importance of this openness to different styles in terms of improvisation:

> In many songs they just go off in a totally unexpected direction.

> The tightness of the playing combined with improvisational looseness.

When asked: "How would you categorize Led Zeppelin: heavy metal, progressive rock, hard rock, something else?" fewer than ten fans answered "heavy metal," and although several were willing to commit to "hard rock," fewer still to "progressive rock," this was with considerable reluctance. The majority of fans said that it was impossible to categorize the band, again because they were capable of playing so many different kinds of music:

> It's impossible to categorize them. There isn't an average sound or style. They don't just dabble with styles, they embody or create.

> Only morons categorize Zep as heavy metal. It's as ludicrous as calling the Beatles "pop" or Dylan a "folkie." They are *sui generis*, a category of one.

> Everybody wants a label in life. It's a phony "safety net" for the masses.

> No, it's not important to classify them. Led Zeppelin can't be defined, easily understood and filed away in some folder or category.

Avoiding easy categorization is important to fans because this is perceived as a mark of the band's willingness to grow musically, to take risks, and especially to shy away from the easy option of repeating themselves. It signals a willingness to engage diversity and to be flexible and fluid in the construction of their identity. Again, these ideas run against capitalist marketplace interests. Theodore Adorno's critique of popular music is centered squarely on the issue of "standardization," of what he perceived to be the sameness or repeatability of the popular music he knew.[13] Although Adorno is regularly criticized for this position, it is nonetheless extremely important in the construction of rock authenticity. Individuality and innovation, musical "depth" (which includes intertextual references), and, as a consequence, the perception that the resulting music and image are "noncommercial" are very much valued in rock culture (in fact, much of this music, certainly Led Zeppelin's, is *highly* commercially successful).

Led Zeppelin's musical eclecticism was a product of, as Jones puts it, "the sheer diversity of the musical tastes of [the band's] members, coupled with the understanding of show/record dynamics that Page and myself had gained through many years of experience." Jones's further reflections on this subject point decidedly in the same direction as those of the fans: musical dialogism is highly valued:

> I have made the comment that bands often form from people who all listen to the same (one) type of music and therefore lack the variety of listening that I think is necessary for a well rounded and interesting musical group. (I actually think that a musician should listen to, and understand the workings of, as many different types of music as possible. All music from Pygmy yodelling through Bartók to Cage operates on the same basic principles.) You also don't get bored playing it! Again, Zeppelin was in contrast to a lot of bands around at the time, who were intent on playing shows full of songs that were virtually indistinguishable from each other.

Although fans spoke mostly to the band's whole recorded output on this question, stylistic diversity and intertextuality was also a hallmark within individual pieces, and "Dazed and Confused," certainly in live performances, is one of the best examples of this. In "Dazed and Confused" intertextuality works on several levels. First, Zeppelin's piece is a cover version of the song by the 1960s American folk singer Jake Holmes, which Page reportedly heard while the Yardbirds were on tour in the United States.[14] In the recording of Holmes's piece, the musical style is a mixture of acoustic folk elements, Eastern influences, and West Coast psychedelia. The form of the tune is similar to Zeppelin's version. The song essentially has two musical parts, the verses and the solo section, so that the piece can be mapped as A (verses) B (solo) A. The descending chromatic repeated bass pattern, or ostinato, that structures the verses, the melodic line, and the solo middle section were all retained by Page. He added the instrumental breaks that occur in between verses and after the guitar solo, a detail that contributes significantly to the drama of the piece, creating enormous tension at the end of each verse before moving on to the next.

In Holmes's version, the instrumentation consists of acoustic and electric guitar, bass, and voice, with percussive effects created during the guitar solos by tapping on the body of the instrument. The acoustic folk style that marks the initial verses is replaced in the middle by an electric guitar solo, in which the instrument sounds timbrally close to a sitar. The pitch material of this solo is mostly Phrygian, with a few quarter-tone inflections added that beautifully color the line, circling around C, with a style of ornamentation that is evocative of Eastern, specifically Indian, melodic styles. The solo is played over a static bass riff in ⅝ time (ex. 1.1).

Holmes's version is, then, an intertextual document in its own right, incorporating various stylistic threads; in fact, there is an additional intertextual reference, more anonymous or general than the others, which is the descending chromatic bass pattern, used, as musicologist Ellen Rosand elucidated some time ago, as a "symbol of lament" from the seventeenth century onward. One of the best-known early examples in classical music is "Dido's Lament" from Henry Purcell's opera *Dido and Aeneas*.[15] That "Dazed and Confused" is a lament is clear from the lyrics, but what exactly Holmes is lamenting is left ambiguous: is he addressing a lover or a friend, or, as some have suggested, is the singer's confusion the result of "a bad acid trip"?[16]

Page clearly understood the potential theater of the piece, perhaps being drawn not only to the musical/lyrical drama of the verse structure but also to the possibilities of the "free" middle section, which in terms of content was what was adapted most radically in the Zeppelin version (adaptations to the verses in terms of timbre and musical space were also radical—see later). Page had already brought the piece into the Yardbirds' repertory, and the general shape of the song as he modified it for performance in that group was carried over to the studio version on the first Led Zeppelin album. The recording on which the Yardbirds' version can be heard (*Live Yardbirds Featuring Jimmy Page*) was withdrawn from the official Yardbirds catalog by Page because of the poor sound quality and also because audience noise had been overdubbed, which greatly compromised the integrity of the recording in Page's view.[17] It is useful, nonetheless, to take this recording into account, partly because so much of the piece as it is heard on *Led Zeppelin* was already formed by this time and partly to illustrate how the differences between the two recordings account for their different semiotic worlds.

In the *Live Yardbirds* recording, called "I'm Confused," one can already hear the two-part solo section. In the first part, Page uses the violin bow; the second part is much faster and in a new meter (4/4), and Page here abandons the bow and

Example 1.1. Jake Holmes, "Dazed and Confused," opening of the guitar solo

plays a traditional virtuosic guitar solo. The lick that ends his guitar solo (the last heard before moving back to 12/8 time) occurs earlier on the album, right at the beginning, functioning as an introduction to the opening track, "Train Kept A Rollin'" (ex. 1.2). This is a trademark device of intertextuality for Page, who loves to find multiple contexts for his riffs, often beginning a piece in performance with a riff taken from another work in precisely this way. In live performance, "Black Dog" often began with the opening riff from "Bring It On Home" or "Out on the Tiles," for example, a gesture that substituted for the guitar strumming on the tonic chord heard at the beginning of this piece on the studio recording. On Page and Plant's tour in 1995, the concert opened with the riff to "Immigrant Song," which after a few repetitions mutated into the riff for "The Wanton Song," a logical combination, considering that the former in its entirety makes up the first portion of the latter. The riff to "Immigrant Song" became, in this context, an open and partial, rather than closed, gesture (see chapter 4 for musical examples).

What is at stake in such musical dialogism? The practice can be viewed in terms of creating a metanarrative: quoting the riffs calls attention to them as belonging to other songs, thus commenting on the interconnectedness of various parts of the repertory or, to put it another way, on its openness or fluidity. It also foregrounds the centrality of the riff in Led Zeppelin's music (see chapter 4). The inventiveness and affective power of Zeppelin riffs is one of the most celebrated aspects of the band's music; recontextualizing them draws attention to this fact as well as to the potency (the virtuosity) of their inventors, Page and Jones, and lending weight, especially, to the already powerful figure of Page as guitar hero. More simply, it creates good theater by setting the audience up to expect one song and then delivering another. In some cases, this recontextualization of the band's music becomes fetishistic, as in the case of "Black Dog," which I will discuss in detail later.

The differences between the Yardbirds' recording of "Dazed and Confused" and the version on *Led Zeppelin* have most significantly to do with the singing, with groove, and with tempo. Yardbirds vocalist Keith Relf's phrasing is square, and his construction of the melodic line tends to reinforce each quarter beat; his tone is consistent and undistorted. He sings in a register that is clearly comfortable for him, with no strain, and with nothing to suggest that this is not the voice of a young white man.

With respect to groove, there are several points to consider. There is much greater subdivision of the 12/8 meter by Jim McCarthy, the Yardbirds drummer, which almost threatens to turn the piece into a relaxed shuffle. During the bow

Example 1.2. Led Zeppelin, "Dazed and Confused," end of the guitar solo

solo, the groove is kept very active by the bass player and drummer, who trade a pattern that consists of four sixteenths and an eighth note at the beginning of each beat. Relf joins in this rhythmic exchange playing the harmonica and tambourine. The rhythmic pattern and the *alternatum* performance come directly from Holmes's version. Relf also interjects other rhythmic/melodic gestures on harmonica over Page's solo. The ensuing complexity of the groove tends to mask the extraordinary sounds being created by Page, and it also keeps the solo too much within the frame of the rest of the song, instead of setting it apart, as happens in the Zeppelin studio version. While the $\frac{12}{8}$ meter is also maintained in the latter version, it is articulated in a less noisy way by Jones and Bonham, which allows Page to be more fully foregrounded. Instead of blues-oriented interjections on the harmonica, Plant uses his voice to spar with Page's bow sounds in a manner that removes the piece stylistically from the blues during this section. The greatest difference in groove, however, comes during Page's guitar solo, when in the Yardbirds' version the drummer moves into a Merseybeat. This pattern is strongly affiliated with a particular genre of pop song. It is partly what defines the Merseybeat style, including early Beatles, for example, not to say the girl-group recordings made in the United States from which the Liverpool groups took it. This makes its use seem stylistically dissonant here (i.e., much too carefree), in the midst of a free form, experimental guitar solo that leans in its seriousness toward the avant-garde as well as the psychedelic. Bonham's driving groove in the Zeppelin version is based on a pattern associated with much hard rock. He supplements this pattern with triplet figures on the first and third beats toward the end of the solo, adding intensity and forward motion to Page's solo.

In the Yardbirds' version, a smooth transition is made from the end of the bow solo into the beginning of the guitar solo, so that even though there is a change of meter, from $\frac{12}{8}$ to $\frac{4}{4}$, a similar tempo is maintained between the two meters. In the Zeppelin version, this differentiation is much more sharply drawn, the fast guitar solo being *very* fast (the eighth note of the previous section becomes the quarter note of this one, making the second solo twice as fast as the first), the $\frac{12}{8}$ sections being much slower than in the Yardbirds' version. Hence there is much greater drama, a much larger emotional soundscape vis-à-vis tempo, in the Zeppelin version.

This is true for other reasons as well. For example, there is no lyrical ambiguity in Zeppelin's studio version, which has turned Holmes's piece of psychedelia into an agonizing blues lament—a musical/textual language distinctly absent in Holmes's original. Holmes's lyrics were changed only superficially in the Yardbirds' version, but with Zeppelin the modifications were much greater, so that there can be no question as to their meaning. They follow a well-developed lyrical trope of the blues: the outpourings of a man under the spell of a woman who toys with his passion but whom he can't leave.[18] The third stanza is completely new (there are only two stanzas before the solo in Holmes's version) and is, perhaps, the one that most recalls the blues tradition. It is thought that the lyrics in

Zeppelin's version were written by Page, but they carry Plant's characteristic trademark of stringing together fragments of text from existing blues songs.[19] In live versions, Plant regularly improvised new lyrics for this song in the blues tradition. The version on *The Song Remains the Same*, for example, intensifies the man's attraction to the woman despite her alleged abuses. In the studio version the lyrics to this verse are:

> You hurt and abuse tellin' all of your lies
> Run 'round sweet baby, Lord how you hypnotize
> Sweet little baby I don't know where you been
> Gonna love you baby, here I come again.

But in *The Song Remains the Same*, the lyrics for this verse are changed to:

> Oh! You babble and talk, Lord, I swear that I been tryin'
> The way that you push push push push me baby, I can't take too much of
>   that.
> So come on, come on, come on, come on, show me the way
> I still wanna make love to you 25, 25 [hours a day, we presume]

In several live performances (*The Song Remains the Same*; Osaka, Japan, 1972; Aeolian Hall, London, 1969; *Classics off the Air*, BBC broadcast, 1969/1971), Plant sings "I try to quit you baby" instead of "I try to love you baby," in verse 3, which references, at least for this listener, the Willie Dixon blues that appears on Zeppelin's first album "I Can't Quit You Baby." The line "I gotta quit you" also appears in "Babe I'm Gonna Leave You" on the first album, demonstrating again Plant's technique of dipping into a stock of blues phrases in composing his lyrics. While I have not discovered further references to specific blues tunes in these lyrics, such borrowings are common in other Zeppelin songs, a characteristic for which the group has been severely criticized as well as sued for royalties, by bluesman Willie Dixon. While there can be no excuses made for denying black blues artists their fair share of royalties, Robert Palmer has written about this phenomenon in Led Zeppelin in a way that recovers it from merely being an action of capitalist greed. Palmer points out that ownership of blues songs was not an issue when they circulated in oral tradition, prior to the advent of recording; indeed, part of the tradition included the incorporation of new elements into existing songs, so that it was a matter of not simply *re*-creating but also creating at the same time. It was only when pieces were recorded that they became fixed and subsequently associated with, or claimed by, a certain artist.[20] Led Zeppelin's use of the blues falls almost completely into this tradition; there are only two instances in which they covered a blues song in its entirety (both on the first album). For the rest, either the lyrics and perhaps melody were used, but the riff changed (as in "Whole Lotta Love"), or fragments of lyrics taken from multiple sources were mixed with new lyrics and music ("How Many

More Times," "The Lemon Song," "Custard Pie"). Plant's often seeming lack of interest in the semantic content of the lyrics he is singing also plays into this kind of composition. In these cases, it is more important for him to experiment with melody and rhythm, dipping into the rich tradition of the blues for the actual words he uses, than to come up with an "original" lyric. As Jones told me concerning the compositional process of the band,

> Songs attributed to all four members were usually worked out in the studio in the "writing period" before recording began. This took place either in a rehearsal room or a rented house before recording equipment was brought in. These songs were often the result of a jam or somebody just experimenting whilst preparing to rehearse. The arrangement was worked out at the same time. Robert would sing along using lyrics from blues songs that he already knew in order to get a melody and/or phrasing and would then rewrite them later (or not!). There would also be partial or complete ideas that Page or myself would bring in to be worked on. Robert would always write lyrics and melody (if needed) last.

This process seems to confirm that creating the instrumental parts to the song, including the melody, was considerably more important than the lyrics—that in the first instance words were simply a means of creating the music (and given Jones's comment that Plant's improvised lyrics were sometimes not modified in the final version, it would seem that what he came up with initially was often considered good enough). It is also telling that lyrics were the last element to be added, so that if they were rewritten by Plant, they were molded to suit the music, not the other way around. This compositional process does not diminish the importance of the lyrics; it simply makes them important in a different way. For example, the repetition of words during the verse of "Dazed and Confused" quoted earlier occurs not only to intensify the emotion but also as complex rhythmic play, that is, for the sake of musical interest: we know the lyrical trope, have heard all about it before, know its source, and therefore can concentrate fully on what Plant does with it musically.

There is a very overt musical connection with the blues made as the beginning of the song merges with the previous piece on the studio album, Willie Dixon's twelve-bar blues "You Shook Me." Both pieces have E as their tonic and they share exactly the same slow tempo. Plant matches the power, vocal quality, and pitch of the vocal/guitar cadenza that ends "You Shook Me" with the opening verse of "Dazed and Confused" (ex. 1.3), establishing a direct connection to the blues. Plant sings in the tradition of the blues shouter, more exaggerated than those he claims as his models, for example, Robert Johnson, Muddy Waters, and even Howlin' Wolf: Plant's style is mannered in comparison with theirs. He sings an octave higher than Holmes. His phrasing is spastic, irregular, "confused"—he doesn't wait until the beginning of the riff to enter, as Holmes does, but comes in on the ninth eighth note of a measure of $^{12}_8$. The corporeality

Example 1.3. Cadenza, end of "You Shook Me," beginning of "Dazed and Confused"

of Plant's voice is overwhelming. It is loud and right up front in the mix, with only a bit of echo on it, so that we can hear his consonants exploding into the mic and the phlegm in his throat that helps produce his distorted tone. The pronounced nasal quality of his voice also gives the body that produces these sounds immediacy, presence. Jimmy Page once characterized this voice as sounding like "a primeval wail," connecting it to the remote past, and the body, as an instinctual, prelinguistic utterance.[21]

In contrast to Holmes's recording, Zeppelin's studio version is marked by the polarities characteristic of the band's sound: the riff is played by bass, doubled an octave higher by guitar and two octaves above that by a second guitar track. Each of these is marked by a timbre that is expressively distinct from the other. The raw sound of the guitar doubling an octave above the bass is contrasted with that of the bass guitar, which uses no distortion, note bending, or other effects but has an almost muffled sound; both of these are contrasted with the synthetic quality of the highest guitar doubling, which sounds completely unlike the "normal" timbres of this instrument. Using different timbres again, including the effects of echo and wah-wah pedal, the guitar also punctuates the cadences of the riff, exploiting different registers of the instrument. These extremes of range, timbre, and the distortion and volume of Plant's voice are certainly symbols of great power.[22] They also create a vast and open musical space, the boundaries of which mark the outer limits of what it is physically possible to achieve with these instruments. The openness of this texture, its bigness, marks it as capable of embracing an enormous expanse of musical experience, while the musicians' desire to work at the boundaries of this large space makes it seem too small to encompass their experience. The openness of the texture parallels the open formal structure of the piece, both technical features serving as possible metaphors for countercultural values of transgression and an openness toward the experience that leads to self-knowledge. Use of the blues here helps deepen the experience, since for the rock musician who was part of the blues revival this was the quintessential authentic music.

As noted earlier, during the first improvisatory section that follows this opening, Page plays the electric guitar using a violin bow. The bow solo will be discussed in detail later, but here it is important to identify the object itself—the violin bow—as intertextual. It acts as a powerful symbol borrowed from the tradition of "classical" Western music, so its presence in the context of a blues-based four-piece rock band is disruptive, more so since it is not being used in an orchestral string section or other ensemble that is part of the arrangement of the piece (the way other rock or pop musicians have used strings) but by the soloist, which gives the object centrality. Page's use of the bow to play his electric guitar connects him not only with progressive rock but also with the avant-garde. He was determined that his use of the bow not be considered a gimmick, but that it be taken seriously as a means for the creation of new sounds.[23] His use of the theremin, which he sometimes employed in live versions of "Dazed and Confused" but more often in other works, such as "Whole Lotta Love," also connects him to the experimental art music tradition. And this is where another layer of analysis comes into play in locating this music culturally. Page was in many respects a quintessential countercultural figure. He came from the bourgeoisie and rejected the values of that class to embrace an alternative lifestyle. But he also went to art school—albeit briefly—and had aspirations of becoming "a fine art painter."[24] He socialized and made music with others who participated in this culture, so important to the ideological development of British rock, as Peter Wicke (and Simon Frith before him) has pointed out.[25]

The mentality of the art school student–cum–rock artist in the 1960s was derived from the nineteenth-century tradition of Bohemian individualism and of the artist as aesthete and struggling genius. "The art school experience," Wicke says, "above all provided rock musicians with the basis of their consciousness of themselves as musicians in artistic and ideological terms."[26] And according to Frith, "Art school ideology casts the self-love of the aesthete and the avant-gardist's sensitivity to the power of form into one style. In this ideology art, in its relation to the individual, is a matter of individuality, of a turning inward, of an obsession."[27] This and other characteristics of the British art school phenomenon are not far removed from countercultural values, for as Paul Willis observes, "[T]he hippies were exploring and broadening a middle-class tradition of the Bohemian intelligentsia—especially as drawn into the lumpen or déclassé urban milieu."[28] One real difference between the two, however, is the art school idea of artist as struggling genius, a role that Page played well. The bow solo in "Dazed and Confused" is a fine representation of this image: the artist experimenting, creating, inventing using unconventional means, as if in a laboratory, right before the audience's eyes and ears. He applies the bow to the guitar as if it is a surgical instrument, raising his right arm, bent at the elbow, in order to place the tip of the bow, carefully, on the uppermost guitar string (see fig. 7). The visual image suggests that great concentration and physical strain are required to produce the sounds in the same way that "difficulty" and "concentration" are enacted by classical musicians in performance. Page's use of the theremin has a similar effect. These sound experiments coincide with those that have been made in "experimental," "avant-garde," and electronic music in the art music tradition. Unfortunately, for reasons that probably have most to do with the pigeonholing of Led Zeppelin negatively as the progenitors of heavy metal, Page's experimentations were taken less seriously than similar attempts made by others—John Cale's in the Velvet Underground, for example. It is lamentable, in fact, that despite his extensive and inventive use of the theremin, Page is rarely, if ever, mentioned in discussions of the instrument.[29] Recovering his sonic experimentations from the realm of dabblings to serious attempts at broadening available sound possibilities is important, and it creates a further intertextual link between Page and the avant-garde.

When Bonham and Jones dropped out just prior to the bow solo, Page and Plant were left to make a sonic journey uninhibited by a steady tempo, meter, or tonality. Intertextual references abounded in this section. In *The Song Remains the Same* and the Earl's Court, London, performance from 1975, Plant sings some of the lyrics from Scott Mackenzie's "San Francisco (Be Sure to Wear Flowers in Your Hair)" (ex. 1.4) and from the Joni Mitchell song "Woodstock," respectively. In both cases, the lyrics are recontextualized into the same musical frame: a slow, balladlike groove, in which Page plays gentle arpeggiations while Plant sings as if in a dreamlike state. This is achieved musically through the invocation of lyrics stripped of their original melodies, sung almost in the style of recitative, and through a change of mode, evoking a melancholy, yearning affect. In the case of "San Francisco," the mode has been changed from Mixolydian to Aeolian, and Plant confines himself to the narrow melodic range of a fifth. One of the most striking differences between the melody Plant sings and that of the original is the first interval: instead of the bright leap of a major sixth, Plant sings a minor third. The lyrics have transported him to a different time and place, both recalling the same utopia: that of the counterculture, as represented by the two powerful symbols of San Francisco and Woodstock. In the Earl's Court performance there is also another intertextual reference, this one purely musical: one of Plant's vocalizations draws on the techniques of classical Indian singing (ex. 1.5), which, together with Egyptian and Moroccan music, became an increasingly more significant influence on Jones, Page, and Plant, (see chapter 3). The "Dazed" guitar solo itself in the 1977 performances begins with heavily distorted guitar, out of which eventually develops a rendition of "The Star-Spangled Banner"—a clear reference (perhaps homage) to Jimi Hen-

Example 1.4. Scott Mackenzie "San Francisco," as heard in "Dazed and Confused" on *The Song Remains the Same*

drix, who performed the anthem in this way at Woodstock—making yet another allusion to that hallowed era.

Beginning in 1977, the bow solo and a few elements of the guitar solo were extracted from "Dazed and Confused" and performed on their own, without any overt reference to the song, although for many audience members the association was strongly present, not only because "Dazed and Confused" was, after the first few tours, the only piece in which Page used the bow but also because some of the musical materials of the solo became fixed and were recognizable as belonging to it. At the Knebworth performances, for example, there were enormous cheers from the audience when Page began to play the central and very recognizable motive that he developed for that solo (see later). This solo was, then, recontextualized, set into a different frame from that provided by the tune. On the 1977 tour, of which I take two widely known performances, found on the bootleg albums *Destroyer* and *Listen to This Eddie*, the "Dazed" solo emerged out of the acoustic instrumental piece "White Summer/Black Mountain Side" and merged, at the end, with "Achilles Last Stand." In the Knebworth performances of 1979, the solo came after "Achilles" and merged with "In the Evening." In both instances, the "Dazed" solo can be viewed, retrospectively, as an extended prelude or introduction to the piece that follows it, but this is an especially strong association or link for the latter example. The reason for this is that the studio version of "In the Evening" begins with an introductory passage that is metrically free and uses atmospheric electronic sounds; in fact, at the Knebworth performance the "Dazed" solo ends with the same flanged drum lick that Bonham plays at the end of the introduction to "In the Evening." This introduction is also the only time aside from the first album (specifically "Dazed and Confused" and "How Many More Times") that Page uses the violin bow in the studio, so the connection to the bow solo from "Dazed" is very strong.

Self-reference such as this occurs earlier in Zeppelin's performances. For example, there is an extended portion of "The Crunge" that appears, without lyrics, in the "Dazed" guitar solo of the Osaka, Japan, performance on October 4, 1972; by the time of the Osaka performance, "The Crunge" had been recorded for the album *Houses of the Holy*, which was released the following

Example 1.4. (*continued*)

spring, so the tune already existed as an entity unto itself at the time of the reference made to it in Osaka.[30] Early on, the band had its own firmly established musical and extramusical traditions, its own signatures and symbols, which could be engaged in play. This kind of intertextual reference worked partly to further promote the mythology that grew up around the band.[31]

Consider the powerful visual intertextuality in the film vignette from *The Song Remains the Same*. The hermit figure that appears in this vignette is the hermit of the tarot cards, the archetypal wise man/woman figure, who carries a lamp to light the path to self-knowledge. The figure, in the same pose, graces the inner sleeve of the band's fourth album cover. The appearance of the figure is symbolically loaded because the fourth album, which contains the group's most popular and enduring epic, "Stairway to Heaven," has been received by many fans as a profound, indeed religious, musical statement. The hermit also references Page's well-known personal interest in the esoteric—he was a student of Aleister Crowley's thought and was known to have other interests in the occult. The conflation of Page's identity with that of the hermit in this vignette not only represents a quest for self-knowledge that takes Page into both his past and his future but also suggests him as supernatural, an appropriate extension of the powerful figure he cuts as a guitar hero. A further connection is made at the end of the sequence, in which the animated version of the hermit waves a multicolored wand in a semicircle over his head; when the viewer is returned to the concert footage and the end of the bow solo, Page makes this same gesture with his violin bow. During the "Dazed" bow solo at the Knebworth concerts in 1979, Page was alone on a dark stage; only the bow was lit, appearing as a phosphorescent beam of light. As a review of the show in *Variety* magazine described it, "[T]he bow was laser-lit along its length and this appeared red; and carried another laser in the tip which shot a pencil-thin green beam over the crowd when Page waved the bow in the air."[32] This image is magical enough on its own, partly owing to the dazzling effects possible through the new laser technology, but to anyone who knows *The Song Remains the Same* it evokes Page's film vignette and his connection with the hermit. This is, then, a powerful—one might say mythological—web of references.

The musicians have continued to make both lyrical and musical references to Led Zeppelin in their recent work. Plant admitted several years ago that after

Heavy Vibrato

Example 1.5. Plant's Indian-influenced vocal melisma in the Earl's Court, 1975, performance of "Dazed and Confused"

trying to detach himself from Led Zeppelin in order to shape a solo career that did not appear to be drawing on that legacy, he finally felt himself able to return to it.[33] But for what purpose? Given what Plant has said in interviews about this return, it is clear that it was a liberating experience for him to make reference to the past, the weight of Zeppelin's tradition and success being lifted in the act of embracing, rather than denying, it. The most overt of these references has been the medley of Zeppelin samples that appears at the end of "Tall Cool One" on the *Now and Zen* album. The medley comes at the end of the song, bombarding the listener with some of Led Zeppelin's most characteristic riffs: "Custard Pie," "Whole Lotta Love," "The Ocean," and a few of Plant's signature lyrics that identify a song immediately (most prominently "hey, hey mama" from "Black Dog" and "Goin' down" from "When the Levee Breaks"). These samples overlap and repeat, breaking into the chorus of the song and rupturing its texture. Backup singers interject with the only line of the chorus, "Lighten up baby I'm in love with you," which has shifted it semantically from a reference to the girl subject of the first part of the song to Plant's past. Plant satirizes both himself and the millions of fans who hold Led Zeppelin's music as something sacred when he ends the piece with a contracted and heavily distorted statement of this line: "Lighten up." The song also contains a sampled guitar lick from the chorus of "Whole Lotta Love," the descending riff (the one Page created using a metal slide and backward echo[34]), that cuts through the texture after every iteration of this line. It also contains a new guitar solo by Jimmy Page. The album cover is a veritable homage to Zeppelin. Plant's feather symbol (each member of Led Zeppelin was represented by a symbol that appeared on the inner sleeve of the fourth album) appears on the front, along with a new symbol (a wolf) that Plant adopted for this and subsequent album covers (it appears on the *Manic Nirvana* and *Fate of Nations* album covers as well), continuing the cryptic self-representation begun in Led Zeppelin. Page's *Zoso* symbol appears next to the songs on which he solos (this symbol can be seen prominently displayed on one of Page's amplifiers in the photograph of the band that appears on the cover of this book and in fig. 11). I suspect, also, that the red flag on the front of the cover of the album is meant to allude to the flag on the boat Plant sails in his fantasy sequence in the film *The Song Remains the Same*.

A central role in this post-Zeppelin matrix of self-allusion has been played by the song "Black Dog," the trademark riff of which was written by Jones. On

Plant's album *Manic Nirvana* two lines from the song appear in the midst of his cover of "Your Ma Said You Cried in Your Sleep Last Night." "Black Dog" was the song Page and Plant performed at the American Music Awards in 1995—a significant event because it marked the eve of their first tour together in 15 years—and it is "Black Dog" that emerges at the end of the *No Quarter* version of "Kashmir." According to Deena Weinstein, "Black Dog" is "one of the most instantly recognizable Zepp[elin] tracks." In her "Listener's Guide to Heavy Metal" Weinstein singles out "Black Dog" as *the* representative piece by Led Zeppelin (not "Stairway to Heaven").[35] The song represents a defining moment in the genre of hard rock, combining the elements of speed, power, an artful and metrically clever riff (one of the most important characteristics of the tune), Plant's high range fully exposed, and a virtuosic display of Page's technical ability in the guitar solo with which the piece ends. The words—boastful, lustful, at some moments sexist—represent a dominant strand of hard rock/heavy metal lyrics.

What happens, then, when *this* particular piece is referenced in the way that it has been by Page and Plant? In "Your Ma Said You Cried," the excerpt from "Black Dog" appears within the context of a slow shuffle groove and melodic/poetic structure that is reminiscent of a children's nursery rhyme. This is reinforced by the stark simplicity of the guitar line that is played (ex. 1.6; heavily influenced by Randy Newman's "Simon Smith and His Amazing Dancing Bear"[36]). The words to the song belie its pop (as opposed to rock) origins:

Your ma said you cried in your sleep last night
Your ma said you cried in your sleep last night
You shoulda seen the look in her eyes
You know I haven't been so true to you [and so forth]

The protagonist in these lyrics is apologetic and penitent. The quotation from "Black Dog" ruptures the poetic and musical structure of the song, shifting from three lines of text, the first two of which are the same, to two different lines of text:

Hey hey mama said the way you move,
gonna make you sweat gonna make you groove.

Plant caps these lyrics with the phrase "'cause I love you." The lines are sung in a subdued tone in keeping with the character of the rest of the piece but in complete opposition to the crude sensibility of Zeppelin's "Black Dog," even though we get the music, as well as the lyric, from the latter.

At the American Music Awards, "Black Dog" was performed *without* the characteristic riff. Instead, a much simpler riff was substituted, consisting only of two straight eighth notes on a bVII chord performed on beat 4, leading to I on the downbeat of the measure and staying there for three beats, with none of

Example 1.6. Guitar line in "Your Ma Said You Cried in Your Sleep Last Night"

the pyrotechnics of the original melody or unaligned rhythm that so defines the original (ex. 1.7). A drone on the tonic was created using two didgeridoos.

The reference to "Black Dog" in the *No Quarter* version of "Kashmir" is the most disarming of these three examples. Before the release of Page and Plant's *No Quarter* album in 1994, I thought I had established that there were two kinds of "epic" musical texts for Led Zeppelin: those that were open, fluid, and intertextual, changing from performance to performance, and those that were closed, that is, that were consistently performed in a manner close to that of the studio version (see chapter 2). "Kashmir" certainly seemed to fit into the latter category. But in the *No Quarter* version of "Kashmir" the band goes into a jam at the end of the song, and what emerges is the third section of "Black Dog" ("hey baby, pretty baby . . . "), complete with music and lyrics. This reference occurs during the climactic moment of "Kashmir": the ascending scale passage that ends with Plant singing, "I can take you there." Two things are particularly startling about this reference to "Black Dog." First, the jam comes at the end of a long piece, which has been formally intact up to this point (with the exception of an extended violin solo that does not harm the integrity of the piece). Exploding the piece formally right at its end is a violent musical gesture that drastically upsets its balance. Second, for about ten minutes the listener has been wrapped in the aesthetic world of "Kashmir," with its Arabic musical stylings and lyrics in celebration of Eastern sensibility (see chapter 3). Injecting "Black Dog" into this musical landscape constitutes a kind of blasphemy—nothing could be further removed musically and lyrically.

All three of these examples bespeak a liberation from any commitment to textual integrity by this group, not to mention a sense of humor and self-parody that fans of the band's music know well but is rarely understood or acknowledged by critics. In the two examples given in which "Black Dog" interrupts another song, the reference is highly incongruous; one might call it flippant or cheeky. In the American Music Awards performance of "Black Dog," adding didgeridoos is another incongruous act and changing the riff—doing away with that part of the song that has been most celebrated as a unique contribution to complexity in rock music—acts to severely undermine the opinion of those who think such things to be of importance. Commenting on the practice of radically changing a piece, Plant has said, "You've got to get the chain saw and cut the song in places and pleat it to make it bleed."[37] As it turns out, not even "Stairway to Heaven" was exempt from this treatment: Plant has reported that in rehearsals the band did "reggae versions" of the tune, not in order to "send the

Guitar

(Bass Guitar doubles one octave below)

Example 1.7. "Black Dog" riff As It Was Played on the American Music Awards 1995
(for the original riff, see chapter 4, ex. 4.5)

thing up—it was just like, here's another way of doing it."[38] This in order to keep
the piece fresh, for both the performers and the audience.

In an oblique way, the manner in which "Black Dog" has been reused can be
likened to sampling, with interesting semiotic implications. Tricia Rose has
argued that sampling locates "'past' sounds in the 'present,'" and Paul Théberge
extrapolates from this that there is, in fact, "a kind of ritual transferral of power
operating . . . where a person takes technical control of sounds that have, in the
past, exerted a certain powerful effect on the individual or on the community."[39] But whereas in rap music sampled sounds have usually been produced
by people other than the artist who is using them, thus creating real dialogism
as well as a transferal of power, in the case of Zeppelin it is monologic: while the
recontextualization of the riff does recall if not necessarily a more distant past
than the song to which it attaches, then at least a differently powerful sonic
experience, it is still a piece of the larger Zeppelin pie, so to speak. Recalling the
riff to "Black Dog" in particular points to the "hardest" rock, or "proto-metal"
side of Zeppelin, inserting a reminder of their power and masculine prowess. So
many references to this song, however, tend to fetishize this particular aspect of
the band. This creates an interesting contradiction, since for the band and fans
alike the moniker of "heavy metal," as indicated earlier, is undesirable.

On Page and Plant's 1995 tour, it was either the Coverdale/Page tune "Shake
My Tree" or Plant's "Calling to You" that was opened up to improvisation and
intertextual reference in the way that "Dazed and Confused" had been during
the Zeppelin days: in this instance, a bit of the beginning of "Dazed and Confused" was relegated to making an appearance "internally," that is, within the
improvisation, as opposed to serving as the frame for improvisation, and was
clearly referenced for the sake of nostalgia.

Spirituality/Ritual

As Jim DeRogatis points out, psychedelic rock "is rock that is inspired by a
philosophical approach implied by the literal meaning of 'psychedelic' as
'mind-revealing' and 'soul-manifesting.'"[40] Members of the counterculture
were "massively concerned with the possibility of transcendence and with fuller
states of awareness."[41] Music served as a powerful means to this end: "Psychedelic rock is open to spirituality, whether it's in the form of Eastern religions,

nature worship, or Christianity."[42] Peter Wicke has said that "rock musicians' self-perception was dominated by the idea that music was the direct result of their particular individual subjectivity and emotions, a creative baring of man's [sic] inner psychic forces, or their belief that liberating these forces also freed man [sic] from the distortions and frustrations which the constraints of everyday life left behind them."[43]

The importance of this view of music is in the *idea* of its spiritual possibilities, the depth of spiritual experience that was thought possible through listening to or making music, its capacity for profound meaning. In this respect, the aesthetic of some progressive rock musicians and their audience is not unlike that prevalent strain of nineteenth-century thought in which music was considered as a substitute for religious experience. In trying to decode this experience it is easy to trivialize it or to interpret it too narrowly. Sheila Whiteley, for example, while acknowledging the relationship between characteristics of progressive rock and "the hippies' emphasis on timeless mysticism,"[44] chooses to locate the meaning of acoustic phenomena primarily in their correspondence with drug use.[45] Allan Moore makes the useful observation that in progressive rock there is "an implicit, but nonetheless strong, ideology which is gnostic in nature,"[46] a gnostic faith being one "based on beliefs that salvation is gained by knowledge rather than by faith or by works or some other means."[47] Instead of allowing some free play of this idea, however, Moore confines himself immediately on two fronts. First, he says that gnostic ideology is the "*single* element [that] can be held to underpin British progressive rock" (emphasis mine),[48] and, second, he locates this gnosticism exclusively in the genre's use of fantasy.[49]

All of these ideas—liberation of psychic forces, the association of drug use with musical structures and sounds, gnosticism, fantasy—can be brought to bear on an analysis of what I would call the spiritual/ritual aspect of "Dazed and Confused." Robert Walser's discussion of the transcendent aspects of heavy metal music can also be brought into play. Since he is talking about music that came long after the counterculture had faded away, he does not link it to that movement but rather to a disenfranchised youth's quest for power and control.[50] For this analysis I wish to focus mostly on Page and the solo portions of "Dazed and Confused," especially as they came to be shaped in live performance, since so much of the transcendent quality of this piece lay in the sounds and the way in which Page shaped them, in his visual image, and in his way of communicating with the audience during this solo.

It is important to account for the *kinds* of sounds that Page chose and the way in which he made them, since it is in these particular sounds that meaning is partly located. In the studio version and early live performances, the bow solo was not extensive; it increased in length as Page's explorations became more sophisticated and interesting enough to sustain a long solo. The studio version is carefully shaped to begin simply, gradually unfolding and building toward a climactic moment. It begins with the least complex sounds and the repetition of a single interval (a descending minor third from g down to the tonic e). These (reasonably) pure tones become increasingly sustained, and finally a small turn motive develops out of the single interval. Eventually Page abandons melody for distorted washes of sound that include the use of the wah-wah pedal as well as the bow. At the height of this, he relinquishes the bow and the fast guitar solo begins. A dramatic visual gesture sometimes accompanied this transition, as in the *Supershow* video from 1969, in which Page holds the bow above his head and then opens his hand to release it, letting it drop to the floor behind him, signifying abandonment.

There are two important kinds of sounds produced in this solo: those that are quite sustained and legato, during which one pitch may mutate into several others, both higher and lower than the first (this sometimes sounds like feedback); and those that do not make use of discrete pitches but consist of highly distorted walls of "thick" sound that slide up and down. Although there is a general movement from simpler to complex sounds, these sounds enter into the texture and slip away again without much respect for beat or meter. They are all made to sound richer through the use of echo and also through Page's placement of the mics in the recording studio. Page and others in the group were keenly interested in "room ambience," which was created by placing the microphones at various distances from the amplifiers and instruments. In "Dazed and Confused" the mics were placed at a considerable distance from the amps—in Page's words, "distance makes depth."[51] Jones nuanced this in his correspondence with me, saying that "ambient/distant mics [were] used mainly on guitar solos and drums to give more depth." The foreign quality of the sounds made, their constant mutation and their distance from the listener connect with the psychedelic, since they take the listener away from common (musical) experience into new sonic territory, which, as DeRogatis has commented, helps to "shak[e] off emotional and intellectual repression."[52]

The studio version of the solo was not reproduced in live performance. Part of the point was to experiment with and develop the sound possibilities, not to reproduce what was on the album. But despite this aesthetic, some of the elements of the bow solo became reasonably set in performance. What I would call a mature version of the bow solo appears on *The Song Remains the Same* and is replicated on other live recordings from 1972–1973 and 1975. It begins with Page drawing the bow across the strings using slow and legato motions at first, creating sustained pitches, beginning in a low range, and getting increasingly higher, with a filling in and extending of the descending minor third motive of the studio version (g–f♯–e; g–f♯–e–c; a–f♯–e; b–f♯–e, and so forth.). Signaled by the use of tremolo and harmonics, another motive of more central importance emerges that consists of four pitches, a–g–d–e (ex. 1.8). He does not use this motive on the studio version of the tune, but it was part of the live solo from very early on, appearing already in bootleg recordings from 1969.[53] For a substantial portion of the solo, this motive served as the unchanging pitch background for Page's timbral experiments. The climactic use of the motive oc-curred when Page struck the bow against the strings of the guitar to create a power chord, leaving a lengthy silence in between each iteration.

Because this motive became set in performance, it came to act as a symbol, with a ritual significance in its own right. In the video *The Song Remains the Same*, the way in which Page performs this portion of the solo makes it unmis-takably ritualistic. He hits the guitar strings with the bow and then extends it out to his audience, moving around in a circle as he does so, as if he intends to deliver—or to share—the power of the music directly, physically, with his fol-lowers. An analogy could be drawn between this act and the sprinkling of holy water by a priest. There is at least one other example of a similar gesture made by Page without using the bow, and that is in the performance of "Nobody's Fault but Mine" in the August 11, 1979, concert at Knebworth. In that perform-ance, after each reiteration of the main riff, during the pause, he holds up his right arm and, moving from right to left, appears to sprinkle the audience gen-tly with bits of sound. One could draw on Moore's concept of progressive rock as gnostic here, viewing Page as the knower, a spiritual guide to his audience. William Burroughs made a similar observation after watching Led Zeppelin in concert in 1975, although he did not mention the bow solo in particular: "A rock concert is in fact a rite involving the evocation and transmutation of energy. Rock stars may be compared to priests."[54] He likened Led Zeppelin's music to what he called the "trance music" of Morocco, "which is magical in ori-gin and purpose—that is, concerned with the evocation and control of spiritual forces."[55] Although it hardly lasts long enough to induce trance, the circling and pointing gesture is repeated by Page, the musical reiteration of the motive get-ting increasingly faster and finally melting away into a frenzied wash of sound, its cathartic quality being expressed physically by Page in his backward-bent frame (see figure 12, which shows both his gesture of pointing the bow out to the audience after playing the central motive and his bent back torso).

Page's use of the bow can certainly have many meanings. As noted previously, it links him to the tradition of classical Western music, perhaps invoking the particular "seriousness" or "weightiness" of music written for the violin. In addition, based on Page's comments about his use of the bow (that it is not a gimmick, that one can employ the bow using traditional bowing techniques) Steve Waksman argues that the bow displays Page's "recourse to a language of proper [i.e., classical] musical technique and that this demonstrates his interest in virtuosity; hence the bow can be viewed as a symbol of this quest for virtuos-ity."[56] It can also be read as a phallic symbol, thus strengthening Page's powerful masculine "guitar hero" musical personality. But Page makes it clear in the way he wields the bow (pointing it out to the audience, waving it over his head) that he also intends it to be viewed as a magic wand. This connection is made clear when Page gives the animated hermit in his film vignette a magic wand that he waves over his head, mimicking the gesture that Page makes during his solo. Lighting up the bow and nothing else during the Knebworth shows refers back

Example 1.8. The central motive from Page's bow solo

to the hermit and his multicolored magic wand, forging another clear connection among Page, the hermit, and the bow as magic wand (to say nothing of the implication of technology as "magic"). In terms of cutting a powerful "magical" guitar hero figure, Page's use of the violin bow was a particularly potent symbol. Yardbirds singer Keith Relf understood this when he referred to Page as the "grand sorcerer of the magic guitar."[57]

The bow is not only a visual symbol for magic; it is also sonically magical, since it drastically transforms the sound of the guitar, taking it out of the realm of what is characteristically possible with the instrument and allowing Page to take an extraordinary musical journey. The sounds that Page chooses to make using this device strengthen the idea that he is creating musical magic in many ways. The sustained tones are an illusion, since even though Page may draw the bow across the strings in a single motion, the pitch is constantly metamorphosing, never stable for a moment, even as his image (and hence his identity) metamorphoses in the film vignette. The use of tremolo and wah-wah further destabilizes the pitch. The way in which the solo grows from simple to complex timbres, from small motives to larger pitch gestures, suggests that Page is conjuring the sounds, coaxing them out of the instrument. Some of the sounds mimic, in a detached and surrealistic way, the agonized groans of a human being, a comparison that is strengthened whenever Plant imitates them, as if he is being pulled into their power.

Paul Willis has made several observations about countercultural spirituality that would have made this musical experience pertinent to that culture. The "now," he says, was more important to adherents of the counterculture than past or future. It contained the "maximum spiritual suggestiveness," since "the precautious promise of the moment kept all the possibilities of consciousness open." "Past or present did not have the same sense of being 'in medias res.'"[58] DeRogatis makes a similar point concerning the importance of the present to psychedelic culture.[59] Even though this music requires patience and close, attentive listening for long stretches of time, there were many who were willing to give themselves over to it, to experience the "now" of the music, and plenty of fans still are—most who commented on the piece on the fan survey expressed their awe at the sonic experimentations and the length of the piece in live shows:

Dazed and Confused is an awesome song. The guitar solos and bass solo in the beginning were excellent. The way Jimmy played the solo in the middle was astonishing!! A great song all together.

Only a few were of the mind that the piece is "too long, with too unbalanced a ratio of noise to music." It was probably because this patience on the part of the audience waned in the late 1970s that the band decided not to perform "Dazed and Confused" during their final tour in 1980. An audience steeped in the punk sensibility was not interested in getting lost in a meandering bow/guitar solo that might go on for half an hour.[60]

Page's bow solo is a particularly rich example of this present-tense listening experience, for in live performance there was no strict meter kept, no rhythm section playing along with Page, and therefore he was not bound to any particular temporal unfolding of the solo. Meter and rhythm (that is, time itself) were virtually suspended. Pitch, too, was indefinite. This is a very different kind of extended improvisation from, say, those of the Grateful Dead, which were also certainly lengthy but grew more logically out of the tune by which they were framed, adhering to the same tempo, meter, and tonality.[61]

The second part of Page's guitar solo (the "fast" solo) brings the piece to a climax. In live performance, this solo was marked by juxtapositions of a wide variety of musical styles—from funk to folk, blues, and rock—with no transition from one to the other. Page loves to try on one musical idea, explore it for a moment, and then abandon it for another, without an intervening transition. A perhaps less violent manifestation of this stylistic juxtaposition is a hallmark of several Led Zeppelin songs, the earliest being "Babe I'm Gonna Leave You" on the first album, which alternates between acoustic and electric sections. Many comments have been made about this juxtaposition, some, significantly, from Page himself, who has said that it was his intention from the beginning to include elements of "light and shade" in the music.[62] In his commentary on "Stairway to Heaven," Robert Walser has interpreted this phenomenon as peculiarly postmodern in that "the narrative juxtaposition of the sensitive (acoustic guitar, etc.) and the aggressive (distorted guitar, etc.) . . . combines contradictory sensibilities without reconciling them."[63] Speaking about later music, such as that of Metallica, Megadeth, and other thrash metal bands, he says that "their songs are formally even more complex, filled with abrupt changes of meter and tempo that model a complex, disjointed world,"[64] but this applies equally well to live performances of Zeppelin's "Dazed and Confused," as well as live versions of "No Quarter," in which it was Jones's turn for an extended acoustic piano solo. In the August 11, 1979, Knebworth performance of this piece Jones's solo occupies only five minutes, but he moves through various musical styles, focusing especially on a jazz style reminiscent of someone like Bill Evans but also adding classical touches and, at the end of Page's solo, a long flourish that draws on a more avant-garde jazz style, playing outside the key and making dramatic shifts in range that utilize the entire keyboard. Paul Willis offers another analysis of this phenomenon that ties it to the counterculture: "[T]he elements of surprise, contradiction and uncertainty in their music—the elements which made it almost threatening to the 'straight' listener—were precisely the elements that were prized by the hippies. They *wanted* conventional meaning to be undercut, *wanted* to be surprised and made uncertain."[65] This is precisely why, in Willis's opinion, pop music was considered to be so vacuous: it was too predictable, contained "too little content."[66]

The whole progression through Page's solos in this piece, then, can be viewed as a journey or quest that begins slowly, cautiously, and ultimately leads to transcendence that comes when Page finally abandons himself to a sustained and virtuosic "fast" solo.[67] Peter Wicke has characterized the "spiritual" element in progressive rock in a way that seems especially appropriate to apply to Zeppelin's "Dazed and Confused": it is "the search for new possibilities of releasing creativity and penetrating to the innermost levels of consciousness and the depths of the unconscious."[68] Robert Plant put it more directly: he saw Led Zeppelin as chroniclers of a "journey, the fact that there are pitfalls and there are trials and tribulations and elations and the end should never ever be in sight."[69]

Gender/Sexuality

There is an extended discussion of issues around gender and sexuality in Led Zeppelin in chapter 5; here I wish to focus specifically on Robert Plant's singing, his onstage relationship with Page, especially during performances of "Dazed and Confused," and the structural characteristics of that piece (especially the studio version) that lend themselves to a gendered reading.

On numerous occasions, Plant has himself characterized his approach to music making in terms that stress the emotional vulnerability that lies at the heart of his singing. He has said that his interest is in "music that I could really bring from my soul and my body to express myself,"[70] which he contrasted with the (in his opinion) shallow pop music he had been singing early in his career (the singles he made for CBS Records in 1966–1967 are perfect examples of this). He has also said that "the wonder of music is that I want to be transported by it. I want something else to think about. I want to be wooed by music. I want something not expensive and not too obstructive. I just want to be taken someplace and dealt with beautifully; and I want to do that too. I want to make music that is sensual and sensuous."[71]

In trying to explain how Plant achieves this, it might be useful to make a comparison with another rock vocalist, Paul Rodgers. Page worked with Rodgers in the mid-1980s and made his own comparison between the vocalist and Plant, one that is useful to this discussion. Page commented that Plant was a "vocal gymnast" and that Rodgers was much more controlled and precise in his shaping of a melodic line.[72] He also commented that this penchant for precision led Rodgers to sing a tune in exactly the same way every time, whereas Plant would always change things, giving in to the expressive mood of the moment.[73] I would describe the difference between the two singers using Roland Barthes's terms: to me, Plant's voice has a "grain," while I don't think Rodgers's does.[74] "The 'grain,'" says Barthes, "is the body in the voice as it sings."[75]

Something is there, manifest and stubborn . . . beyond (or before) the meaning of the words, their form . . . the melisma, and even the style of execution: something which is directly the cantor's body, brought to your ears in one and the same movement from deep down in the cavities, the muscles, the membranes, the cartilages . . . as though a single skin lined the inner flesh of the performer and the music he sings.[76]

In my description of Plant's singing at the beginning of the studio version of "Dazed and Confused" I tried to characterize something of the *literal* grain of his voice, if you will: the high range, phrasing that stays away from the beat and was regularly changed in performance, the disjunction of the melodic line (less extreme in this case than in others), the intensity and volume, the distortion that allows us to hear and feel his body. Especially in live performances, Plant utilized a wide dynamic and expressive range especially in "Dazed and Confused." In the *Song Remains the Same* version, for example, his vocal begins in a completely opposite manner from the studio version, subdued, lazy, quiet, matching the expressive quality of the bass guitar, some of the features of his singing resembling the scat singing of jazz. Deena Weinstein's generalization that "[in heavy metal singing] as in other features of the genre, softness, irony and subtlety are excluded"[77] simply does not hold true, especially when examining a singer such as Plant.

It is not, however, these characteristics per se that create the grain. It is, rather, that Plant's emotional core is held out to the listener through his voice. While he may assert his control visually, as many of those who have written about "cock rockers" suggest they do, musically he often teeters on the brink of being purposefully out of control. He achieves this not only through the characteristics described earlier but also by his use of dissonance, including sometimes singing outside the key, and through his ornate style of singing. On the studio version of "Dazed and Confused," at the beginning of the last verse after the guitar solo, on the words "Been dazed and confused for so long it's not true," he sings "out"— that is, instead of ending the first phrase (on the word "true") with the expected descending pitches g–e, he almost (but not quite) makes them g♯ and f, against the prevailing E Aeolian modality (he has also sung the first part of this line completely on one pitch, the fifth scale degree, instead of following the shape of the melody as heard the first time these words were sung, creating more tension). There are many examples in which Plant uses dissonance for expressive effect. For example, at the end of "D'yer Mak'er," over the harmonic progression I–vi–IV–V in C major, he sings a sustained and piercing b♭, which is resolved not at the tonic, when the progression is repeated, but on vi. At the end of "The Wanton Song," the bass and guitar play the descending pattern of pitches D, D♭, C, B♭ in the key of G (minor), ending the piece on the unresolved ♭3 scale degree. Plant enters coincidentally with the B♭ on the pitch c and moves downward to b♭. He is left by himself on the latter pitch, the rest of the band having faded out. He makes the resolution to the tonic, himself, but it is much less emphasized than the previous dissonant pitches, and in a very effective production Page fades the singer out during this resolution, so that the listener just barely hears it. A more recent example from Plant's "Memory Song (Hello Hello)" (*Fate of Nations*) finds him singing an anticipation of the tonic over subdominant harmony that is sustained, with rhythmic variation, over four measures. Most of the dissonant pitches that Plant plays with are blue notes (the flatted third, fifth, and seventh scale degrees), but he takes risks in using them that most other rock singers do less often or not at all (especially with the flatted fifth, which is a tritone away from the tonic—there is a powerful example of Plant's bold use of this note at the end of "Whole Lotta Love," where he enters on this dissonance full force, singing a long sustained "ooh" on this pitch just before he repeats "oh, oh, oh oh"). Although there are moments through the Zeppelin repertory when Plant clearly sings "out of tune" (especially on some of the live recordings), most of the time his use of dissonance is deliberate, intended to heighten expressivity. Critics have sometimes been miffed at this bold manipulation of dissonance. Jim Miller, for example, reviewing the album *Physical Graffiti*, remarked, erroneously, that several of the tracks "suffer from Plant's indefinite pitch."[78]

Plant's vocal gymnastics also stem from the ornate singing style he sometimes uses, which was influenced by Indian and Arabic music. I have already mentioned his vocal melisma that was derived from these non-Western sources in the Earl's Court performance of "Dazed and Confused," but there are many other examples. His vocal during the outcourse of "Four Sticks" is a case in point (Plant has said that this song was intended to have a "raga vibe"[79]), as is the melisma that he sings at the end of the line "Trying to find where I been" in "Kashmir" (see chapter 3). The effect of teetering on the brink of control in Plant's singing also comes from his timbral fluctuations, his occasional use of vibrato, and his slipping from song into speech and vice versa. In general, then, he allows himself great freedom with respect to melodic invention in order to express himself, about which he has commented that he thought it acceptable to "lose the melody" when experimenting in performance to make himself vulnerable to the musical experience.[80]

How can these musical gestures be tied to gender? It can be argued that we are culturally conditioned to read them as gender-coded, since they have been treated that way historically. As Susan McClary has argued, resistance to tonal stability and closure, which so marks Plant's singing style, has traditionally been considered a "feminine" musical characteristic in Western culture.[81] Robert Walser's discussion of masculinity in heavy metal music begins by citing the legend of Orpheus, the god of music, who "must sing in such a way as to demonstrate his rhetorical mastery of the world, yet such elaborate vocal display threatens to undermine Orpheus's masculine identity. Flamboyant display of his emotions is required as evidence of his manipulative powers, but such excess makes him into an object of display himself and suggests a disturbing similarity to the disdained emotional outbursts of women."[82] The Greeks (specifically Aristotle) differentiated between Dorian and Phrygian modes, coding Dorian as calming, strengthening, and "virile" and Phrygian as inducing frenzy and being "effeminate," on the basis, it is now thought, that the latter contained semitones while the former did not, that is, that the tension produced by semitone movement from dissonance to consonance was emotionally destabilizing and even erotic.[83] The medieval traditions of Gregorian and Old Roman chant have been coded masculine and feminine, respectively, because Old Roman melodies are more ornate than Gregorian ones.[84] Indeed, we need only go back to 1978, to Simon Frith and Angela McRobbie's description of the music of "cock rock" as hard, in control, and virtuosic, which they say are masculine characteristics.[85]

The other way in which Plant betrays a feminine musical persona is through his partnership with Page. Deena Weinstein has discussed the relationship between singer and guitarist in heavy metal bands in a way that accords them equal importance:

> In heavy metal there is an intimate connection between the vocals and the instruments, with the voice participating as an equal, not as a privileged instrument. The voice is an instrument that challenges the prominence of the guitar. . . . Vocalist and guitarist are each accorded importance but neither is allowed to eclipse the other. The two are dual foci, like the twin foci of an ellipse, around which the music is described. The relationship between the guitar and vocals is one of tension; they dynamically contend with one another for dominance but never allow this continuous competition to result in the defeat of either guitarist or vocalist.[86]

Weinstein cites Page and Plant as among the most famous of such duos.[87] She is right that guitarist and vocalist are twin focal points in a band, but with Page and Plant, at least (and perhaps with other bands as well), the relationship is not equal. Page is always clearly the dominant force, clearly the one who controls the musical flow, and most often the one who is in the limelight with his extended solos (see chapter 4 for further discussion of how he achieves this). Page is also the one who displays technical control and virtuosity in the way we most often think of it; that is, he has mastered an instrument (that is, mastered technology, a masculine domain) and can play reams of fast passages on it that wow his listeners. Plant's virtuosity lies mostly in different spheres: in the power of his voice, his ability to sing in a high range, and his use of dissonance as described earlier, characteristics less associated with the concept of virtuosity than is technical mastery of an instrument.

The interplay between the two musicians reflects their respective approaches to the music, their status within the band, and their relationship with each other. In "Dazed and Confused" this interplay is extended and especially well developed. During the bow solo in *The Song Remains the Same* version, Page is the first focus of attention; Plant's role is supportive. Plant vocalizes instead of singing words, so that he moves closer to the instrumental world of his partner.

The musical dialogue that occurs between Page and Plant during this section of the piece is an intimate and sensual exchange in which, I would argue, Plant is cast musically in the role of a feminine other to Page's masculine guitar hero. Most of the time Plant imitates Page's licks, offers him sympathetic encouragement, or complements him, in any event creating a supportive musical environment for Page. Plant sometimes uses a tone that is remarkably clear, at other points employing a highly distorted timbre in imitation of some of the effects that Page achieves with the bow, and so joins in Page's sonic experimentation, following him into uncharted territory. The extremely high range in which Plant sings here—especially when his tone is clear—also evokes the feminine, which some male fans, interestingly, have pointed to as one of the desirable characteristics of his voice.[88] In fact, although he has never openly acknowledged it, I would argue that one of Plant's strongest influences as a singer must have been a woman, Janis Joplin, since they share a similar emotional plane in their singing and since Plant draws on Joplin's specific licks and technical vocabulary, including all the characteristics of his singing that I described earlier. A typical visual manifestation of the intimate relationship between Page and Plant in performance can be seen in figure 2, where singer and guitarist lean into each other, sometimes (although not in this photograph) actually making physical contact as a sign of their bonding through the music. In fact, this kind of physical union between singer and lead guitarist in rock music performances has become typical and clichéd (performers from Jagger and Richards to Bono and the Edge engage in it) but nevertheless remains a crucially important opportunity for intimacy as well as the creation of community.

In the studio version of "Dazed and Confused," during the fast section that follows the bow solo, all musical elements are subordinated to the dominance of the guitar. On the studio version and also often in performance, this solo would begin with Page playing a pitch, which Plant would imitate, this being repeated at increasingly higher intervals, forcing Plant to the uppermost reaches of his range. During one performance from 1969,[89] this contest ended with Plant conceding, "I can't do it no more." Waksman argues that the vocal exchange between Page and Plant "reinforce[s] both a sense of fraternal bonding and camaraderie among musicians and . . . the homosocial content of cock rock" (he doesn't acknowledge the sexual implications of the exchange),[90] but there is actually a more subtle kind of relationship occurring here. Plant is at once mentored, musically, by Page, stretched to his limits, coaxed to go further and further, and also, ultimately, controlled by the guitarist. Plant also often ended this contest between himself and Page by saying, "Push; push" (which he was wont to do during many other of Page's solos as well), not only encouraging Page to push his playing further—to exceed the limit—but also making the connection between male sexual ecstasy and the ecstatic musical moment. It is possible to hear this comment as an imperative to Page, casting Plant in the role of receiver of sexual pleasure during intercourse, the "woman" who is asking for more, thus strengthening his role as feminine other to Page.[91] Throughout the rest of the solo, Page becomes the sole focus. In the studio version the singer makes several interjections, but his voice—that incredibly powerful instrument heard at the beginning of the piece—is relegated to the background, barely audible in the mix, rendered impotent. In live versions Plant has very little to do with the solo from this point on. Perhaps this is simply an enactment of hegemonic male–female relations, even as Plant's gestures earlier in the piece—his following of Page's melodic and timbral improvisations with the bow and sympathetic and emotionally charged encouragement to Page—are enactments of these relations.[92] Other musical elements are also subordinated to the powerful guitar in this part of the solo: there is no harmonic movement, the solo being played over a static dominant pedal (manifoldly increasing the intensity by shifting from the tonic to its harmonic axis), Jones repeating the same arpeggiated chord over and over again. Only Bonham changes his pattern, adding, as was noted earlier, triplet figures toward the climax of the solo, to generate more excitement for the soloist. In the twenty-odd performances of "Dazed and Confused" that I have heard, Page never quoted another piece during this solo or alluded to a specific musical style. This was his moment for invention without the reference to other music that pervaded the bow solo. The guitarist has broken out of the confines of the piece and also of specific musical allusion

At the end of the piece, however, the four musicians are on the most equal footing of the entire work. After the final verse has been sung, the musical gesture that began the solo section is reiterated (four sixteenth notes and an eighth), suggesting that there may be another foray into improvisation. Instead, the piece comes to a conclusion, with the four musicians unified in playing variants of the same gesture (bass and drums stay steady on the four eighth notes plus sixteenth, Page plays a descending chromatic lick that echos the riff of the piece, and Plant interjects with "oh" on each beat of the measure). This is a particularly erotic conclusion to the piece: the regular repetition of the gesture that mimics thrusting, Plant's moans that occur with some force on the beat, these beginning as soft and short and becoming increasingly longer and more intense, and the rising volume all suggest a movement toward sexual climax. A great deal of harmonic tension is generated by the use of bVII throughout this section, which finally, on the last beat, resolves upward to the tonic. This conclusion presents an interesting balance to the guitar solo, which was so dominated by Page. As opposed to the solo, in which the other musicians were subordinated to Page, here there is unity among them, and, in fact, Plant is foregrounded in the mix, so that this climactic moment seems to belong especially to him (her).

On the 1977 tour, as mentioned earlier, only the solo portions of "Dazed and Confused" were played. Instead of dialoguing with the singer in this decontextualized solo, Page turned to his electronic companion, the theremin, to act as a sparring partner. This change meant that Page was in complete control of both the sounds he produced on the guitar and those that come out of the theremin (which he had to invoke by waving his hands around the instrument—another way in which he could play magician). There was no more human interaction; Page's musical journey became solitary, and as a result the intense energy, much of it sexual, between the performers was lost. There is a probable reason for these changes to the solo. By 1977 Page's addiction to heroin was complete, and this altered the dynamic between him and Plant considerably. Page had at this point turned inward and was less interested in communing with his partner than in making solitary explorations.

Although the erotic quality of the musical dialogue between Page and Plant is particularly strong, a similar dynamic is present between musicians in other rock groups. Rock music performance is one of the few venues in our culture in which heterosexual men can be openly, sensuously expressive with one another, in which gender lines can be safely transgressed not only in terms of dress and other visual display but also in the performance of a musical text. Same-sex friendships between heterosexual men in the twenty-first century often do not allow for the expression of deep affection, sensuality, vulnerability, or other characteristics that may be seen as threateningly "feminine." But within the musical dynamic of the rock group, such emotion is allowed to be openly indulged.

THE FLUID APPROACH to text in Led Zeppelin, and especially in this piece, requires an equally fluid, polysemous approach to analysis, one that shuns unities or fixed homologies. I therefore do not wish to attempt to draw together the three ways in which I have analyzed "Dazed and Confused" except to point the reader's attention to some of the interesting intersections among them. The visual image of the violin bow, for example, acted as an intertextual reference to classical music, as a means through which Page turned his performance into ritual, and as a phallic symbol. The second part of Page's guitar solo was also interpreted in two different ways, first as representing a moment of spiritual transcendence and second as symbolic of the guitarist's male dominance within the group. There are also interesting tensions that obtain more broadly among the three views of the piece. The collapse of the spiritual and the physical in the discussion of transcendence with respect to the guitar solo is one such tension; spiritual and sexual ecstasy are analogous in this interpretation. Equally interesting is the role of intertextuality within the spiritual quest (see chapter 2 for further discussion of this). Not only are the musicians and audience taken on a sonic journey in which they experience an openness toward musical form and timbre, but they are also encouraged to leave the confines of the text itself and wander freely in what may seem to be unrelated musical material on their "journey." And finally, there is the slippery issue of gender construction, in which Plant's powerfully masculine voice and vocal style, partly appropriated from the black male blues tradition, take on feminine musical characteristics through a particular approach to the construction of melody and through the musical relationship forged between singer and guitarist.

TWO

Stairway to Heaven

Myth, Epic, Ritual

I am watching the video of Led Zeppelin playing at Knebworth August 11, 1979. It is near the end of a concert that lasted two hours and forty minutes.[1] The final song before the encore is "Stairway to Heaven," and the moment that prompts me to begin writing is the introduction to the guitar solo, a majestic, militaristic fanfare played by guitar, bass, and drums. At the Knebworth gig (and also in *The Song Remains the Same*), Page plays this fanfare as if he might be a warrior offering his guitar up to the gods. He points the neck of the instrument straight upward and holds the body away from his own, turning it outward, much like he does in Marty Perez's photograph from the 1977 Chicago show (fig. 9). The musical and physical gestures taken together are powerful symbols. A musical fanfare signals the beginning of an important event, usually one that is solemn, ceremonial, ritualistic. At least one part of the music of this fanfare—the flourish of triplet figures—has been used for centuries in Western culture to signal an auspicious occasion, so an aural connection is made with tradition, a direct link with decisive moments in the culture. In fact, the genre of the fanfare—especially the blowing of trumpets to signal events of great significance, which Page's ringing guitar timbre is clearly meant to mimic—is rooted in biblical tradition (a trumpet blast signaled the beginning of the meeting among God, Moses, and the Israelites when the Israelites were given the Ten Commandments; the events of the apocalypse unfold as seven angels sound their trumpets) and Greek and Roman literature (the blowing of trumpets at Agrippina's funeral in Tacitus's *Annales* 14,10; the sky "sound[ing] as with trumpets" during battle in Homer's *Iliad*, Book 21, I; the use of a trumpet blast to call a conference in the midst of battle in Julius Caesar's *Commentaries on the Gallic Wars*, 8.20.2).[2] It is, more recently, connected with high culture (with coronations or weddings of royalty, for example) or still with the military and generally then with events of mythical proportion, those that reach beyond the individual to affect the collective movement of culture in momentous ways. Page's physical gesture, with arms raised and a firm stance, has also been used repeatedly in Western culture in visual depictions of victory (the Nike of Samothrace from the early second century B.C.; Andrea de Castagno's depiction of David after slaying Goliath [1450–1457]; Francois Rude, *Monument to Marshal Ney*, 1853, to name a few).[3]

There are those for whom such an image of grandeur in rock music, and perhaps also my explanation, which draws it into the weighty tradition of historical/mythological discourse, is much too serious for rock and roll, and pretentious to boot. Critics such as Simon Frith and many others have pointed out that the development of *rock*, with its artistic ambitions, including "deep" lyrics, other symbolisms, and musical experimentations, as distinct from rock and roll and pop in the mid-1960s, was, as Frith puts it, "the beginning of the end."[4] But for those who love Led Zeppelin, the mythological, epic, and ritualistic aspects of the band and their music are very significant parts of the experience, ones that deserve critical commentary, not cynical dismissal.[5] Indeed, listening to Led Zeppelin's music and connecting with aspects of the band's image and what they had to say—about music or anything else—is for many fans part of a spiritual life that may have begun in their teens but stays with them well beyond that, probably for the rest of their lives. Far from being a pretentious claim, this simply suggests that Zeppelin's music and image is one expression of living mythology in contemporary culture, and fan responses to this are a clear indication of the necessity of such mythology in many people's lives. In his study of the Led Zeppelin fan community, Christopher Williams discusses this in general terms, arguing that avid fans usually consider themselves to have undergone a transformation because of their connection with the band; Williams calls their relationship with Led Zeppelin ritualistic, a concept to which I will return momentarily.[6]

While an intense connection with Zeppelin's music, or with the music of any band or artist, can be spiritually transformative for the listener, Led Zeppelin consciously constructed a certain kind of "mythology," one that has become a particularly important part of the culture of this band. When asked on the fan questionnaire what they liked best about the band's image and lyrics, the majority included some comment about "mythology" or "mystical" aspects or alluded simply to the "mystery" of the band.[7] The first response given here is interesting not only for what it says but also for *how* it is said: the author tries to capture something of the spirit of mythological discourse by using poetic, formal, and slightly archaic language ("virtues of a bygone day") and by pointing to metaphysical concepts such as force, illumination, angelic source, and so on:

The dark and light concepts represented by Plant and Page both in personality and presentation. Plant and Page combine the forces in their work as well as their appearances and lifestyles. Both harbor darkness that's irresistible because they are, at the same time, illuminated. They represent the paradox of mysteries, even appearing androgynous and effeminate while remaining symbols of testosteronic superiority and control. They are messianic as well as satanic. They are utterly corrupt but childlike in their expressions of pure belief in virtues of a bygone day. They are consummately modern with cores of ancient and original spirits. Page, like Mozart, is possessed knowingly, by an angelic source, who flows through him like the wind through the trees. He has written some of the most "otherworldly" music.

Other responses are somewhat less poetic but no less indicative of the importance of the spiritual or mystical aspects of the band:

I enjoy the sense of magick [sic] in the music as they obviously are consciously raising power.

Jimmy Page & his mystique.

Power, mystery, emotion.

The lyrics work so perfectly with the music, adding spirituality to the passion.

A lot of their lyrics portray far off, mystical lands, castles, oceans, etc. The band's image was known as being mystical and somewhat secretive. I also like how they can change their mood with every song, from romantic ballads to loud rock, and still make it sound great.

In every song there is a message. Sure you think the song sounds pretty. Like "Stairway to Heaven" for instance. Everybody thinks that that is the most beautiful song, but there are so many messages that one can pick up from it. Their music brings out a part of me.

Comments that concern the powerfully transformative nature of Led Zeppelin's music also dominated the responses to "Your comments on: the epic quality of pieces like 'Stairway to Heaven' or 'Achilles Last Stand'":

These songs are about big ideas, big feelings. For some of us, they are the closest things to hymns that we have.

Do we really need to talk about this? These are the songs that change people's lives. They should be part of history like the Gettysburg Address.

"Stairway [to Heaven]" especially, changed the world. Songs that were written without great human intervention. Great music seems to flow, from somewhere else, anyway. It never seems to come from the person themselves. Zep always had a connection to a certain timelessness. In fact, timeless, or eternal is how their best material sounds.

It isn't just hype. Those are songs to stir the soul.

They epitomize humanity in a way. We are such a magical race and yet we don't realize our potential and they also reflect the sadness of humanity with lines like "as we wind on down the road our shadows taller than our souls [from 'Stairway to Heaven']."

Epic isn't a big enough word. They change lives.

What do fans mean when they use the words "myth," "mythology," and "epic" in the context of Led Zeppelin's music? In the preceding comments, there have already been elucidated three uses of these terms: The first is the mythological or epic character of some of the lyrics, including, importantly, the idea that the lyrics simply deal with "big ideas," not with the narration of a myth per se. The second is the mythical status of the band itself, created not through a coherent narrative but through symbol, image, and attitude that either have an immediate mythical significance or cause a mythological discourse to be generated by the press, by the band members themselves, or by the fan community. Fans locate the mythological in all kinds of iconography and discourse that surround the band, including the obvious, such as the "four symbols" found on the inner sleeve of the fourth album cover and Page's associations with the occult, as well as things that might seem less likely candidates for mythologizing. On this matter one fan wrote:

Jimmy Page's appearance, with his famous "dragon pants,"[8] double necked electric guitar and use of the violin bow, in combination with some of the "otherworldly" graphics that appear on Zeppelin albums all contributed to creating a mythology and mystique surrounding the band which exists to this day and is arguably stronger than ever.

While Page's use of the violin bow, as I argued in chapter 1, seems a likely practice to play into a mythology given its potential association with ritual, the double-neck guitar might at first seem less obviously "mythological." Page had the double-neck made especially for him, however, and he was one of the first rock guitarists to use the instrument. Like the violin bow, then, this instrument is identified with Page; that is, both objects have come to symbolize him in all his complexity as a performer (quiet, dark, virtuosic, and so forth). The double-neck is also tied to Page's mythology because he had it built in order that he alone could cover multiple guitar parts in concert, instead of hiring another guitarist to assist him. It therefore magnified his potency as a guitar hero. I will have more to say about this later.

Fans also point out that the music itself is epic or mythical and that the experience of listening is part of their spiritual lives. They link band members' ability to compose with some "otherworldly" force or with a tradition of inexplicable musical inspiration that links Page to icons of classical Western music such as

Mozart (the number of times Page was compared to Mozart—the only classical composer mentioned—on the fan questionnaire is remarkable and points to the status Mozart has achieved in some corners of popular culture as the quintessential representative of musical "genius"). I would add to this that some of the pieces, certainly "Stairway to Heaven," are constructed in a way that can be read as suggesting a mythological or epic narrative; I make such an analysis of "Stairway" later.

Definitions of myth and epic are highly contested among scholars of these genres. Indeed, the distinction between the two is not entirely clear,[9] except that "epic" usually suggests length, which is how fans often use it to describe some of Led Zeppelin's pieces. Some clarification of how these terms are used in this context is therefore in order. What fans seem to be suggesting in their comments is that certain lyrics, imagery, discourse, and music combine in such a way as to suggest the sacred. By sacred I mean, with Catherine Bell, "not explicitly a religious claim to divinity, [but] a quality of specialness, not the same as other things, standing for something important and possessing an extra meaningfulness and the ability to evoke emotion-filled images and experiences."[10] As one fan put it,

From ages 15–23, Led Zep was my religion. Whether I was happy, sad, mad, stoned, drunk, sober, dazed or confused, Zeppelin had a song for me. Some people go to churches, synagogue, etc. Whatever mood I was in, when I needed to search within myself, when I needed answers, when I was on top of the world, I would go to my "faith" and absorb my emotions within Zeppelin.

Myth and the sacred are overtly linked by Paul Ricoeur, who believes that the "symbolic function" of myth is "its power of discovering and revealing the bond between man [sic] and what he considers sacred."[11] Ricoeur writes further that through myth "experience escapes its singularity," that "[t]hrough the figure of the hero, the ancestor, the Titan, the first man, the demigod, experience is put on the track of existential structures: one can now say man, existence, human being, because in the myth the human type is recapitulated, summed up."[12] "[Myth] signifies an indivisible plenitude, in which the supernatural, the natural, and the psychological are not yet torn apart ... a cosmic whole."[13] Ricoeur's idea that myth unites us is particularly important, for it is one reason that the mythology of Led Zeppelin is so powerful to many fans. When fans say that Led Zeppelin's music is "timeless" or that it "epitomizes humanity," this is, I think, what they mean. The feeling of connectedness to other people, to history, and to a supernatural world is profound, especially for those who feel alienated in their daily lives.[14] As Ricoeur observes, "If myth making is an antidote to distress, that is because the man of myths is already an unhappy conscious; for him, unity, conciliation, and reconciliation are things to be spoken of and acted out, precisely because they are not given"[15] (think of how this resonates with the comments from the fan who spoke of the inherent "sadness" of the human race). For a certain segment of the population in contemporary culture, Led Zeppelin, in one of its guises, offers a performance of this kind of mythology to its fans.[16] The performative aspect of Zeppelin's mythology is important to stress, for much of the construction of a mythology lies in the *act* of hearing the music, seeing them live, or on a video, or in constructing a discourse around the band. The idea that the performance of myth is critical to its power came originally from anthropologist Branislav Malinowski, who wrote about his study of myth in Melanesian culture: "[T]he interest of the story is vastly enhanced and it is given its proper character by the manner in which it is told. The whole nature of the performance, the voice and the mimicry, the stimulus and the response of the audience mean as much to the natives as the text."[17] It is not in a written (or notated) text that the myth has power but in its reenactment. Further, it is the performance or reenactment that brings myth into the present, that makes it living. As Eric Daredl writes, "The mythic . . . is present because the original event, by repetition, is once again 'presently' produced."[18] I would suggest that the centrally important notion of reenactment in this definition of myth was manifested in Led Zeppelin's performances in two ways. First, fans came to expect certain elements to be part of every performance (the bow solo, the use of the double-neck, and so forth). Second—and this is critical not only to Led Zeppelin performances but also to much stadium rock—the stability of the set list on a specific tour makes the entire concert a ritual act that is repeated again and again. Through my participation in Internet discussions of the 1995 Page and Plant tour, it became evident to me that through the near-daily descriptions of concerts by fans, which detailed the same set lists, solos, between-song dialogue by Plant, and so forth, that the event had become a ritualistic ceremony. When I finally saw the show myself, I reveled in knowing what was coming next. In this context, incremental changes—the substitution of one song for another, for example—take on incredible significance, changing the shape and nature of the ritual for that particular audience (hence one feels privileged, singled out, especially blessed).

Performing myth is, of course, ritualistic.[19] In his study *From Ritual to Theatre*, anthropologist Victor Turner theorizes that performance media in industrialized societies often take the place of what we would consider to be more traditional rituals (initiations, for example) in the sense that these are liminal events; that is, theater or music performances (including listening to recorded music) remove one from the flow of everyday life (from, as Turner characterizes it, "the indicative" into "the subjunctive") into "a time and place lodged between all times and spaces," which he likens to the subjunctive mood in language.[20] "Here the cognitive schemata that give sense and order to everyday life no longer apply, but are, as it were, suspended."[21] The singularly most important aspect of this kind of liminality, or of being in "the subjunctive" for Turner, is the potential for transformation—to emerge from the experience a changed person. The state of liminality allows for this because "the fixing and ordering processes of the adult, sociostructural domain are liminally abandoned and the initiand submits to being broken down to a generalized prima materia," so that s/he can be "reshaped to encounter new experiences."[22] A similar point of view, focused not on performance media but on the rituals of "everyday life," is given by Mary Douglas in her fascinating study *Purity and Danger*:

[S]ymbolic enactment does several things. It provides a focusing mechanism, a method of mnemonics and a control for experience ... a ritual provides a frame. The marked off time or place alerts a special kind of expectancy, just as the oft-repeated "Once upon a time" creates a mood receptive to fantastic tales .... Framing and boxing limit experience, shut in desired themes or shut out intruding one.... The mnemonic action of rites is very familiar. When we tie knots in a handkerchief we are not magicking our memory, but bringing it under control of the external sign. So ritual focuses attention by framing; it enlivens the memory and links the present with the relevant past. In all this it aids perception. Or rather, it changes perception because it changes the selective principles. So it is not enough to say that ritual helps us to experience more vividly what we would have experienced anyway ... It can come first in formulating experience. It can permit knowledge of what would otherwise not be known at all. It does not merely externalize experience, bringing it out into the light of day, but it modifies experience in so expressing it.[23]

Chris Williams offers a similar account of the transformative experience that avid fans have with Led Zeppelin's music: "When fans refer to the effect that Led Zeppelin has had on their lives, I interpret them as referring to the way its music has led them across a threshold of emotion and meaning. The listening experience has left an indelible mark on their lives."[24] But Williams, a sociologist whose aim is to centralize the Led Zeppelin fan community as the locus of meaning, views the activities of this community—tape trading, collecting of memorabilia, discussion on Internet lists, and so forth—as the rituals around which this intense experience is maintained, arguing that without the community, interest in the band would not continue: "[T]he life-change caused by contact with the band's music would soon whither without community support."[25] My personal experience, as well as the comments that I received from fans, lead me to believe that this is not the case. My life-changing experiences with Led Zeppelin (and various other music, too) began to occur when I was fourteen (see chapter 5). Although I occasionally read rock magazines such as *Creem* and *Hit Parader*, I had no contact with fan communities, for either Led Zeppelin or other rock artists with whom, at various times throughout my adolescence, I was significantly engaged. The only items I collected were studio albums and posters, and I did not trade these with anyone (they were much too valuable). In fact, the only other person around me who was interested in Zeppelin was my older sibling's boyfriend, with whom I only rarely discussed music (and never Led Zeppelin). Still, once I had heard the music and been so powerfully moved by it, it remained an incredibly important part of my life, in fact, my identity. Because of various pressures (among them a graduate school environment in which rock music was seriously frowned upon), I stopped listening to the music for several years; I came back to Led Zeppelin with a vengeance in 1990, when I heard "Whole Lotta Love" on the radio. I felt the same power, the same kind of liberation, the same kind of spiritual and physical connection to it as I had years before, and this remained with me as I began listening to the music regularly again, without any contact with any part of the fan community. The ritual that allowed me to have transformative experiences revolved around listening to the music itself, by myself. The ritual of listening was framed by two events: it began at the moment I decided I would listen to a recording and lasted while I was choosing which one it would be and until I took the album off the turntable and slipped it back into its jacket. The experience of going to concerts was (and still is) similarly ritualistic and transformative for me. Hearing the announcement that musicians important in my life will tour, buying the tickets, getting to the concert, and, finally, seeing the performance can, depending on how much I admire the artists, serve as important frames in my life, setting those experiences off from "the indicative" (and witness the fan whose comment is offered later, whose memory of buying tickets for a Led Zeppelin concert many years ago still excites him, still brings him into "the subjunctive").

We can turn to fan comments for confirmation that my experience is not singular. For many, seeing Led Zeppelin or Page and Plant in concert or listening to their music was indeed a powerfully transformative experience that did take them into the "subjunctive"; although I did not ask about this specifically, I get no sense that this experience is contingent upon being part of the fan community.

In answer to the question "Do you listen to Zeppelin casually, fanatically, somewhere in between?" many fans elaborated on their own rituals of listening:

I am a fanatical listener . . . I listen to Zep at least 30 minutes a day, and I go to bed with a CD of theirs on every night . . . Almost everything they ever did is a piece of musical genius.

I might not listen to them everyday, but when I do, I think I am pretty fanatical about it. Especially when I haven't listened to them for a little while, and then I put like "IV" (the zoso album) in or something, I just get chills.

I listen to Zeppelin in a fanatic rage, jammin' with Jimmy Page all the time. I would be classified as an aggressive Led Zeppelin listener.

23 years of listening to them appreciatively.

I listen to Zep now like one would drink a fine wine. I bring it out occasionally, enjoy it immensely, then put it away till the next time. Having heard the music for the better part of 20 years I don't have the need to hear it daily. However, growing up this music was part of my daily life. It helped me through bad times and I celebrated with it through the good!

I guess it must be fanatically. This doesn't mean all the time but I tend to listen to at least 5 Zep concerts every week, bootlegs, that is (DAT, cassette or CD). Nowadays, the official studio albums don't spin that much at my turntable. I'm too familiar with them, every note, every little nuance, so there is no challenge or excitement anymore. Don't get me wrong here, even the worst Zep album is superior to any other album by any artist/group. It's just that the music from these masterpieces is "planted" in my head, I can hear it without putting the actual record on, so what's the point? The only reason would be to confirm that the music inside my head is true to the albums.

[I listen][r]eligiously, as therapy; I'm one with them.

In answer to the question "If you ever saw the band live, describe your experience," fans responded:

Powerful, elemental, like a pagan celebration

I saw them in a small club in Miami [in 1969], and was blown completely away. My life has never been totally without Zep in some way ever since.

I felt like I was in a different world . . . my senses were overloaded and I experienced synthesthesia

Again Page and Plant came to our town this month, once again I was taken to Kashmir.

It was the most religious experience of my life. I have never been so engulfed in a band's music as I was when I saw them.

I've never missed Jimmy play in the 30 years [that he's been playing]. Very electric energy bouncing back and forth between the band and audience. It was a wild feeling. You could almost see the energy, that strong. It was rushing, goose bumping experience. Never with any other band [have] I experienced this.

During "Kashmir" I had my eyes closed and hands outstretched to receive the power. I heard a voice saying "Do you feel it?" over and over. I opened my eyes and Robert was standing directly in front of me. He put his hand with the microphone on his hip and pointed directly at me with his other repeating "do you feel it?"

San Diego, '69, Atlanta '77 and '73. They took you someplace you'd never been before — an intense emotional experience.

Saw Zeppelin on 7.23.77. I left the show feeling it was the single greatest experience that could ever happen to me. It changed my life. The show itself wasn't one of their best but it was the vibes, THE VIBES MAN!! The magic, the "electric presence" and the charisma.

In a word—intense. In more words—a complete musical experience. First they hit you hard and loud, and then they give you a chance to calm down, although never completely. They knew how to keep you interested. When you were at a Zeppelin show there wasn't usually much talking going on—people listened to the band. Near the end of the show, they just didn't let up—you felt physically drained at the end of the evening, having been taken through every facet of their music—from soft and sweet to bone-crunching electric blues and rock. They did it all. In the end, we were left screaming for more, even though we may not have been able to take any more—they would drain you.

I saw them at the Pontiac Silverdome on 4/30/77. It was a highlight of my life. I remember thinking how I could feel their presence, even though they were so far away from me . . . the feeling of being there with them was really something.

Saw LZ in 1977 for a mere $7.50. I was 13. Hard to put into words. Actually, kind of a vague memory for me. I remember Jimmy doing his bow solo and the lighting around him was spinning from above. It appeared he was in a cone. Totally awesome. (I wasn't totally ripped, either.) The Bonham solo was powerful. JPJ and his triple-neck!! Can't tell you a set list. But do remember getting tickets, and the anticipation before the show. Making my heart pound now as I am typing this. Still have the ticket stub in a photo album!!!

It tears me up that I never got to see all four of them. I survive, though, because I have seen Robert Plant on 3 solo tours, Jimmy Page on both Firm tours, and both Page/Plant tours. Every time has been a magical, near religious experience. I swear to Bonham, the first time I heard Plant/Page do "Going To California" live I had tears in my eyes.

Saw Page and Plant in May [1998] on tour. It gave me a glimpse of what they were like in the heyday. at the end of "how many more times," Plant asked the audience, "Can you feel it?" If you were there, you'd know exactly what he was talking about.

Yeah, I saw them [Page and Plant]. I'm only 18 and have never had sex before, but I don't see how that can possibly compare to seeing Zep in concert.

While sharing one's love of a band or artist with others who feel similarly can be an important part of the experience, the individual response to the music— its transformative power (and, clearly from these fans' comments the power to continually renew)—is paramount. Similar accounts of the potent and trans- formative power of popular music have been written by fans of other artists— Fred and Judy Vermorel's book *Starlust* is full of them, not to mention various e-mail discussion lists, for Zeppelin and other bands, that I have visited or been a member of.[26] These experiences not only represent powerful and important junctures in fans' lives when they are young but also, as can be seen from several of the responses written by fans who saw the band or began listening to them in the 1970s and are now in their thirties, forties or fifties, stay with them.

THE MUSIC, THEN, whether live or recorded, lies at the heart of this powerful experience: it is the sound of the music, even according to Williams, that first draws people to the band and is responsible for their transformative experience.[27] It is difficult to know whether particular pieces are responsible for this experience, whether it is immediate upon first hearing the music or whether it is the repertory as a whole and the slower accumulation of knowledge about it that account for this experience; this undoubtedly varies from person to person. It is also difficult to say whether those pieces that can be called "epic" or "mythic" because of their length, lyrical subject matter, and various kinds of musical structure and complexities are more likely to generate this transformative experience than, say, "Whole Lotta Love." This, too, must vary, but an argument can be made that while an initial powerfully transformative experience may happen while listening to any song, the idea of the music as "mythical" or "epic" probably does not derive from songs such as "Whole Lotta Love" in the first instance.[28] That is, had the band not produced a range of songs that more obviously cultivated mythic and epic traits, there would be little reason to consider "Whole Lotta Love" as having such traits in and of itself or to use words such as "mythical" and "mystical" to describe the music and the band. A conscious cultivation of such traits is of paramount importance.

The collection of songs that belong to this mythic/epic category obviously includes "Stairway to Heaven" (the archetype for such songs in Led Zeppelin), "Achilles Last Stand," "Kashmir," "No Quarter," "In the Light," "The Song Remains the Same," and "Carouselambra," all of which are lengthy, multisectioned pieces with lyrics that allude to the mythological/spiritual/philosophical spheres to varying degrees. Furthermore, songs such as "Battle of Evermore," "Ramble On," which includes references to J. R. R. Tolkein's *Lord of the Rings* in the lyrics, and "What Is and What Should Never Be," as well as "Immigrant Song," which are not very long and are less complexly structured than a song such as "Stairway," should certainly also be put into this category because of the lyrics, which in all cases suggest an epic hero protagonist on a quest or positioned as a "seeker." There are those who would call a piece such as "How Many More Times" epic due to its length, but I would not include it here, since both the lyrical content and the musical structure are primarily taken from the blues, whereas in what I would call the "true" mythic/epic pieces (such as "Stairway" and "Kashmir"), the blues influence is less significant—at least, it is not the primary structuring music. I do not intend for this list to be complete or definitive—there are undoubtedly many lengthy debates to be had among those knowledgeable about the band's music as to which songs should and should not be included here.

There are only a few lyrics in which Plant actually uses a narrative mode–"Achilles Last Stand" is one of the best examples—which is generally considered to be a fundamental requirement of myth. Yet all of Plant's protagonists in songs such as these correspond loosely to Vladimir Propp's characterizations of the folk tale hero as well as definitions of the mythical/epic hero by writers such as Masaki Mori, both of whom stress the importance of a "lack" that propels the hero into (necessarily difficult) action or a struggle of some kind (either physical or psychological).[29] This, together with poetic language that often seeks to evoke the archaic, creates a material link with mythic/epic stories of the past, of which these songs form a part. Indeed, this is what makes them so powerful: they resonate with the listener because Plant performs mythic ideas that have circulated for centuries, at once narrating the myth and positioning himself and, by association, the other band members, as the hero protagonists. What brings his lyrics further into the mythic/epic tradition is that, as Bakhtin states it, "the absolute past is closed and completed in the whole as well as in any of its parts. It is, therefore, possible to take any part and offer it as a whole."[30] In other words, the listener seems to get parts of stories that remind us of the mythic/epic while telling no myth in particular. As Robert Walser says with respect to the lyrics of "Stairway to Heaven," the "images seem not to have any historical coherence, but they are all available in the present as sources of power and mystery."[31] Unlike many lyrics in progressive rock, which "draw on mythology, fantasy literature, science fiction, and sacred texts of the past to suggest a model for an ideal society towards which we might strive,"[32] the mythologies constructed by Led Zeppelin are meant to evoke the extradaily, especially the past or the magical, in a much more general way, and this was a conscious decision on the part of the band. As Page put it, "I still feel that some so-called progressive groups have gone too far with their personalized intellectualization of beat music. I don't want our music complicated by that kind of ego trip—our music is essentially emotional like the old rock stars of the past. It's difficult to listen to those early Presley records and not feel something. We are not going out to make any kind of moral or political statement. Our music is simply us."[33] This last statement suggests, of course, that there is no artifice or constructedness in Led Zeppelin's music, which is untrue but a powerful signifier of rock authenticity. At the same time, however, the statement does point to an important aspect of the band's music, which is away from the kind of intellectualization that occupied many progressive rock bands toward greater physicality and undefined (or at least underdefined and therefore more interpretively open) spirituality.

The music of each of these pieces deserves close analytical attention in order to determine how the mythological has been created through the use of sound. Here I want only to begin such a project through an analysis of "Stairway to Heaven." The fanfare in "Stairway" to which I directed attention at the beginning of this chapter is a good place to begin exploring mythic, epic, and ritualistic aspects of Led Zeppelin's music. I have already tried to demonstrate how, taken in isolation, this fanfare taps into the mythological through the historic association of this musical genre with ceremony, pageantry, war, and other events of "deep" cultural significance. Within the context of the piece these associations are strengthened through the fanfare's position at a critical musical juncture: it signals a definitive break with the music heard up to that point and introduces the guitar solo (the guitar hero), the new central voice in the narrative. It is a kind of musical crossroads in a piece that has been marked, up to this point, by harmonic, timbral, and structural instability—a constant trying on and then calling into question of the chosen mode of discourse, features that may be what has led many, including John Paul Jones, to characterize the piece as a "journey."

Robert Walser notes that the opening phrases of the piece are "reassuringly square," and on the surface this is certainly true. The instrumental part uses a very traditional musical construction, which consists of four phrases, each four measures long, about as regular a formal design as is found in Western music. These four phrases of music are repeated several times, until, in fact, the electric guitar is introduced, at which time the music changes significantly. The rhythm of this opening music, predominantly straight eighth notes that occur regularly with almost no syncopation, reinforces this squareness and regularity. This formal and rhythmic design also suggests simplicity and, when the timbres of the instruments are considered (acoustic guitar and recorders), the pastoral and the archaic as well. When Plant enters after the sixteen-measure instrumental introduction of the piece, the melody he sings is simple, too. It consists of only one phrase, which is constantly repeated with only slight variations, and it reflects the square rhythmic and metric design of the rest of the music. Example 2.1 reproduces the first texted phrase of music in which these features are illustrated (measures 17–20 of the song); the instrumental part given in this example is essentially the same as that with which the piece begins.

But the simplicity of the opening is deceptive. Just underneath the surface of the melodic and rhythmic squareness is a harmonic and formal openness and irregularity that is highly significant in terms of the semiotics of the piece. We can take the relationship between vocal and instrumental parts at the beginning of the piece as a first example of this irregularity. Example 2.2 maps the relationship between instrumental music and Plant's vocal line from the point at which Plant enters (measure 17) through what I would call the end of the first section of the piece (just before the first iteration of the line "ooh it makes me wonder"). Each horizontal numbered line represents a phrase of music, there being six phrases in this section altogether; this is the first departure from the regularity of phrase construction suggested by the opening four phrases of instrumental music and the four-plus-four phrase construction generally observed in tonal music .

The other feature of the relationship between voice and instruments in this section that I have tried to depict in the diagram is that even though Plant's melody repeats, there is no regular verse structure to the vocal line, and this creates an interesting disjunction between it and the instrumental part. In fact, some of the regularity of the instrumental music is undermined by Plant's irregular poetic construction, which at the beginning seems to consist of two lines ("There's a lady . . ." and "When she get there . . .") followed by a line that sounds as though it might become a refrain, although it doesn't return until the

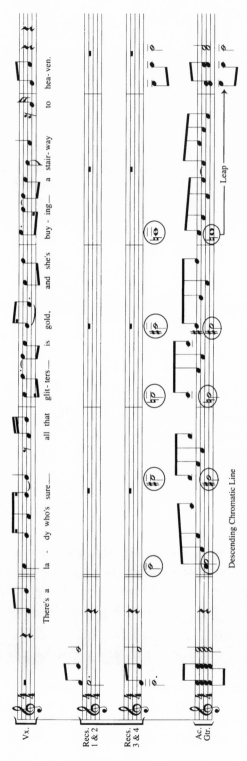

Example 2.1. "Stairway to Heaven," first texted prase

vocal	__1__ __2__ __3__ __1__ __2__ __silence__
instrumental	__1__ __2__ __3__ __4__ __1__ __2__

Example 2.2. "Stairway to Heaven," phrase relationship between vocal and instrumental parts, measures 17–40

end of the piece ("oooh, and she's buying a stairway to heaven"). This much takes up three phrases of music. The next line seems to begin a new stanza of poetry ("There's a sign on the wall"), but the instrumental part continues with the fourth phrase of music. In other words, the text seems to begin anew, but the music does not. This initial section of music then ends with one more line of text ("In a tree by the brook") and a reiteration of the first phrase of instrumental music: this time the music starts over while the vocal line continues. A final phrase of the instrumental music (the second phrase, cadencing on the tonic) brings this section to a close, but at this point of closure we simultaneously move ahead, since the guitar part changes, adding sixteenth notes to the texture. The verse form becomes more regular at this point: the refrain line "ooh it makes me wonder" alternates with two-line stanzas of text, all of which have the same poetic construction, up until the fanfare music.

The harmonic structure of this opening is also important to consider. The first two phrases of music cadence on the tonic, A, making them sound conclusive and "stable," but this stability is somewhat hard-won, since the harmonic progression that leads to the final cadence is built on a chromatically descending melody from A down to F♮ (these are the long-held notes heard in the acoustic guitar and recorder—see ex. 2.1). The chromatic scale is an unstable musical construct—it has no "center," no clear set of hierarchical relationships within it. Short segments of a descending chromatic scale also have a clearly established affective character, one to which I referred in chapter 1, that is as a musical signifier of lament in opera. Here the music also has a plaintive character, enhanced by the timbre of the recorders. This plaintiveness is important to the narrative, encoding the weightiness and uncertainty of spiritual journeys. In other words, this musical construction signifies struggle. The final cadence of each of these phrases is approached by a large leap—the long-held F♮ moving suddenly downward to a B, which quickly resolves to an A (see ex. 2.1). This is a jolting musical gesture, especially coming after the incremental movement by half tone that precedes it. It is as if the bottom has dropped out of the melodic line, forcing one to risk a leap to reach the safety of closure. There is also a great weightiness to this cadence—because of the large leap downward—which signals a kind of resignation to the inevitability of the tonic at this point. There are at least two semiotic readings of this cadence, then, one that views the leap to the tonic as daring, the other that views it as a gesture of resignation.

The third phrase cadences on the subdominant, D, leaving it tonally open, and the fourth phrase, which normally in such a "regular" kind of musical construction would bring another cadence on the tonic to balance the openness of the third phrase, cadences instead on an F major 7 chord, which creates a wonderful harmonic ambivalence (see ex. 2.3). F major 7 contains the complete tonic chord (A, C, and E) above its root, F, and one can really hear this tonic, but sounding displaced, its finality having been thwarted by the addition of the F underneath it. In the language of tonal theory, this kind of cadential movement, that is, to the sixth degree of the scale (F) instead of the tonic (A), is called deceptive because the harmonic movement that precedes it makes the listener expect the tonic. Here the deception is magnified by the addition of the seventh to the chord (E), so that we hear both the complete tonic and the submediant (F, A, C) sounding simultaneously. This doubleness of the cadence suggests choice as well as uncertainty; or, as Susan McClary has articulated it, "[the deceptive cadence can] rob the piece of certainty, yet create . . . [a] sense of nostalgia" or *desire*.[34] The changing cadential patterns of the phrases change the character of the repeated vocal line. For example, the cadence on D coincides with the repetition of the line "and she's buying a stairway to heaven," which, only one phrase earlier, cadenced definitively on the tonic. The refrainlike repetition of this line suggests that it should come with musical closure, but instead it has been musically recast, calling into question the certainty of its previous iteration, suggesting that there may be more than one way in which to interpret this lady and her quest. The line of text sung to the musical phrase that cadences on F is "'Cause you know sometimes words have two meanings"; the deceptive movement of the music and the two ways of hearing the F major 7 chord underscore the sentiment of the text very effectively, by literarily painting its meaning in sound.

But even without text, the cadential structure of these opening phrases is significant to take into account, because the tonal openness of the last two phrases and especially the deceptive movement and ambiguous nature of the last cadence point to a structural openness that supports the reading of this song as a "journey" or that might be said to fulfill the expectation of the hero-seeker of mythicological/epic tradition. Tonal closure indicates finality, a solution, an answer to a question; tonal openness suggests that there is more to come (or to learn), and the deceptive motion calls into question that which we think we know or can expect, challenges our assumptions, and forces us to open up to new possibilities.

The unexpected harmonic movements of the opening phrases are echoed later in the song in important ways. The fanfare begins with an unexpected harmonic move to the subdominant (D). Instead of continuing the two-measure progression III–VII^6–i (C–B–A in the bass guitar), which has been used to structure the music for a considerable time (since the words "There's a feeling I get"), the tonic A is replaced by D, the subdominant. The structuring pattern and cadence on the subdominant are illustrated in example 2.4.

Earlier I called the fanfare a musical crossroads, the point at which the musical discourse changes irrevocably, so it makes sense that in addition to the music of a fanfare marking this point there should be a striking harmonic move to set the music off from what has come before, one that, once again, suggests a ques-

Example 2.3. "Stairway to Heaven,"
a) cadence on the subdominant, third phrase (measures 11 and 12)
b) "deceptive" cadence on F major 7, fourth phrase (measures 15 and 16)

tioning of the status quo. This crossroads is also marked by a rhythmic questioning, if you will (see ex. 2.5). On one hand, there could not be a more decisive
gesture than the rising triplet figure of the fanfare, all instruments playing it in
sync, with a sweeping pickup to the downbeat of the measure, the melody rising
in stepwise movement from D to G, suggesting a dominant–tonic relationship.
On the other hand, there are constant metrical shifts that work to undermine
the forcefulness of the gesture. In the notated score, the section has been tran-
scribed as moving from $\frac{4}{4}$ to $\frac{7}{8}$ back to $\frac{4}{4}$, to $\frac{9}{8}$, $\frac{4}{4}$, $\frac{7}{8}$, and then finally resting on $\frac{4}{4}$
time. Basically, the addition and deletion of eighth-note beats here creates slight
hesitancies or anticipations (someone holding back and then jumping the
gun): in which direction do I move next? what turn do I take?

Finally with respect to harmony, there is one further playing with notions of
closed and open between the grooves that accompany the verses leading up to

Example 2.4. "Stairway to Heaven," six measures before fanfare, piano and bass guitar parts only

the fanfare and that which follows it. Both involve three-note descending patterns, but before the fanfare the pattern ends each time on the tonic, A, suggesting closure (see ex. 2.4), while afterward, during the guitar solo and the verse that follows, the pattern *begins* on the tonic A, moving down through G to F (again, the sixth degree of the scale, on which deceptive cadences are built), moving outward from closure to openness (see ex. 2.6). The instruments end the piece, in fact, on the F of this repeated harmonic pattern, leaving Plant, alone, to bring final harmonic closure. The way the change in the riff is effected is worth noting. The three-note pattern prior to the fanfare is C–B–A. At the point of the fanfare, the movement is C–B–D, as noted earlier. At the end of the fanfare, the movement is from C down to B and then A, the closing note of the riff, but this A now becomes the first note of the new riff—A–G–F. The tonic is a kind of pivot in this construction, at once the closing or end point of the old riff and the beginning of the new one.

The harmonic, formal, and rhythmic instability just outlined are important ways in which a sense of growth or striving is achieved musically, in that a process of openness and questioning is constantly at work in the music. But there is another way, perhaps more obvious to the average listener, in which the concept of growth is constructed in this piece, and that is through instrumentation. *Rolling Stone*'s Jim Miller has observed this concept of growth in the song, which he views as building intensity through the addition of instruments, the piece "finally . . . blossom[ing] into an epic rocker," which he calls transcendent.[35] While it is true that instruments are added—the recorders, voice, electric guitar, bass, and finally drums—it is also significant that instruments are "replaced" by the electric guitar. Although the acoustic guitar remains part of the timbre throughout the piece, the electric guitar *takes over* from it upon its entry—it dominates the timbre—and is responsible for reshaping the discourse of the piece. The recorders drop out of the texture at the same time as the electric guitar enters. The electric guitar begins, upon its entry, with arpeggiated

Example 2.5. "Stairway to Heaven" fanfare, opening measures

gestures similar to that of the acoustic guitar (if slightly less complex), mimicking until it finds its own voice at the beginning of the solo. What happens, then, is a *replacement* of the acoustic with the electric. Since this happens fairly smoothly, I would diverge from Robert Walser's opinion that there is a "narrative juxtaposition" of the two and that they "combine contradictory sensibilities without reconciling them."[36] Rather, there seems to be an incremental movement away from the pastoral/archaic toward the electric/contemporary (the instruments added after the electric guitar include electric piano, electric bass, and drum kit). Part of the journey, then, has to do with moving from the rural/folk/archaic to whatever we might equate with the electric instruments— certainly something more contemporary, technological, and perhaps also urban. There are several interesting implications in this reading. Eero Tarasti has suggested that in general, when references to "archaic" or "folk" music styles are overtly made in a contemporary piece, this points to the mythical in that it brings the "mythical" past into the present (again, this suggests the importance of the performative in mythology).[37] Whether or not this is the case must depend on who is doing the listening. As a trained musicologist with a fairly good grasp of historical styles of Western music, I hear traces of sixteenth- or early seventeenth-century Tudor music in the opening of "Stairway to Heaven," and this situates it not in mythological time for me but in a particular historical moment.[38] The stylistic features that signal this to me are the timbres of the instruments (especially recorder), the contrapuntal lines, the quite static rhythmic texture (comprised primarily of straight eighth notes), with a few ornamental melodic gestures, the tonal language, and the square construction of the phrases. To many listeners, however, the opening of this piece may well suggest a kind of archaic music that is not linked to any particular time or place and hence may well signify the mythological. This is perhaps what Dave Lewis means when he writes about "Stairway" that "it has a pastoral opening cadence that is classical in feel and which has ensured its immortality."[39] Here "classical" music of any kind signifies "timelessness," a characteristic of myth (as Ricoeur put it, "we can no longer connect [mythological] time with the time of history as we write it . . . nor can we connect mythical places with our geographical space").[40] The narrative that is suggested by this piece, then, becomes the move-

Example 2.6. "Stairway to Heaven" harmonic patterns, last two measures of the fanfare, and beginning of guitar solo

ment away from myth or mythological time into present time. Given the interpretation of this song as a journey with the implication, or the overt acknowledgment, that the journey is about "a search for spiritual perfection"[41] or that it "seem[s] to embody the individual's prevailing quest for a spiritual rebirth,"[42] it is an interesting reversal, in musical terms, of the usual retreat into the archaic, away from the technological present, the past generally considered to have had more "depth" of spiritual force, especially for the counterculture.

In any event, the important mythological/ritualistic notion of transformation is certainly inherent in the formal characteristics of this piece. Spiritual/intellectual openness and questioning are suggested by the harmonic openness. Not only do we move from the acoustic to the electric (perhaps from mythological to historical time), but there is also the continual sense of growth through both the replacement and addition of instruments. Growth is also suggested by the unsettled form of the piece, the movement out of one music and into another, and, significantly, in never returning to the beginning. One might say, as Robert Walser does, that "Stairway" ends by "return[ing] to the solitary poignancy of the beginning,"[43] that is, with Plant's unaccompanied voice, but I would argue that this is not a very literal "return." Rather, because of the changes in the melody, the production, the complete lack of accompaniment (no acoustic guitar, no recorders, no "reassuring squareness" of the phrases), and the rubato way in which Plant sings (adding poignancy and a reflectiveness to the line), it is a clear indication of the transformation that has been undergone. One could argue that the idea of (extreme) transformation is also present in the drastic change in Plant's voice as he uses it after the guitar solo (from ballader to rock screecher). There is also a consistent textural movement away from counterpoint and toward homophony throughout the piece. In the first two sections there are various independent voices that are intertwined (listen, especially, to the independent movement of the bass during the "ooh it makes me wonder" refrain in the second section of the piece). During the guitar solo, of course, a single voice emerges as predominant in the texture, but significantly, it does not remain unsupported for very long: a second electric guitar track is added toward the end of the solo, which repeats a simple four-note descending motive in answer to the final phrases of the solo. This accompanying gesture, a descendant of the baroque "sigh" motive, is full of pathos; it answers each phrase of the guitar solo with the same plaintive wail. Following this, in the final section of the piece, all the instruments play the riff together, in complete unity. These textural changes suggest movement from a kind of community individualism (a working together), to the extreme individualism of the guitar solo, to the extreme community (Ricoeur's mythological unity and connectedness) of the ending. One of the respondents to the fan survey, Cynthia Kasee (who holds a Ph.D. in American Indian studies), pointed to a way in which at least some of the musical changes that one might construe as "growth" in this song also correspond to rituals that "are intended to draw participants closer as they progress (such as rites of passage which seek to include participants in a new life-phase or 'society'); [these] sound/appear to get faster and either louder or higher-pitched" (Plant raising his voice an octave, the intensity of the groove that accompanies the guitar solo, and so forth).[44]

Mary Douglas stresses that in ritual, "[e]vents . . . acquire meaning from relation with others in [a] sequence,"[45] and so it is important to consider that on the original LP "Stairway" was the last song on the first side of the album. This placement is significant to the semiotics of the piece because, on the one hand, it meant that the song was followed by silence that allowed for reflection—one had to turn the record over in order to hear any more music. But on the other hand, it is not the final song of the album—the last song of side 2—which might have been a logical positioning for the "gem" of the album. Getting to the end of the song that materializes the idea of the gnostic journey does not mark the end of the journey, only the midway point.

THE FOURTH ALBUM, on which "Stairway to Heaven" appeared, is certainly the most overt and celebrated document in terms of creating a mythology around the band. The album cover appeared with no title and without the group's name anywhere on it (not even the spine). The front of the jacket offers a portrait of an old man posed in the countryside, bent under the weight of a bundle of sticks carried on his back, which hangs in a battered frame on a dilapidated wall; the back offers a bleak urban landscape. A bit of the torn wallpaper from the front bleeds onto the back cover, suggesting that perhaps the wall belongs in one of the buildings portrayed on the back. In any case, the juxtaposition of the two environments, rural and urban, raises more questions than it answers: the rural landscape, green, luscious, is inviting but clearly requires strenuous labor (the man's back bent under the weight of the load he carries); the urban landscape is simply gray and dreary and seems to offer nothing at all, except alienation.[46] The jacket opens up to reveal some relief in the form of escape: a drawing of the hermit of the tarot cards, looking down on a little walled medieval city; a young man is climbing up the mountain toward the hermit, presumably to partake of his wisdom. The inner sleeve carries, on one side, the four symbols, each of which is meant to represent one of the band members, as well as the song titles and some other information, such as where the album was recorded. On the opposite side are the lyrics to "Stairway to Heaven," printed in an archaic script.[47]

This collection of images works in various ways to create the mythological. The hermit is a spiritual or occult symbol. Even if one did not know he was the hermit of the tarot cards, his status as a guardian of wisdom would be clear from his antiquity and the symbolic lantern (the light, the way) that he holds. This is one means by which the sacred is brought into play. The notion of a spiritual quest is symbolized by the youth climbing toward the hermit and the light. The four symbols that represent band members are also important in creating myth and a sacred realm. As Catherine Bell says, "[W]ith regard to objects as sacred symbols, their sacrality is the way in which the object is more than the mere sum of its parts and points to something beyond itself, thereby evoking and expressing values and attitudes associated with large, more abstract, and relatively transcendent ideas."[48] That these symbols are meant to stand for or at least be associated with the band members is extraordinary, since it at once tends to immortalize them and draw them into a sacred and mysterious realm (since we have little idea where their symbols come from or what they mean), one that appears to be ancient (since we imagine that symbols such as this are not invented in the present but are "timeless") and exclusive (since they seem to be part of something that we are not and about which we have little information). Printing the lyrics to "Stairway" but no other song on the album marks its specialness and frames this song as important; in fact, this is the first time the lyrics to any song were reproduced on a Led Zeppelin album cover so they are especially privileged. And because the lyrics are philosophical, as well as mysterious, choosing to print them points to the importance of these qualities to the band.

Although the fourth album is by far the most complex and developed collection of symbolisms that suggest the mythological or the sacred, there are many other examples. Page's interest in Aleister Crowley led him to inscribe Crowley's credo into the vinyl masters of the third album ("Do what thou wilt" is scratched into the last band of the vinyl).[49] The cover art for *Houses of the Holy* depicts young children climbing up what could be ancient runes. The cover of *Presence* includes "The Object" or obelisk, which was meant to reference the monolith in the film *2001: A Space Odyssey*. The remaining band members attempted to maintain this connection with the mythological or spiritual symbolism when they released the boxed set recording in 1990, which features a photograph of crop circles on the album cover.

The kinds of symbolisms used on Led Zeppelin's album covers are important for creating a mythology, but equally important is the complete lack of explanation for them, and especially the obscured identities of the band members. The dearth of information is extreme on the fourth album cover, but giving as little information as possible about themselves was typical. After the third album their pictures never again appear on album covers, and on the second album they appear only on the front cover, their identities fairly disguised by costumes—in fact, the photograph is of the Jasta division of the German air force, the original faces replaced with those of band members, managers Peter Grant and Richard Cole, and various other personalities, the large group of people helping to further obscure the band members' identities. On the third album cover tiny pictures of them in drag appear as part of the spinning wheel, but clearer photographs appear on the back. On both the second and third album cover photos, however, the color and quality had been manipulated so that they looked more like portraits than photographs—in other words, less real, more distant, and more stylized. Aside from the reproduction of the lyrics to "Stairway," only *Houses of the Holy* contained lyrics. And there was only ever the most limited information given concerning production, recording locations, engineering, and so on: the written information was kept to a bare minimum.

In addition, Led Zeppelin's media exposure was more limited than their stature would have warranted, although this was (and still is) exaggerated, in order, I would argue, to position them as something along the lines of misunderstood genius (and thus also important in constructing their mythology).[50] Press coverage in their native United Kingdom was, from the beginning, extensive and largely positive, especially in the magazine *Melody Maker*, where journalist Chris Welch became their champion. It was in the United States, where the band garnered a huge following immediately, that the press was much more lukewarm. *Rolling Stone* in particular had no use for them, publishing scathing reviews of the majority of their albums and, despite the band's enormous popular success, neglecting to publish a major story on them until 1975.[51] This story, by the young reporter Cameron Crowe, who became the band's defender at the magazine, already begins to mythologize their relationship with the press. The piece opens with the story of John Paul Jones overhearing a New York radio disc jockey vilify Led Zeppelin, who are scheduled to play Madison Square Garden the following night: "Let me just say that Led Slime can't play their way out of a wet paper bag, and if you plan on seeing them tomorrow night at the Gardens, those goons are ripping you off."[52] Crowe frames this in the following way: "It was a familiar battle, as Jones saw it. Although Led Zeppelin has managed to sell more than a million units apiece on all five of its albums and is currently working a U.S. tour that is expected to be the largest grossing undertaking in rock history, the band has been continually kicked, shoved, pummeled and kicked in the groin by critics of all stripes."[53] This becomes a familiar trope in the discourse about Led Zeppelin, one that aligns them in fans' minds with the unfairly downtrodden, as well as ensuring that they remain antiestablishment, "of the people." Still, the band *was* relatively reclusive: Page made it a point to speak with the press much less after some scathing reviews of the third album (and the relatively poor reception of this album by the press was one of the reasons that Page decided to put out the fourth album with no information about the band, confident that the music would "speak for itself").[54] Manager Peter Grant was fully cognizant of the powerful effect the band's absence from touring and putting out albums could have on its audience. *Billboard* magazine reported in 1979 on "the pattern of widely-spaced tours," noting that since establishing itself in 1969–1970 through extensive touring in the United States, the band had toured only four times, the last tour having occurred three years prior to the writing of the article. Grant is quoted as saying that "one of the keys to Zeppelin's longevity is that its appearances have been well-spaced, preventing overexposure."[55] The band's decision not to issue singles plays into this same idea of limiting exposure but also into notions of artistic integrity: one element of the album cannot be separated out from the whole. It also helps ensure that fans have to make a real investment in terms of searching out the music and then listening—to the whole album, not just one cut—if they want to come to understand the band, thereby differentiating insiders' knowledgeable about the band from those on the outside. As Robert Plant put it in retrospect, "From the beginning, really, it was a group policy that singles were not to be considered, that the whole game would be that if you wanted to find out about Led Zeppelin, you had to get into the whole thing. We would not put out singles as calling cards."[56] I would argue that the lack of what could be called programmatic titles for the first four albums also played into the band's desire to limit the amount of information available about them. Titles, like the printing of lyrics and other information on album covers, connect us to the artists; they open an interpretive window on the music and reveal something about the people who made it. Not giving programmatic titles to the albums also connects them to the tradition of "absolute" music: in the nineteenth century there was a school of thought that considered instrumental music, devoid of extramusical associations, to be the most serious and the most "transcendent" (that is, it was considered to be above any association with culture). Many composers named and numbered their works according to genre, as in "Symphony No. 1," so that the listener would not have a preconceived notion of how to listen to the piece or, indeed, that there was any extramusical (i.e., cultural) connection with the piece whatsoever. Numbering albums carries with it this same distance from the poetic, from the extramusical, from "pre-conceived" notions of what the music is "about."

The distance created between the band and fans through this lack of access and information, photographic or discursive, is very significant in creating their mythology, which can be better understood by using Marshall McLuhan's concept of hot and cold media.[57] McLuhan argues that a hot medium is one "well filled with data" while a cool medium is one that supplies little data: "The low definition of cool media requires the audience to 'fill in' the gaps. . . . Since hot media provides a substantial amount of information, it requires far less participation on the part of the audience in order to define or explain its meaning." In his essay "Aren't They Going to Turn That Down? Led Zeppelin, *Rolling Stone*, and the Thoughts of Marshall McLuhan," Simon Wood suggests that McLuhan's concept of hot and cold media can be extended from his limited definitions to include the way in which Zeppelin presented "a cool media image."[58] Their decision to keep a distance from the print media, especially after several bad reviews of the third album, and the titillating bits of information given on album covers required fans largely to invent the band for themselves. There are several ways in which this works to help create a mythology. First, the fans can imagine fantastic or extraordinary lives for their heroes when they do not know very much about the real-life situations. Second, when information is gleaned, its rarity makes it a precious commodity, and knowledge of it makes the fan an "insider."

This information vacuum manifested itself in performances as well. Very few words were ever spoken onstage, and those that were almost exclusively by Plant. He limited himself to introducing songs, sometimes with a small story attached, inviting the audience to sing along, or acknowledging one of the band members before or after a solo, but there was no extended dialogue. One way in which Plant helped to mythologize Page in concert was by calling out his name during a solo ("Oh, Jimmy!") or, as at the end of the performance of "Since I've Been Loving You" in *The Song Remains the Same*, saying, "Jimmy Page, electric guitar," as if Page needed this form of introduction, ever, but especially at that point in the concert; it was clearly intended to draw attention to the *wonder* of his playing.[59] The relatively small amount of dialogue was probably intended to signal that it was the music that was meant to convey band members' ideas, not their words, that, in fact, words just get in the way of the music. But it also has the effect of mythologizing band members, since the speaking voice—not only language but also the sound of a specific voice, the inflections used, the particular turns of phrase, and other mannerisms—is one of the ways we come to know something intimate about a person. Without that, again, we are left with only the few words that Plant ever uttered and must expand on those in our own minds in order to shape him into a human being.

None of the other three band members spoke during concerts, but this carries the most significance in terms of Page's persona. However much the other members of the band contributed (and their contribution was significant), Page was publically positioned as the virtuoso, the composer, the producer of the albums, the leader (see chapter 4). From the very beginning of Led Zeppelin, the discourse around him was intent on showing Page as the frail, perhaps slightly eccentric genius, and Page himself cultivated this image. Some early interviews took place at Page's boathouse in Pangbourne, and pictures from those interviews show him with hair draped around his shoulders, sporting plaid pants and maroon silk shirt, a lace throw on the couch and various antique objets d'art surrounding him—a snapshot of a Bohemian lifestyle.[60] The discourse around Page's personal life has tended to focus on his status as a loner (he was the only unmarried and childless member of the band) and on his interest in Aleister Crowley and the occult. In that 1975 *Rolling Stone* article, Cameron Crowe romanticizes both traits. In a brief biography, Crowe writes:

> Jimmy Page, now 31, grew up in Felton, a dreary community near London's Heathrow Airport. An only child, he had no playmates until he began school at the age of five. "That early isolation," says Page, "probably had a lot to do with the way I turned out. A loner. A lot of people can't be on their own. They get frightened. Isolation doesn't bother me at all. It gives me a sense of security."[61]

Stephen Davis repeats these exact words in the opening chapter of his sensational biography of the band.[62] Elsewhere in that same *Rolling Stone* article, Crowe asks Page about living in Aleister Crowley's house and what attracted him to the place. "The Unknown," Page replied, "I'm attracted by the unknown."[63] At the beginning of the film *The Song Remains the Same*, band members are shown receiving word that a tour is about to begin. Plant, Jones, and Bonham are shown with their families; Page is shown alone, sitting on the grass of his country estate playing a hurdy-gurdy, his back turned to the camera. When he turns around, his eyes glow an inhuman orange color.

It was logical, then, that Page should also have cultivated an isolationist persona onstage, keeping silent in terms of speech (or song—he only sang backing vocals during one song, the chorus of "Whole Lotta Love") and allowing the guitar to be his only voice, to, as it were, speak for him. The only notable exception to Page's silence onstage was during the 1980 tour, when, at least in the shows from Frankfurt and Berlin, Page appropriated Plant's customary greeting to the crowd ("Good evening"), told the crowd that it was nice to see them and it was nice to be seen, and introduced the song "Black Dog."[64] So extraordinary was this that it elicited comment from a number of sources. Steve Gett, who reviewed the Munich show for *Melody Maker*, commented "[I]ncredible, but true, Jimmy Page actually speaks on stage!"[65] Davis notes that "[Page] actually spoke to the audience, even introducing songs occasionally in his peculiar nasal voice. This had never happened before."[66]

Furthermore, Led Zeppelin was a closed and highly structured social organization, relatively isolated from the rest of the rock establishment, seemingly marked off from other performers and from the musical flexibility that is found in other groups. There are only three instances of "guest" appearances by musicians outside the band on their studio albums, the most exposed of these by a woman, Sandy Denny, who sings with Plant on "The Battle of Evermore"(the other acknowledged guest is Viram Jasani playing tabla on "Black Mountain Side"; Rolling Stones keyboard player Ian Stewart plays, unacknowledged, on "Boogie With Stu"and "Rock and Roll"). In live performances of "Battle of Evermore," however, Jones sang Denny's part, partly, it must be assumed, in order not to have someone outside the band appear on stage, since it would have been easy enough to hire a woman to sing Denny's part on tour. Although Page created multiple guitar tracks on many of the studio recordings, he never allowed another guitarist onstage with him. In order to play "Stairway to Heaven" live without the aid of a second guitarist, Page had built for him his famous Gibson SG double-neck guitar, which includes both a six- and a twelve-string guitar. It was apparently of utmost importance to Page that he be the only guitarist onstage—that he be able to manage the live arrangements of the most complexly orchestrated studio tracks on his own, that a "foreign" presence not pollute the purity of the band or break into the closed society, or, for that matter, dilute the appearance of Page's mastery over the instrument and consequent status as the powerful guitar hero. Commenting on this, Page said "There are times when I'd just love to get another guitarist on [stage], but it just wouldn't look right to the audience."[67] And although part of Page's mythological status certainly resides in his abilities as a soloist, it is interesting that he often chose not to solo within a song: Page's first consideration was the "mood" of the song, and he clearly felt that in many instances it was not in the best interest of creating the appropriate mood that a guitar solo be incorporated into the piece.[68] The song—the "work of art"—comes before the musician, who is positioned as the medium through which the work manifests itself (this interpretation corresponds to the way in which several fans characterized Page and the music earlier in this chapter). Page himself helped create this kind of mystique about his playing with comments like the one he made in 1975: "I'm not a guitarist as far as a technician goes. I just pick it up and play it. Technique doesn't come into it. I deal in emotions."[69]

While Plant would overdub his own vocal line or sometimes create a backing vocal for himself on an album (it is more usual in Led Zeppelin's music that he sings alone), backup singers were never used on albums or in concert (Plant began using an Eventide Harmonizer to create vocal effects in the studio and harmonies in performance at the time, according to Jones, of *Presence*). When Led Zeppelin began headlining shows, there was no opening act, which was highly unusual. The band was the sole focus of a show. When I asked Jones about these matters, he replied:

> As far as other musicians were concerned, Zeppelin was a tightly-knit unit, everything onstage was "in-house." Other players were simply not considered. Guests were invited on albums as and when we felt like it or when an instrument was required that nobody (me) could play, e.g., tabla on *Led Zeppelin I*.
>
> Opening acts were more trouble than they were worth. You couldn't get them on [on] time, then you couldn't get them off! Most people only wanted to see the headline band anyway, especially if it did a three hour set.

These characteristics set Led Zeppelin apart from contemporary British bands, for example the Who and the Rolling Stones, in which it was common for group members to change their roles within the band. Both Roger Daltrey and Pete Townsend sing, for example, and the Stones have always had two guitarists. Outside musicians commonly appear on Stones albums and in live performance.

As the fan who commented on Page's dragon pants earlier in this chapter noted, stage costumes are also important in the construction of a mythology. Costume has the effect of distancing the performer from audience members, of setting the performer apart. The more extraordinary the costume—the less likely one would be to wear it on the street—the more pronounced this effect is. There was little consistency among band members in terms of whether or not costumes would be worn or what kind of costume it would be. On this subject, John Paul Jones commented:

> Page and I were from the old school of "it's a show so wear something different," as opposed to the "honest" anti-show "come as you are" ethos. In fact, it is not true that Plant and Bonham did not have "stage clothes"; they may have been less obvious, (apart from Bonzo's *Clockwork Orange* boiler suit and bowler hat of later years!). Plant did in fact wear a fur-lined cape on

the first tour but it mysteriously disappeared one night. . . . It became a Zeppelin tradition never to discuss clothing before a tour, sometimes resulting in one member turning up in a white suit with the others in T-shirts and jeans, keeps ya smiling! As you can see, no significance whatsoever.

Although Jones is quick to dismiss costumes as having no particular significance from the band's point of view, they certainly made an impact on the audience. Page's visual iconography is partly defined by the costumes he wore on the 1973 and 1977 tours, on the former a black suit emblazoned with red and gold glittering serpents and on the latter a white satin suit with large red poppies (the white suit can be seen in Marty Perez's photographs, the black suit in the film *The Song Remains the Same*). Although Jones wore a spectacular costume in 1973, it was Page who mostly stood out in this respect, further entrenching his isolationist position but also, together with his spectacular movements onstage (see chapter 4), drawing the eye's gaze toward him.

A KIND OF epic length was, from the beginning, an important element not only of songs on the studio albums but also of performances. As one fan remarked, the length of some "epic" pieces "allowed the band to really stretch on stage and improvise, which is so much a part of their legend." In popular music, the length of a song has long been equated with substance, or lack thereof: the three-minute single has been repeatedly slagged as superficial, supposedly because it is not really possible to say something meaningful in such a short amount of time. We tend to make this association between shortness and superficiality, even though numerous examples exist that suggest otherwise (most people would not think the Beatles' "A Day in the Life" to be superficial, even though it is little more than 4 minutes long). This equating of length with substance is a holdover from the nineteenth century, during which time art works of epic length came to be associated with profundity. Several fans have clearly accepted this paradigm. The long songs, some say, "really make people think since they are so long and narrative. They are like short stories sung by bards." Long songs "usually show the band as a cohesive unit of virtuosos making a large statement." The epic songs require "patience" on the part of the listener: "If one has the patience to sit through these, it is amazing how the songs change and evolve to keep the listener interested." The ability to write these lengthy pieces is also tied to the musicians' ability to sustain musical ideas without losing the listener's interest, which one fan links to power and which has obvious (male) sexual connotations as well: "I have yet to hear a band that could produce an epic, to keep the power up over 10 minutes and not lose an ounce of grunt." The ability to compose long pieces as well as short ones demonstrates the band's versatility, and this serves as "evidence to how great the band is. They can compose long masterpieces as well as great three-minute singles." The composition of long songs that did not fit into radio playing formats is evidence that "Zeppelin didn't make music for radio or singles, they made music because they loved it and this resulted in them writing songs and not dropping any of the music just because it was to long to play on the radio"; hence the perception is that they did not "sell out" to commercial interests.

In epic pieces such as "Stairway," "Achilles Last Stand," and "Dazed and Confused," length is accompanied by musical complexity, which is manifested in two distinct ways: in structure and in the use of improvisation. The use of improvisation in concert performances of songs such as "Dazed and Confused," and "How Many More Times," and the improvised medley of song excerpts that occurred during "Whole Lotta Love" is extremely important to fans and has garnered much attention in writings on the band; length is one of the most critical issues around the use of improvisation. In his track-by-track listing of Zeppelin songs, Dave Lewis comments that "Dazed" "became a vehicle for extensive improvisation. . . . It also often stretched to 30 minutes in length."[70] Charles R. Cross, in his opening essay to the book *Led Zeppelin: Heaven and Hell*, mythologizes nearly every aspect of the band's existence; but on the question of length he writes: "During the 1975 tour they would occasionally stretch their concerts out for upwards of four hours but in that time they would only play 15 different songs."[71] The length of the show is mentioned three times in the same 1969 concert review in *Melody Maker*:[72]

Zeppelin play their marathon sets, which often run well over two hours, with a drive and intensity that demands your attention. . . .

Fans leapt onstage to grab lead singer Robert Plant as Zeppelin piled climax upon climax during the two hour plus shows that went on until after 2 am.

[Jones] We played over three hours without a break in Boston once. You get to the stage where you don't want to get offstage!

And in a 1990 interview, this concert in Boston, according to Jones, becomes four hours instead of three.[73] *Variety* magazine reported after the Madison Square Garden concert in 1973: "The only act on the bill, the Atlantic disk artists performed for 275 minutes with the sole pause being between the finale and encore."[74]

The stretching out of songs through improvisation in concert is important because it once again suggests movement away from the formulaic, toward the "spontaneous" creativity that is clearly highly valued by Led Zeppelin fans. Improvisation as it was manifest in Zeppelin meant not only lengthy solos but also veering off from the tune to explore bits of songs or grooves that often started and stopped without transition; as discussed in chapters 1 and 5 with respect to the songs "Dazed and Confused" and "Whole Lotta Love" respectively, extended improvisations were often free form, not very structured. According to Mary Douglas, what makes this attractive—indeed what perhaps makes the whole issue of length so attractive—is that form or order implies limitation or restriction, whereas disorder suggests potentiality: "This is why, though we seek to create order, we do not simply condemn disorder. We recognize that it is destructive to existing patterns; also that it has potentiality. It symbolizes both danger and power."[75] It is a risk but also thrilling to allow disorder into the music, and the musicians are credited as great risk takers for doing so. The power that Douglas sees in disorder comes from its perceived potential for leading the one who allows himself to enter into disordered mental states to untapped sources of power and wisdom: "In the disorder of the mind, in dreams, faints and frenzies, ritual expects to find powers and truths which cannot be reached by conscious effort. Energy to command and special powers of healing come to those who can abandon rational control for a time."[76] Further, Douglas speaks of this kind of formlessness as being a transitional or marginal state, again suggesting, with Victor Turner, that such states are transformative.[77] Experiencing the lengthy improvisational sections at Led Zeppelin shows, or now via bootleg recordings of those shows, is like experiencing someone in transition, in a liminal state: the potential for transformation comes through these improvisational moments. Hence they have a ritualistic importance that cannot be underestimated. Perhaps this is why so many Led Zeppelin fans collect bootleg recordings of live performances and why many of them insist that after digesting the studio recordings, listening to the bootlegs becomes a much more rewarding experience for them. As Douglas says, "To have been at the margins is to have been in contact with danger, to have been at the source of power."[78]

Coda: Ritual, Intimacy, and the Acoustic Set

The evocation of the "pastoral" and "archaic" in the opening of "Stairway to Heaven" is only one example of Led Zeppelin's "acoustic" side, a side of considerable importance when it comes to issues of mythology and ritual with respect to this band. Nothing, first of all, threatens the perceived stability of Led Zeppelin's identity as "proto-metal," as "cock rock," or as participating in the gnostic peregrinations of progressive rock as much as their acoustically based music and, especially, the acoustic set that became part of many performances in 1970 and after. The acoustic music moves the band into the realm of the folk or, more specifically, the folk revival of the 1960s, the ideology behind which Neil V. Rosenberg has neatly summarized as the "authentic democratic (or regional, or ethnic, or individual) expression in the shape of a natural, unpretentious art, [which has] frequently . . . been touted as an antidote against the alienating and meaningless modern popular music of the times."[79] In other words, evocation of the "folk-" or acoustic-based music in Led Zeppelin in general helps shape the band's mythology in terms of linking them to ideals of (perceived) noncommercialism, simplicity, the feeling of intimacy that came with such musical means, and "meaningful," sometimes "serious" texts.[80] It makes them "of the people," by employing a simpler style of music, by singing lyrics that related quite innocent visions of life ("Bron-Y-Aur Stomp," "Down by the Seaside," "That's the Way") and love ("Tangerine," "Ten Years Gone," "Going to California"), and by setting aside the visual theatrics that tended to make them larger than life, to distance them from their audience and render them mythological in a "heroic" sense. For some fans it also proved the band's musicianship: "[Y]ou know a band has really good music when they play acoustic and don't have to rely on fancy electrics, this is true with Led Zeppelin."

That acoustic music is found on every Led Zeppelin album save *Presence* and *Coda* (the latter an album of outtakes in any event) suggests how important it was to the band. Indeed, Jimmy Page has often commented that he wanted Led Zeppelin's music to comprise both "light and shade" (a phrase that has acquired its own kind of mythological status with respect to the band: almost every writer uses the term to describe their music, and it was repeated countless times on the fan survey), both acoustic and electric music. John Paul Jones said to me that "[the band] did not look upon ourselves as 'heavy,' at least not without the presence of balancing 'light.' The heavy image was largely a result of the press not paying attention! There were, after all, two acoustic songs on [the first] Led Zeppelin [album]." In chapter 3, I discuss Zeppelin's many and varied musical influences partly in terms of the importance they and their fans place on the perceived "depth" that such diversity signifies. Here, however, I think it is important to note that the importance of these "opposite" musical utterances indicates a desire for "wholeness," or, as some fans expressed it, it was "one of the things that made them Zep, the balance"; "[The acoustic music] balances the harder electric songs in a good way"; "[It] completed their stage performances." Balance is important not only to create an interesting show or to create musical variety but also as a signifier to fans of the band members' complex and multifaceted identities, which are capable of embracing opposites. And the notion of balance or all-encompassing identity is an important concept in diverse spiritual traditions—yin and yang or the alpha and omega, to name two—deep-rooted cultural concepts to which the balancing of the acoustic and electric in Led Zeppelin's music may be tied in fans' minds, even if subconsciously.

While acoustic music played an important role in Led Zeppelin's music from the outset, it hadn't previously been featured as prominently as it was on the third album. On the first two albums, acoustic elements are, except for the instrumental "Black Mountain Side," juxtaposed with heavy, electric sections within the same song. With the third album, and subsequently with the acoustic sets within live performances, this juxtaposition was manifested on a larger scale: on the album, moving from the mostly electric songs on side 1, to the more acoustically based songs of side 2, and in performance, shifting from an opening segment that began with heavy electric music to the acoustic set, back to electric music to end the show. Of the many acoustically based Led Zeppelin songs, "Tangerine" is a particularly powerful example of their musical intimacy and vulnerability. The lyrics relate the story of an innocent love that has been lost—a rare example of Page's lyric writing, one that reveals him to be capable of articulating the sentimental. The studio recording begins with a "mistake," which Page allowed to remain on the album. He plays the first two measures of the introduction but abandons it (in a later interview he admitted that the tempo was too slow). He begins again after he audibly counts himself in—taking a long two and a half measures to do so. We hear him whispering into the microphone and tapping his foot. The listener is given a window into the musical process here, as well as a glimpse of the artist (who was so guarded and inaccessible) at a moment of fallibility. The melody of the verse is comprised of three short phrases, all of which descend, poignantly depicting the loss of an innocent love ("Tangerine, living reflection of a dream; I was her love, she was my queen"). Page learned to play pedal steel guitar specifically for this piece, and it is one of the few times the instrument appears in Led Zeppelin's repertory. It enters during the chorus and evokes a soundscape seemingly antithetical to the musical personality of Led Zeppelin, given the instrument's association with country and western music (in fact, it should simply point up the fact that no musical style is antithetical to them). Perhaps the most striking feature of the piece, however, is the electric guitar solo that is heard in place of the chorus after the second verse. The solo is a surprise, first because instead of the expected G-major tonic chord and a reiteration of the chorus, a deceptive harmonic motion is made to an A-minor chord and the guitar solo. It is the first and only instance of the electric guitar used in this piece, a fleeting sign of power and confidence. But the solo is too short—it climaxes too soon, reaching a fevered high point without sufficient development (one fan calls it a "pseudo solo"), and the acoustic chorus, which has been delayed by the guitar solo, now appears. Page's usual ability to create a transcendent guitar solo within a piece has been curtailed here, demonstrating frustrated desire, perhaps also impotence, in any case fallibility, imperfection, and vulnerability.

The inclusion of a greater amount of acoustic material into something that can eventually be called an acoustic set was a gradual process. Page had included the acoustic "White Summer/Black Mountain Side" as part of the set in the first concert at the Fillmore West in San Francisco on January 10, 1969, and it was a staple of many concerts thereafter. By the time of the watershed Bath Festival Concert on June 28, 1970, there was a three-song segment that was more-or-less acoustic: "Thank You," "That's the Way," and "What Is and What Should Never Be."[81] This was later expanded to include songs such as "Bron-Y-Aur, "Going to California," "Tangerine," and, on the 1977 tour, "Battle of Evermore," with John Paul Jones singing the part of the Queen of Light.[82] Given what John Paul Jones told me about the acoustic set, however, it is not entirely clear that it was consciously developed as such:

I don't think that the acoustic set was ever discussed as such. "Going To California" and "That's The Way" were both written/rehearsed and recorded just sitting in a semicircle, and it seemed an obvious way to present them live. Page [had] already included a seated version of "White Summer" [in earlier shows]. It was also nice to have a rest in the middle of the show and worked well for the dynamics of the act.

As Jones describes here, the acoustic set in performance involved band members sitting across the front of the stage (see figs. 1 and 10), physically narrowing the gap between themselves and the audience and losing the readiness of "action" that comes with standing and, especially, moving—of commanding, dominating, owning the performance space by using all of it. By sitting down, band members became passive, vulnerable, much less powerful. When asked to comment on the acoustic set, fan respondents to the survey made it clear that they understood the playing of acoustic music and sitting down while doing so as gestures of intimacy and also risk (the band making themselves vulnerable in the process):

> A chance to become acquainted with individual members of the group instead of Led Zeppelin the machine.
>
> Made the band seem less remote.
>
> That other side of Zeppelin that was never really mentioned in the press. That time to relax a bit, chew the fat, and sing around the campfire—only there's an audience.
>
> It showed a delicate side instead of the Rock and Roll/Stairway hard rock music.
>
> The biggest risk, can you keep the attention and energy of an audience that came to ROCK? They could and they did. Every band should do an acoustic set. It forces the band to come out from behind the protection of feedback and play honest music.

At least for some fans, then, the acoustic music is perceived to expose the core of the band, stripped of the protective aural shield of amplification and the visual shield of high drama. In these situations, the heroes demonstrate how similar they are to you and me. Further, the acoustic set—or even Page sitting down to play "White Summer" in early gigs—begs to be viewed in terms of ritual. The moment was marked in concert by physically changing positions on the stage, not necessary in order to play the music but clearly viewed as important by the band in order to mark off the acoustic music from the rest of the concert. The intimacy of the music and the seated positions of the musicians created a confessional atmosphere, as well as one that suggests that private (domestic) as opposed to the public sphere.

Other bands, such as the Rolling Stones and the Grateful Dead, included acoustic sets in their concerts during the 1970s as well. It is still a feature of many hard rock concerts today, and the MTV *Unplugged* series derives from this idea. Those who consume rock music clearly want it to be part of their experience, for many different reasons, which range from simple "variety," to its significance in indicating something about the band's superior chops, to the opportunity it seemingly creates for feeling a closer bond with those musicians we admire.

THREE

Over the Hills and Far Away
Difference and Representation

[We were influenced by] a lot of stuff left and right of center . . . a lot
of West Coast stuff which really had caught me and saved me from
ending up being the typical English pub singer, because I found
that the Californian musical scene was the spearhead or the great
indicator of how music should have some bearing on . . . social
behavior or social awareness . . . The fact [is] that Led Zeppelin was
bold and brave and chaotic and honest. . . . It captured all the
elements of the kind of wondrous music that we'd all been exposed
to. . . . It's like we were a filter for all the good things. We filtered it
and we begged, borrowed and stole, and we made something
that was particularly original, by which a lot of other music has
been measured.
—Robert Plant, Interview on *Led Zeppelin: Remasters*

T he comments in the epigraph, made by Plant on the occasion of the retrospective four-CD boxed set release of Led Zeppelin's music in 1990, touch
on many ideas pivotal to the band's aesthetics.[1] It is a critically important aspect
of the music for band members and its reception by fans that not only were the
influences diverse and multiple but also, as Plant puts it, they were "left and
right of center," away from the mainstream—or at least that there was (and still
is) the perception that some of these influences were on the margins. The often-
told story goes that these were four people with eclectic musical tastes, all of
them steeped in various traditions, experiences, and influences. "We all had
ideas, and we'd use everything we came across, whether it was folk, country

music, blues, Indian, Arabic," recalled John Paul Jones.[2] In one of the finest essays written about the band, Robert Palmer works hard to get at this very point: Led Zeppelin was not only influenced by the blues, and their only product was not the raunch of "Whole Lotta Love": "Zeppelin's stylistic and emotional range were as broad and encompassing as those of any other band in rock's history."[3] Further, Plant suggests in the epigraph that music should have a purpose beyond entertaining, that it should be about "social awareness," something that is reflected fairly consistently in his lyrics ("The Song Remains the Same," "Kashmir," "The Battle of Evermore," and "Immigrant Song," to name a few in which the ideals of peace, brotherly love, and the futility of war are explored).

Most of Plant's comments, as well as those made by Page and Jones in retrospective interviews, point to the idea of Led Zeppelin's musical "depth," arrived at through the richness of their experience with various musics, their imperative constantly to engage in musical exploration—to go "beyond" the mainstream and to incorporate their many and various influences into their own music. This notion of depth has to do partly with questions of rock authenticity, partly with a much broader cultural trope that hinges on the importance of dense knowledge as a measure of seriousness as well as wisdom. I will return momentarily to this important notion of depth and how it might be interpreted in music, but it is the last of Plant's comments that requires problematization first: Led Zeppelin as a filter through which various musics are passed and then offered up, in an "original" way, to the listener. Plant clearly views this in a positive light, expressing what I understand as his genuine enthusiasm for and love of the many different kinds of music by which he was influenced. While there is much about it that is, indeed, positive (various fans have commented that it was Zeppelin who made them want to listen to bluesmen Muddy Waters and Howlin' Wolf, for example), there are certain aspects of it that will trouble students of culture. "Filtering" psychedelia or the folk/Celtic music popular in Britain in the 1960s has different political implications from "filtering" Indian and Arabic musics and the blues. Psychedelia and folk were being made by white middle-class youth, the same racial and economic group, coming out of similar cultural conditions and with some similar ideologies to those held by the members of Zeppelin. As well, the folk/Celtic influence connected them, however tangentially, to their own ancestry. But blues, Indian, and Arabic musics were radically other. Those sounds and lyrics come out of cultural experiences far removed from those of the white, Western middle class. "Filtering" in these instances carries with it the politically messy notion of "speaking for," because, unlike West Coast psychedelic musicians in the 1960s, the black blues musicians and largely anonymous Indian and Arabic musicians on whom Led Zeppelin drew did not have the same economic advantages, the same clout in the music industry to have their own voices heard, in short, the same cultural or economic capital.[4] The idea of filtering also resonates uncomfortably with Edward W. Said's notion that Westerners have often wanted to "invent" "the

East [or in this case the African-American experience]" for their fellow Westerners; to Said, it is an act of power to "discover," to re-create in this way.[5]

It would be easy to proceed by simply condemning Plant and the rest of the band for what might be viewed as a hopelessly colonial perspective. This would not take us very far, however, in understanding the band's use of these musics, the historical and cultural circumstances under which the appropriations were made, or, in fact, what they tell us about Led Zeppelin or the fans who consume these influences in their music (see later in this chapter for their comments). What kind of "East" is created by Zeppelin, how have they appropriated the blues, and why do these borrowings resonate with fans? Is it, in fact, too simplistic to separate the appropriation of these musics from that of others, to, in fact, politicize some borrowings but not all of them? On this subject, John Paul Jones has said, "It never occurs to me personally that one type of music is really any different from any other music. But other people can't understand it. They think you've really gone out on a limb to do something that's Arabic, or like a fifties rock and roll thing."[6] Similarly, Jimmy Page when asked about his and Plant's incorporation of Moroccan music into rock replied, "I don't like all those categories myself, putting things in pigeonholes: it's all music to me."[7] Are these comments naive or conveniently evasive, or do they reflect countercultural ideals of global unity, the ideal of some intrinsic sameness of all music and therefore all peoples? Do they reflect an idealistic desire to hear sounds as sounds, stripped of their cultural and political resonances? Should we view the various appropriations Led Zeppelin made in terms of Frederic Jameson's concept of postmodern "pastiche," which is either, as Jameson believes, "neutral mimicry, ultimately signifying nothing"[8] or, as Robert Walser suggests, "eclectic constructions ... [which can be] consulted, appropriated, and combined, used to frame questions of and answers about life and death."[9]

Appropriation of the blues and Eastern musics and images began to be made by British bands in the early 1960s and continue to be made in rock and pop music (in the 1990s witness the new white teenage blues guitar phenomenon Jonny Lang or Madonna reinventing herself as a geisha),[10] but as Timothy D. Taylor suggests, "Writing around these concepts without oversimplifying or mistaking a particular musician's subject position" should be the goal, which means that the distinctive way in which such borrowings are manifest in an artist's work and attitude should undergo careful scrutiny.[11] Much has been said about Led Zeppelin's relationship with blues music. The essay by Robert Palmer that accompanies the boxed set recordings of Led Zeppelin addresses the persistent criticism the band has faced with respect to their appropriation of the blues, and Dave Headlam has written about the issue of authorship in Led Zeppelin with respect, mostly, to the blues. He has engaged in close musical analysis in an attempt to determine what Zeppelin borrowed and what was original in several songs (see bibliography). I address aspects of the band's use of blues in chapters 1 and 5. Here, then, I want primarily to focus attention on Zeppelin's borrowings from Eastern musics.

THERE ARE ONLY a handful of Led Zeppelin songs in which elements of Eastern musics are used overtly. There is the use of tabla in "Black Mountain Side" (the only song to use a non-Western instrument), as well as the various melodic and rhythmic elements in "Friends," "Four Sticks," "White Summer," "In the Light," and of course "Kashmir." Page also claimed that "Achilles Last Stand" was influenced by "the local music" he had heard on his travels to Morocco in 1975, and it is possible to hear some of this influence in the melodic turns and ornamentation in the guitar solo.[12] Partly because of its title, but also for musical reasons that I will explore later, "Kashmir" stands as the most overt example of this influence. It is also the piece responsible for foregrounding the band's interest in Eastern musics, because Plant has made such a point, in retrospect, of saying that it best represents what the band was about, a remarkable idea considering the diversity of their output. In 1988, Plant commented:

> ["Stairway to Heaven"] is not the definitive Led Zeppelin song, "Kashmir" is.... It's the quest, the travels and explorations that Page and I went on to far climes off the well-beaten track. Of course we only touched the surface. We weren't anthropologists. But we were allowed, because we were musicians, to be invited in societies that people don't normally witness. It was quite a remarkable time, to open your eyes and see how Berber tribesmen lived in the northern Sahara. My interpretations lyrically are not that fantastic; they never have been. But that's what it was like for me then. That, really, to me is the Zeppelin feel.[13]

For the sake of balance, it should be noted that John Paul Jones's view of things is almost exactly opposite: "As much as I like 'Kashmir' (one of my favourites) I would have thought that 'Stairway To Heaven' is closer to defining what Zeppelin was about, with its acoustic/electric dynamics and long journey-like form." But note that for both musicians it is the idea of "the journey" or "quest" that makes these pieces significant in terms of defining something essential about the band (see chapters 1 and 2 for more on this).

This points up the other crucial factor in foregrounding the band's interest in Eastern musics: the Page/Plant reunion in 1994, which produced the *Unledded* concert video and tour and the album *No Quarter*. Whereas the use of Indian and Arabic musics in Led Zeppelin had always been fairly covert—almost no use of exotic instruments, the influences coming through the use of particular modes and rhythms instead—here the idea was to bring these and other influences to the surface, to point to them in a much more direct way. For the performances of "Friends," "Four Sticks," and "Kashmir," an ensemble of Egyptian musicians was used, and the form of "Kashmir" was opened up to include a brief introductory *taqsim*[14] on the electric guitar and a lengthy violin solo by one of the Egyptians, Wael Abu Bakr. In the performance of "The Battle of Evermore," Indian vocalist Najma Akhtar took the part of the Queen of Light, originally sung by folksinger Sandy Denny on the fourth Led Zeppelin album. Page and Plant wrote and performed two pieces with Gnawa musicians from Morocco (on location) and also played an original Arabic-influenced piece in a square in Marrakech. The decision to make non-Western music and musicians so central a part of this project, which, although not touted as a Led Zeppelin reunion (John Paul Jones did not take part), consisted to a large extent of reworked Zeppelin songs, necessarily strengthened the link between their music and the East, setting it apart as a particularly important influence and romanticizing and mythologizing it in the process (see later).

Still, the idea of these influences being particularly significant and of bringing them to the fore in a similar way to that done by Page and Plant on their 1994 album seems to have been in the works in the 1970s as well, at least for Page and Plant. They traveled to Morocco and India together after the 1975 tour and made attempts to record with local musicians. Page recalled in 1990 that "[the recordings of 'Friends' and 'Four Sticks' made with members of the Bombay Symphony] were something that we were going to work on.... The actual master plan after having [made those recordings] was to maybe do a tour through the Far East, going through Egypt and Bombay, then on to Thailand ... and then recording in those places."[15] There is also evidence to suggest that these musics were significant for more than their sounds alone. In 1975 Page told *Rolling Stone* reporter Cameron Crowe, "I think it's time to travel, start gathering some real right-in-there experience with street musicians around the world. Moroccan musicians, Indian musicians." When asked by Crowe what he hoped to gain from these travels, Page replied, "Are you kidding? God, you know what you can gain when you sit down with the Moroccans. As a person and as a musician. That's how you grow. Not like this, ordering up room service in hotels."[16] Plant, too, was drawn into the otherness not only of Indian and Arabic musics but also of the emigrant Indian and other ethnic populations in 1960s Britain: "When I was 17, I began dating the consequent mother of my children [who was Indian]. She lived in an East Indian area, so I was constantly surrounded by Indian film music ... And five blocks from that was the Jamaican neighbourhood, where I used to hang out when I wasn't working, eating goat stew and listening to ska records."[17] Plant discussed these influences at greater length, in the context of his plans to travel to Kashmir, in a 1975 interview in *Circus* magazine: "It's my ambition to go to Kashmir, and I'm saving that as the last trek.... Then I'd like to just disappear for about four or five years.... Of course it's not wine and roses or even the spiritual aspects of life there that I'm interested in. It's day to day experiences.... There's so much to learn there, so much that we here in the West have lost."[18] Jones has always expressed the influence in musical terms alone, relating that as a child he listened to Arabic music on shortwave radio: "[W]e could pick up North Africa, so I spent many hours listening to Arab music. I loved it—and still do."[19] In my correspondence with Jones, I pressed him on the issue of how he viewed the appropriation of these musics, especially on the issue of whether there was for him a resonance with the cultures from which they came:

It is true that I heard a lot of what must have been Algerian/Tunisian music on my father's radio. My father was a pianist/arranger and my mother a singer and dancer. Together they did a "variety" act, what you would know as vaudeville. I would tour with them when I was young and would therefore be exposed to music from other acts on the various bills they played. These would include acts from all over the world, jugglers, acrobats, trapeze, animal acts, as well as singers, dancers, etc. They all had their own music which I would hear night after night! East and Western European, Arab, Chinese, North and South American, I must have absorbed it all from the ages of 3 to 11.

My [musical] interest was probably ignited through the jazz of John Coltrane/Yusef Lateef/George Russell before the British blues revival/countercultural stuff, but it is also true that around the time of the Beatles more and more "Eastern," especially Indian, classical music was being heard in England. . . . I think that with the increased access to these musics it seemed natural to expand one's musical vocabulary by incorporating modes, rhythms, form, etc. into our own music. Indian pop music (for instance) of course did the reverse! There was of course, at the time, an interest in other cultural/spiritual/religious aspects which had arisen fashionably but were being more seriously explored by musicians and artists generally, but for me the music was the main focal point. Friends of mine in the jazz field (John McLaughlin) were also investigating Eastern musics at the same time. . . . In terms of musical culture I didn't see what we were doing as so wildly different. . . . Whilst I appreciate some of the "cultural appropriation" arguments, as I'm sure you know, things aren't quite as simple as they are made out [to be]. The constant flow of musical (and cultural) influences around the world throughout history is one of the aspects that makes it all so interesting and exciting.

These comments express something of the producers' perspective; from the point of view of the consumers, there is almost always an extramusical association made and almost always the same kind of association. Fans are generally enthusiastic about Zeppelin's use of "Eastern" elements, commenting mainly on how this adds to that all-important characteristic of the band, their musical diversity, and, once again, to the notion of depth: "I like the sound of this, especially in 'Kashmir.' It shows how the band is becoming more diverse and is not afraid to go in different directions"; or, "I enjoy the 'eastern' sound in their music, I think it gives us a taste of how culturally rich they are." But many of the fans' comments suggest that "Kashmir" or the use of Eastern elements in their music gives it a "mystical" or "mysterious" quality, and some take this further, suggesting that there is something "ethereal," "otherworldly," and "timeless" about these elements as used by Zeppelin:

> ["Kashmir"] A beautiful and innovative exotic song that takes me on an ethereal journey to a far away land. Perhaps Zep's finest moment.

> Epic, mysterious, beautiful—paints a perfect picture of utopia.

> It makes the music mystical.

> Very important as it enhanced much of what they did and brought a mysterious, unearthly feel to their music.

> "Kashmir" is a timeless masterpiece, one which cannot be defined.

> Eastern elements are very welcome as I practice meditation and love the vibe.

> Brings their music to a new level. "Kashmir" is classic. Eastern elements give their music a timeless quality, while at the same time giving it an exotic, ethereal, otherworldly feel.

> I love the eastern sound. I liked it in some of the Beatles songs, too. Both groups implemented it well into their music. I like the mystery of it. It's so un-American, and it gives the song a spiritual quality which it otherwise may not have.

These comments clearly signal that the use of these characteristics is positive—that they enhance the music in a significant way. Only three fans suggested that there might be something problematic about this use of Eastern elements, one suggesting that it was "revisionist history," another simply commenting, without further explanation, that it was "not right." The third fan was more specific: "Early 'worldbeat' or Western cultural imperialism? Hmmm. I've been around the university too long...."

All of the comments made by fans indicate that they hear the sounds as signs of radical otherness, which they characterize in fairly stereotypical ways; they have, indeed, internalized the exoticism of othering. They make, for example, a general association between the East and spirituality, including mysticism. They perceive a kind of continuity found in these cultures ("timeless") absent from the West. I would suggest that this has to do with romantic notions of the rural (pastoral) and a perceived absence of the alienation of industrialization and modernity; perhaps this is what makes these cultures "utopian." That the Eastern elements suggest something "otherworldly" to several of the fans indicates perhaps the continued perception that these cultures are extremely remote from them. Clearly in some cases the global culture in which we now live has done little to remedy this situation.

The ideas expressed by fans and by Page and Plant were born during the late-1960s countercultural moment. The members of Led Zeppelin were in their late teens or very early twenties during this time, and in many respects they carried the impulses of that movement with them throughout the 1970s. They were, of course, among many musicians from about the mid-sixties on who came to discover Eastern musics and who began to incorporate Eastern sounds into their music. Their attraction to the East came, at least in part, from the countercultural impulse to look somewhere other than the dominant culture for their spiritual and social truths. As Paul E. Willis put it, there was a widespread belief that "Europe [had been] worked out, [that you] had to get to the East if you want[ed] anything real" (a sentiment that one can hear ringing loud and clear in Page's comments about sitting "down with the Moroccans" quoted earlier).[20] And further:

> Identification with underprivileged groups is a much noted characteristic of the hippy movement, most clearly represented, of course, by the espousal of the American Indians by the San Franciscan hippies. The basis of this interest and identification was not simply curiosity, not the desire to be different and colourful, not a romantic association with the outsider and his style. The aim was to feed on dense experience: to be with the smell of real human bodies before the dehumanizing juggernaut of material society squashed out the real human juices. Oppressed cultures were used as a set of forms, a milieu, within which to express their criticism of the ratio-technical order and what *it* suppressed or no longer had.[21]

The perceived "depth" of non-Western peoples is what is at issue here. Willis chooses to align the notion of dense experience with the body, with "smells" and "juices" that are imagined by Westerners to have been erased from their culture. He makes the important point that the countercultural impulse to look toward non-Western cultures was not a simplistic, superficial yearning for the other but rather occurred in order to engage in a process of recovery: of body, spirit, and community. As Plant said in 1977 about listening to Bulgarian folk music, "[I]t's what you might call mass singing, like village singing when a village gets together at various times of the year when they hope for this, that and the other to happen ... all that we in Britain have almost lost."[22]

What references to Eastern musics can be heard in Led Zeppelin and how are these heard? Can we know from listening to the music alone what philosophical or political point of view the musicians had toward these musics and cultures? Can we hear these points of view in *any* music where such borrowings are made? Since it has become so central a document in Led Zeppelin's output, I will begin an exploration of these questions through an analysis of "Kashmir."

The title to this song might suggest that it is intended as a representation of the place, although when the album appeared band members pointed out that none of them had been there.[23] Plant recalls, in fact, that he wrote the lyrics to this song as he was traveling in Morocco,[24] far removed from the Indian subcontinent, and so one has to wonder why the piece wasn't called "Marrakech" instead (the existence of the Crosby, Stills, and Nash song not withstanding). Does "Kashmir" suggest greater remoteness and exoticism? Furthermore, the lyrics do not describe anything specific about Kashmir the place. In fact, quite the opposite: Plant's most graphic imagery is of the desert as a geographical metaphor for remote otherness (the burning sun, the dust and sand of "this wasted land"), and the harshness of such a landscape serves as a metaphor for his arduous gnostic journey (the mountains of Kashmir probably wouldn't evoke the same kind of "difficulty" or "remoteness" in a listener's mind). The lyrics characterize a generalized cultural other through their use of "incomprehensible" language and further suggest that this cultural other is not Western by using the word "elders" to describe members of it. This word is used, especially, in tribal societies (and so it also references the nonindustrial), as well as Protestant churches, in which it suggests religious authority and wisdom, and so here it suggests a kind of generic spirituality. Only near the end of the song do we get the specific reference to the place: "moving through Kashmir." "Kashmir" stands for "other" in the broadest sense, invoking remoteness, strangeness, and the exotic to the Westerner in its very name,[25] and for "the East" in a slightly less broad sense. After describing the profound experience he has in his encounter with this other, Plant ends the song by singing, repeatedly, "Let me take you there," as the song fades out. This is a vexing statement with which to contend: is this Plant the idealistic hippie, eager to share his "dense" experience with fellow Westerners, an experience that has, after all, been largely about encountering a radical other who is "gentle," through whom "all will be revealed," who speaks with "tongues of lilting grace," with "sounds [that] caressed my ears," whom the singer has eagerly encountered with "no provision but an open face"? Or is this Plant the imperialist, discovering (constructing) an "East" for other Westerners with whom he wishes to share it—"let me invent this experience for you through my lyrics and through the evocative music"? Or does he literally want to take his fellow Westerners to the "real" East, to have them experience what he perceives as the wonders of it themselves, in all its richness, "unfiltered" by Western notions of what the East should be? From my position as a white middle-class Westerner, with residues of countercultural idealism still running through me, Plant's imagined encounter with an extraordinary place and people, far removed from the modernized West, resonates strongly with me. But I am simultaneously made uneasy—guilty, perhaps—by his inventions, his characterizations, made by an outsider, observing from his privileged position, me consuming his imagery from mine.

There are similar tensions to be found in the music. In fact, the cultural, ideological tensions to be found there are perhaps even more problematic to sort through than in the lyrics because there are so many issues to consider with respect to the sounds heard. There are no "exotic" instruments used in this piece, so Eastern elements are melodic, rhythmic, and perhaps also structural. Concerning the absence of "exotic" instruments in Led Zeppelin, Jones says, "We did not like to use instruments that we could not play to a reasonable standard," suggesting, importantly, that "dabbling" with the instruments (that is, their superficial use) was not acceptable. Further, Jones stresses that the "structural as opposed to surface use [of Eastern influences] was perhaps more a result of understanding rather than imitation," again emphasizing the musicians' construction of what might constitute "deep" knowledge of the music.

For the purposes of my discussion, I have mapped out the formal structure of "Kashmir" in the diagram that follows. There are three distinct sections of music, which I have labelled A, B, and C, respectively. Both A and C sections are repeated.

Section A: main riff: intro/ Verse 1/transition/Verse 2/ transition (with brass)
Section B: new riff (octaves) "Ooooo, baby I've been flying"/ transition
Section C: "All I see"/mellotron and string melody
Section A: main riff: verses 3 and 4/transition
Section C: "When I'm on my way"/more mellotron/ascending scale to fade

The prevailing references to Eastern music in this piece suggest Arabic, not Indian, sources, although there is a certain amount of ambiguity with respect to this and the two might well be intermingled in the mind of a Westerner with limited exposure to or experience with these musics. This further stresses that the word "Kashmir" is invoked to represent "the exotic" in a general way and, in fact, that for some Westerners differences between Kashmiri culture and those of North Africa are insignificant in painting a picture of the exotic for Western listeners. While it is easy to point to North African musical influences in some cases (the mellotron/string melody in section C of the piece, for example: see analysis later), in others the very notion that something Eastern is being referenced is in itself ambiguous to the Western ear. For example, the pervading rhythmic gesture throughout much of the piece, including the riff, is comprised of unsyncopated sixteenth notes or combinations of straight eighth and sixteenth notes, and this strikes me as a reference to a similar rhythmic structure often found in Egyptian music. It is possible to see these rhythmic similarities in example 3.1, which reproduces the main riff and turn figure of "Kashmir" (ex. 3.1a) as well as the opening of the piece "Gannat Naimi" as performed by the Egyptian singer Oum Kaltsoum (ex. 3.1b; this introduction is played by a classical Egyptian instrumental ensemble consisting of 'oud, nay, strings qanun and percussion). Although it is possible to find this rhythmic structure in much Egyptian, as well as other Arabic, music, my choice of example here is not random: Plant has often cited Oum Kaltsoum as an influence. She is, in fact, the only non-Western musician important to the band who was actually named by them.

This kind of rhythmic gesture also references Western classical music, in particular the motor rhythms of the late Baroque (the riff) and the ornamental figures of the Classical period (the turn). For many people in the West, the use of strings and brass playing figures like this would probably reference Western

Example 3.1a. "Kashmir" riff; turn figure

Example 3.1b. Oum Kaltsoum, "Gannat Naimi," introduction

classical music, but strings are also used in Egyptian ensemble music, making the cultural significance of this instrumentation within the piece ambiguous as well. The riff to "Kashmir" is played in octaves or unison by the instruments, which is characteristic of Egyptian ensemble music; but it is also characteristic of some rock music. A further ambiguous element is the drone and slightly heterophonic texture created by Jones in the bass guitar part. While he mostly mirrors the rhythm of the other melodic instruments, he does diverge from it slightly, dropping an octave at the end of every measure of $\frac{3}{4}$ instead of resting as the others do. This slightly heterophonic texture is fairly typical in rock music, however, and very typical for Led Zeppelin, where instead of drums, guitar, and bass doubling a part exactly, there is often some melodic and/or rhythmic variation made (see the discussions of riffs in chapter 4). In addition, as the other melodic instruments play the ascending chromatic line of the riff, Jones stays fixed on the tonic, D, creating a drone, a musical device often used in both Indian and Arabic musics (although it is not particularly associated with Egyptian ensemble music); but he also participates in the rhythmic structure of the riff, so that this stasis on the tonic loses some of its dronelike quality.

While the specific cultural or historical reference might be difficult to point to with any specificity, it is clear that the rhythm of the riff especially, as well as its melodic shape—chromatically ascending—lie very much outside the sonic norms of the blues, R&B, or other Western popular musics usually drawn upon in rock. In other words, whether or not the listener consciously identifies the riff as resonating with Arabic or classical Western musical gestures, s/he probably recognizes its otherness from the rock tradition. In fact, the musical design of the riff points up the otherness of the rhythmic/melodic structure of what strings, guitar, and bass are playing by pitting this against the groove of the drums. The drum groove is very much tied to rock tradition, the measure of $\frac{4}{4}$ time being articulated by the bass drum on beats 1 and 3, the snare on the backbeat. As has often been pointed out, the guitar/strings/bass riff is, in fact, in $\frac{3}{4}$ time against this. Four measures of the guitar/strings/bass riff equals three measures of the drum groove. In other words, the two coincide at the beginning of each new statement of the guitar/strings/bass riff (when it reaches the top of its chromatic ascent). This not only creates an interesting sonic landscape, one in which the relationship between the parts is constantly changing, but it also works semiotically to point up the otherness of the guitar/strings/bass riff from the rock tradition—how it fits only partially and most of the time uneasily within that tradition. Page has said that his experiments with rhythm and meter were influenced by his interest in Eastern musics, where asymmetrical groupings are common, but again, it would be difficult to pin the opening of "Kashmir" explicitly to this influence.[26] The musical construction of the riff has further semiotic significance with respect to the lyrical message of the song that has nothing to do with its musico-traditional associations. The metrical ambiguity, the changing relationships between the two parts of the riff—the blurring, in effect, of clear relationships between the two—suggests the alien environment in which the singer finds himself; and the rising chromatic fourth of the riff, which moves from the fifth scale degree to momentary closure on the tonic, taking considerable time to accomplish this rise to the tonic, creates a sense of striving for a goal that is only reached momentarily before sliding back down to the starting point of the riff (the goal of tonic is, in fact, elided with the beginning of a new iteration of the riff, so there is an elusiveness about having reached the goal at all).

There are three musical elements of this piece that are much more clearly derived from Arabic sources: the riff to the B section, the mellotron melody in the C section, and Plant's vocal melisma, also in the C section. There is a tonal shift away from the tonic, D, for both of these sections, to the dominant, A, for the B section and to the subdominant, G, for the C section. This means that those characteristics furthest removed from Western music occur during moments of tonal instability, so that they are placed within a "foreign" tonal context, thereby reinforcing their otherness. The riff to the B section consists of a falling octave, marked by a glissando in the strings, and both the descending motion and the glissando clearly reference similar gestures made in Arabic ensemble music. Note the downward tendency of the melody in example 3.1b; on the recorded performance, the musicians almost always add glissandos between notes of the melody.

Jones's mellotron melody in section C is perhaps the clearest reference to the East in the piece. It is a sustained presence, and there is some development, as opposed to mere repetition. The scale (ex. 3.2) belongs to the *nakriz* genre of *maqam*, or Arabic mode, with its characteristic cadential pattern that includes—in descending order—a semitone, an augmented second, another semitone, and a whole tone, or, in the parlance of Arabic music theory, "the descending sequence of seconds—minor–augmented–minor–major.[27]

About the knowledge of modes, Jones told me: "I don't know about Jimmy, but my modal knowledge came from generally listening to the music and using my 'ears' to use appropriate modes over harmony. I didn't study them formally. I was, however, used to utilizing modes whilst playing jazz before Zeppelin, with John McLaughlin." Although Jones stays with Western tuning, avoiding the

Example 3.2. Scale used for the mellotron melody in section C of "Kashmir"

three-quarter and one-quarter intervals characteristic of the Arabic tone system, the timbre of the mellotron, with its shaky pitch, helps to create the illusion of that nuanced system. Again, Jones's melody has the characteristic "straight" (unsyncopated) rhythmic shape of so much Arabic melody, and the particular melodic gestures he makes—turns, descending sequences, and so forth—help to link the melody further to that musical language. Plant shares part of the mode with Jones—mostly the three notes B♭, A, and G—but, importantly, he does not make use of the augmented second that appears between the third and fourth scale degrees, which is what assures the listener that this mode does not belong to the West. Significantly for the semiotics of the mellotron melody, it always follows Plant's entry, usually beginning with the same three-note descent and then veering off into an ornamental elaboration (a characteristic heterophonic construction for Arabic music). It reinforces Plant's musical direction—is the source of this direction—but is tonally and melodically much richer and "other."

The second "exotic" element that appears in section C is a vocal melisma sung by Plant; this comes at the end of the section, with the lyric "trying to find where I've been." It is the only time in the piece that he vocalizes without using lyrics for a fairly extended period of time, the only occasion on which he ornaments the melody (he adds a shake twice in the melisma), the ornaments carrying the melody into a new tonal range, one that becomes jarringly dissonant against the riff (at the end of the melisma he is singing an F♮ against B in the riff, creating a tritone—the F♮ pulls him further into Jones's mellotron melody and the *nakriz* mode). Even though it lasts only a moment, the stylistic shift is jarring. Semiotically, Plant has moved into another musical language and, by association, into the other culture, finally going beyond a verbal description of it to try something of it out through his own voice, his own body. This is a decisive moment in the song—perhaps its defining moment—when cultural lines are crossed within a single melody. What gives this moment its particular power is the way in which Plant sings as well as the particular production values, which include the heavy use of echo on his voice to make it sound increasingly distant. He *drifts* into the melisma, as if in a dream state. The expression he uses throughout the piece has much the same quality to it—often behind the beat, with deliberately slurred articulations, a generally slowed-down approach to the delivery of the lyrics—indicating the physical impact that his encounter with otherness has had on him. He has left behind the rat race of the West, has embraced a slower, more thoughtful, enchanted realm.

FIGURE 1

FIGURE 2

Figure 3

FIGURE 4

FIGURE 5

Figure 6

Figure 7

FIGURE 8

FIGURE 9

FIGURE 10

FIGURE 11

FIGURE 12

FIGURE 13

FIGURE 14

FIGURE 15

FIGURE 16

FIGURE 18

Plant's characterization of this profound experience is marked in other ways as well. For much of the time he uses a tone that is reasonably free from distortion. There are only two points at which distortion becomes an important element: during the B section and during the repetition of the C section. These moments in the piece are rhetorically different from the others. While in the verses sung during A and first mention of the C section Plant is describing the details of his experience—where he's been, what he's seen—in the B and final C section he is describing the emotional effect these experiences have had on him. If the presence of distortion in rock singing often signals power, its absence throughout much of the song might reflect his deference to the experience he is describing, his lack of power in the face of these experiences, or, in fact, a certain unwillingness to assert power or ego; the relative weakness of his vocal tone during the verses also points to this kind of interpretation. We should not lose sight of how powerful a voice Plant has and how deliberate an attempt this is to make his instrument sound feeble. It is when he turns inward to describe the effect of his experience that he conveys its power over him through the use of distortion and his more characteristically powerful tone, especially at the end of the song, beginning with the words "when I'm on my way," at the beginning of the repeated C section. The structure of the lyrics also conveys this sense of deference to the overwhelming power of the experience. During the A section, there are two verses. The first of these is regular: eight lines of text per stanza in which (more or less) alternate lines rhyme. But the second stanza in each case has only four lines of text, after which Plant sings "woa, woa," instead of text. Lost to the power of the experience, he can find no more words to describe it. This also occurs during the entire B section of the piece, where there are few lyrics, most of them incoherently expressed.

Other elements of the piece, too, encode the lyrical theme and evoke the Eastern other, but without making reference to Eastern music. As Ralph Locke points out in his article on the use of Eastern elements in nineteenth-century opera, musical manifestations of Orientalism are in no way limited to overt references to Eastern musics, just as literary Orientalism has little to do with using formal elements borrowed from Eastern poetry or prose styles. Echoing Said, Locke argues that "the primary aim of nineteenth-century Orientalism was to 'represent' the East to the West: precisely how this was done varied a great deal, and did not always involve non-European stylistic means."[28] For example, the asymmetrical form of "Kashmir," which I have mapped ABCAC, denies closure, suggesting a loss of self to the other throughout the progression of the piece. This interpretation is strengthened by the fact that clear, overt references to Eastern music are made as the piece progresses, and the most "developed" use of them (the mellotron/string melody) appears in the C section with which the piece ends; there is no return to the more ambivalent use of these elements in the riff. Not only are the melodic materials of the closing section different from those at the beginning, but it is tonally open as well, ending on the dominant of the piece, not the tonic. The mellotron/string melody changes at the end of the piece, further exaggerating this openness: it turns into an ascending G Dorian scale that, near its end, tonicizes A major, the final chord of this ascent, which occurs on the downbeat, ornamented with part of the turn gesture that has been heard throughout, both signifying a kind of triumph. This "triumphant" ascending scale is repeated over and over as the piece fades out and as Plant begs to take his listener "there," somewhere "else," to the other.

There is also a grandeur to the piece that comes partly from its pace—the unhurried tempo—but also from the way the groove is set up. As is so often the case with Led Zeppelin's music, it is John Bonham's drumming that does so much to crystallize the feel of the piece ("['Kashmir'] works because of Bonham's drumming," wrote one fan, and several others noted the crucial role it plays in this song). Although the groove set up by Bonham is regular, it is very simple, articulating only each quarter note of the beat, occasionally adding two sixteenths on the first or third beat to mirror the rhythmic pattern of the riff, leaving much of the beat empty, creating the effect of wide open space. This sense of space is magnified in the B section, where the third beat of every second measure is left completely empty, by Bonham and everyone else. This marks the end of each new iteration of the riff, the pause coming directly after the descending string glissando.[29] No doubt in part because of the slow tempo of the song and this simple, unchanging drum groove, one fan described the piece as "hypnotic," another as "a powerful machine that went forward no matter what stood in its way. There's just no stopping it." I have also heard the groove described, again because of its slow pace, its regularity, and the heavy sound of the bass drum, as a particularly apt sonic depiction of someone walking through the desert, determined to forge ahead yet burdened, weighted down by the elements. One fan captured something of this interpretation when he described the "lyrics and rhythm" as "indicat[ing] ever onward, further and further into the unknown, leaving the West behind."

Several fans also described this piece as "majestic" or "grandiose." This effect is created in part by the slow tempo and regular drum groove but also, of course, by the orchestration—the use of strings and brass—and the "cinematic" quality of Jones's mellotron melody, as one fan described it. The brass instruments have a commanding presence in this song. They are introduced during the transition between verses, where, reinforced by guitar and keyboard, they interject a new harmonic, melodic, and rhythmic gesture overtop of the main riff. Robert Palmer wrote that at this moment in "Kashmir" "both guitar and brass lose their identities."[30] While he is certainly right that this transition has to do with blurred, if not lost, identities, it is not so much that the sounds of the brass, guitar, and keyboards are sometimes difficult to distinguish (but not impossible—the power of the brass still certainly comes through) but rather that the insertion of this gesture threatens to overwhelm the main riff, which continues to be played, continues to fight its way through this barrage of powerful sound with which it is hit. And it is certainly not only the power of the brass and other instruments that nearly engulfs the main riff. There is also a tonal struggle that ensues. Pungent harmonic dissonances are created against the main riff by the brass and guitar, through their series of chromatically descending chords. Plant's laid-back vocal style is echoed in the performance of these chords, which are often (but not always) played slightly behind the beat, an effect that makes the blurring and dissonance even more prominent. This transition, then, is a powerful site of struggle for identity.

PERHAPS IT IS possible to see (or better hear) more clearly, after having now worked through this piece in some detail, the ideological tensions referred to earlier, but this hardly makes them less vexing to deal with. For example, one of the issues that must be revisited is that of depth and its association with authenticity. Some who have written about the appropriation of Eastern or other musics by rock or pop artists make a distinction between whether the borrowing seems to be "superficial" or "deep," usually implying that "deep" is better because it reflects a more profound understanding of or respect for the culture. This is the position taken by Gerry Farrell in his book *Indian Music and the West*. Farrell's concern is mostly to describe not to problematize the use of Indian music in the West, which is unfortunate; he also tries hard not to deliver judgment on the use of Indian music in pop and rock, but the language he uses betrays him. He comments about Page's approach to the sitar (never played on record or in concert), saying that his "concern for technique, the mechanics of the instrument, and its careful, discriminating use was probably not wholly typical [of those in pop music in the 1960s] and many other bands were content to use the sitar just as a fashionable accessory to their image."[31] Implicit in this statement is the idea that to use the instrument "decoratively" is problematic (indeed this is also Jones's position, given his comment that members of Led Zeppelin did not wish to use instruments over which they had little technical command). Farrell makes this clearer when he talks about George Harrison's use of Indian music in the Beatles, describing how Harrison "progressed" from a superficial use of this music in "Norwegian Wood" to a much more complex use in "Within You Without You," with the clear implication that complexity is better.[32] But Farrell complicates this judgment by suggesting that in the end Harrison's relatively superficial use of Indian music is acceptable because he was "sincere" in using it and that this is why "the Beatles'" 'Indian' songs remain among the most imaginative and successful examples of this type of fusion."[33] This trope of superficiality is used again in an article by Ellie M. Hisama, where she says about David Bowie's "China Girl" that the music "is introduced . . . with superficial notions of what constitutes 'oriental' music—here parallel fourths played by the guitar."[34] Robert Palmer makes a similar kind of comment that hinges on the notion of depth, arguing that Led Zeppelin's blues influences became "more deeply assimilated," that they "incorporated the blues language more organically into their own creative processes" as they "progressed."[35] But Timothy Taylor makes a different argument that concerns the issue of depth in discussing Peter Gabriel's use of non-Western musics.[36] In the song "Come Talk to Me," for example, Gabriel begins with a tape of African drumming, which he uses as a foundation over which he composes new music. In other pieces where he has used non-Western musics, they similarly serve as a beginning or point of entry but then become subservient to Gabriel's own musical ideas or to the codes of Western music, such as strict meters, which are imposed on them by Gabriel. Here an argument can be made that the non-Western music is serving at a "deep" level, as the foundation, but as Taylor observes, this is problematic precisely because Gabriel seems to be colonizing these musics for his own use; here "deepness" equals a certain loss of identity and consequently the subservience of the other.

It is of course obvious that greater knowledge of something, including a particular kind of music, indicates a certain commitment to and engagement with it: if one has taken the time and effort to understand a musical culture in detail, then chances are there exists a personal investment in that music and culture that brings with it considerable respect, tolerance, and perhaps also admiration. One is less likely to stereotype, to misunderstand, to demean. But how should this investment and respect be manifested in the music that results out of it? Farrell's argument concerning Harrison's experiments with Indian music centers on the importance of structure. No matter how many details of Indian music Harrison eventually uses in songs like "Within You Without You" or "Love You To," he never, according to Farrell, succeeds in using these elements structurally, and this, according to Farrell, is problematic. The references to Indian music in "Love You To"are called formulaic: "[Harrison's] knowledge at this time did not allow him to explore fully the structural possibilities."[37] Similarly, Hisama is troubled that Bowie begins his song with a clichéd musical gesture, one that lies exposed on the surface of the music and is not further developed. Palmer, on the one hand, argues that an "organic" use of musical materials, by which he means that the borrowings or influences are tucked away so that they are barely recognizable, represents a "deeper" understanding, one more mature (Zeppelin "progressed" to this kind of use); there is the suggestion here that these musical materials have been internalized to become part of one's personal musical culture, as opposed to recognizably belonging to an other, and there is a clear indication that this is, in fact, desirable. Taylor, on the other hand, argues that a deep or foundational use of non-Western musical materials in effect colonizes them.

These discussions of depth versus surface and, indeed, what constitutes "depth" in music are problematic in terms of coming to understand musical/cultural borrowings. "Superficial" gestures such as the one that begins Bowie's "China Girl" are troublesome in large part not so much because they are short or nonstructural but because they have become associated with essentialist portrayals of Oriental peoples, and for Westerners in the twentieth century this association has occurred largely through film, television, and perhaps to a lesser extent opera. It is in films and television especially where formulaic bits of music have been used to indicate that the setting is now Cairo, Baghdad, or

Peking, making the association for the viewer in the shortest time possible and with the clearest possible means, turning the East, as Said argues, into "a set of representative figures or tropes . . . stylized . . . [attempting] to characterize the Orient as alien . . . *for* Europe."[38] Since it is so often the case that Oriental cultures have been negatively portrayed in these films, the superficial use of music has come to be associated with these negative portrayals. Several examples come easily to mind: the opening of *The Pink Panther* (undisclosed location in India), of the James Bond film *Live and Let Die* ("An Island in the Caribbean"), and of the musical *The King and I* ("Siam, 1862"). The association of these musical fragments with an essentialized East has become so strong for me, at least, that it is sometimes difficult to hear them used within their original contexts without flinching (the opening of Oum Kaltsoum's "Gannat Naimi" transcribed earlier is one example: the mode and descending sequences of straight eighth notes, some of them repeated, have been heard countless times as musical signifiers for "Arabic"). But would having longer, more developed examples of music or more of the structural elements intact change the situation? I think not. Unless the Western musician plays a complete raga, for example, the charge of essentialist characterization may be justified. And if the raga is being played by Western musicians, complete or not, the appropriation may still be bothersome. If the entire side of a Beatles album had been devoted to Harrison playing a complete Indian raga, it would still have been Harrison playing, and it still would have been a Beatles album: the music would still have been "filtered" through the West, if only through the positionality of the musicians as Westerners. But such a purist approach has rarely been the objective of rock musicians in any of their borrowings (the blues is exceptional in this regard) or of other Western musicians who use Eastern or other "exotic" elements. They have always sought to *incorporate* new sounds and styles, not copy them verbatim. In an attempt to make this point, Jonathan Bellman writes: "Exoticism is not about the earnest study of foreign culture, it is about drama, effect, and evocation."[39] The last part of this statement may be true, but Bellman equates evocation (as opposed to imitation?) with a lack of "earnestness" about studying the foreign culture, far too easy an assumption to make. In the case of Led Zeppelin, there is plenty of evidence that Page and, especially, Plant are genuinely interested in and knowledgeable about North African and Indian culture, and musical culture in particular, and while Jones has said less about the cultural influence, his musical interest is certainly genuine: how this "earnest" interest manifests itself in the music—again, whether it is deep or on the surface—is not necessarily an indication of how much respect the musicians have for the culture. Likewise, earnestness or, to use Farrell's word, "sincerity" does not erase issues of essentialism, Orientalism, or other cultural politics from the equation.

Robert Walser has theorized the appropriation of a variety of musical and visual iconography in heavy metal, including "the mystique of vanished Egyptian dynasties," as important "sources of power and mystery" for both the producers and consumers of this music.[40] The "depth" of the reference—in terms of length of musical excerpt, its development, whether it is structural, and, indeed, how it is juxtaposed with other elements—makes little difference in terms of its powerful significance, the weightiness of its impact. Indeed, the emergence of a "foreign" musical element in an otherwise "Western" musical frame points very specifically to difference, to a separate identity, in a way that cannot be mistaken. The suggestion that "organic," structural, or developed references are somehow better indicates in one way elitist notions about ownership of knowledge and the power that comes from it. Organicism, the importance of structure, and development in music are ideas that come largely from classical Western music, not from pop or rock. It would be wrong to minimize or slight powerful experiences that people (those making it as well as those listening) have with this music on the basis that the reference to difference has been quick. As Paul Willis explains, "[T]he easy use of the reference [to Eastern ideas] should not disguise the desperate authenticity and importance of the experience beneath."[41]

In the case of "Kashmir," beyond the song's having a title that may indicate a desire to signify the East in a broad way it is difficult for me to characterize Plant's lyrical depiction as essentialist in a traditional sense. In fact, it misses or completely contradicts many of the elements that so often appear in Orientalist depictions of the East. Plant describes the fictitious people he encounters on his travels as a "gentle race this world has seldom seen," stressing the rarity and importance of their gentility, and he acknowledges their wisdom by calling them elders. The sound of their words "caresses" his ears, and although he cannot understand what they say, there is a bond between him and these people that transcends spoken language. It is made clear that their common goal is profoundly spiritual—that they wait for a time when "all will be revealed." These people are not represented as primitive, frightening, or curious, although one could certainly argue that Plant stereotypes them in other ways, which might potentially be just as alienating. Significantly, there is no woman in Plant's fantasy, no Eastern "seductress." In fact, there is no woman referred to in any of the other Zeppelin songs that draw on Eastern musical influences; all of Plant's lyrics to these songs are about spiritual quests or nonsexual human relationships. Since, according to Jones, Plant always wrote the lyrics after the music had been composed, this seems to signal a connection for him between Eastern musics and questions of spirituality and humanism rather than sexuality.

Furthermore, I have tried to argue earlier that much about the way the music of "Kashmir" is put together speaks to the issue of blurring identities, and I think this is one of the most interesting and important things about it. There is one further point to make that underscores this, and that concerns the role of the guitar. Not only is there no guitar solo—no blatant assertion of the Western ego—but there is also very little typical guitar timbre heard. Page uses a synthesized guitar sound that blends seamlessly into the texture of strings and mellotron for the riff; the guitar is slightly easier to hear during the brass transition sections and at the beginning of the C sections, but it is still only acting as one timbral layer within a dense texture. Although Page plays throughout the entire piece, the sound of the guitar stays very much in the background, one identity among many.

ALTHOUGH IT MIGHT at first seem less problematic when Western rock musicians actually "collaborate" with non-Western musicians, as opposed to simply borrowing musical gestures from another culture, I think the presence of the non-Western musicians makes the situation more politically complicated, and for this reason I want to turn momentarily to the video performance of "Kashmir" from the 1994 *Unledded* concert by Page and Plant. The performance features the two rock icons—reunited fourteen years after Led Zeppelin disbanded—standing front and center. In a gesture that points to the construction of their equality in this long-awaited reunion, they share the spotlight. They are flanked to the side and behind by the rest of the "core" band, bassist Charlie Jones and drummer Michael Lee. Stage left sits a group of "classical" musicians, string and brass players from the Metropolitan London Orchestra, in their concert blacks, there to fill out the texture of riffs and punctuate various other musical lines but otherwise remain peripheral. Stage right is a group of Egyptian musicians led by percussionist Hossam Ramzy, a classical ensemble that consists of strings, nay 'oud, and percussion. All of them except Ramzy are dressed in tuxedos, mimicking the western Classical musicians to their right. This could not be in deference to Page and Plant, who would little value this gesture since they do not subscribe to the mores of the classical Western tradition. In fact, the appearance of tuxedos is one sign of the uncharacteristic formality of this concert—something that would have been anathema to Zeppelin—all aspects clearly planned, the musicians rather reserved in their movements, slightly nervous and stilted in their performance. These are clearly the outward indications of the tentativeness of this reunion, which both musicians had resisted for so many years. The tuxedos add something mechanistic to the scenario and make a political statement as well: the Egyptians must be wearing them in order to appear equal in stature to—to be taken as seriously as—the Western classical musicians, the latter having exerted their authority vis-à-vis their tradition visually, if not musically. By virtue of his casual dress, Ramzy reinforces his difference from all the musicians who "support," both British and Egyptian. He takes himself out of the background, visually, and aligns himself with the core band. He also leads, albeit a supporting group of musicians.

The Egyptians, however, accompany in a much more integral way than the Western classical musicians. "Kashmir" begins with the nay on its own for a moment. At one point the piece virtually stops to make way for a gripping violin solo by Wael Abu Bakr. Near the end of the piece, the Egyptian percussionists become the focus of attention when they trade licks with the four-piece rock band, and ultimately the percussionists are left jamming on their own while the stars leave the stage (during this final section of the piece the Western classical musicians did not play and many of them were captured on film enthusiastically, if uncharacteristically, clapping and otherwise moving to the music). Of this scenario, Page later commented: "We already knew that we wanted to be totally enveloped, Western orchestra this side, Egyptians this side, feel this whole force that was going on, this joy and jubilation; it was wonderful. It was transmitting between the Egyptians and the Western string players who are usually very, very reserved, you know, in their playing."[42]

This scenario is remarkably complicated to interpret. On the one hand, cultural identities seem to be neatly eked out. Territory is marked off through the use of the performance space, a geography of clearly demarcated zones that represent certain musical, cultural, and aesthetic interests. Eastern and Western classical traditions are on opposite sides of the stage, while the rock musicians occupy the center. Difference sits on the periphery, waiting to act, to be called on, to "envelop," to be redefined and absorbed into the culture of rock music, always on the borderline, always in a kind of identity crisis. But there is no economic crisis here. The core band of Page, Plant, Charlie Jones, and Lee is the capital that makes this excursion possible, the rock foundation that has drawn the crowds in the first place. One could argue that this is a typical way to set up a stage for a performance of this kind, that there are acoustic reasons for keeping the Egyptian musicians separate from the Western orchestral players and perhaps even for positioning both sets of players to the back of the stage (although it is also customary to place the orchestra in front and below, in a "pit"). But even acoustically, these are not the only options available. What does Page's wish to be "enveloped" by different musical traditions mean? This word he chooses is significant, indicating his desire to be engulfed, perhaps suggesting a willingness to relinquish part of his identity to this experience. He also suggests that the Egyptian musicians might offer an alternative way for the classical Western musicians to experience music—one that is less restrained, more "joyous" and "jubilant" (and certainly the Western players seem to be expressing both of these emotions at the end of the concert). Yet there is something about the various roles that are being played out here, something about the politics of "main" and "periphery," "East" and "West," that is being articulated. But what *is* this something? What *are* the politics?

From my Caucasian middle-class Western perspective, it is difficult, on the one hand, not to feel a certain discomfort, a small pang of guilt, concerning questions of representation in this scenario. After all, there are Page and Plant, economically privileged white rock icons and citizens of Great Britain, with its heritage as a colonizer. Theirs is not the only such scenario to consider, of course. Paul Simon with Ladysmith Black Mambazo and Peter Gabriel with Youssou N'Dour—one cannot help but be struck by the problematic cultural politics of such enterprises. The glaring imbalance of power in the concert setting between the white pop music icon and the non-Western musicians seemingly colonized for the performance is striking.[43] I have felt the same discomfort about white rock stars who have invited their black blues idols to perform with them: the Yardbirds and Sonny Boy Williamson, the Stones and Howlin' Wolf, U2 with B. B. King, and, perhaps the most problematic example, Muddy Waters as Eric Clapton's *opening* act on his 1979 tour. This last example is particularly problematic to me because of the inherent power imbalance between opening and headlining acts and how this rubs against Clapton's apparent reverence for Waters. Opening acts are subservient to the headliner. They are there to warm the audience up for the "main" act and are therefore invested with considerably less importance, a fact the audience acknowledges by often not showing up until the headliner appears. Clapton acknowledges that Waters has had a profound influence on him and that he is a seasoned master of blues music. It is difficult to reconcile this with Waters's relegation to opening act—there in Clapton's service—unless one understands that this is a decision based on Clapton's enormous cultural capital, which is, in turn, based in part upon his race. George Lipsitz has articulated the same kind of discomfort about such scenarios, writing:

> Intercultural communication does not automatically lead to intercultural cooperation, especially when participants in the dialogue speak from positions of highly unequal access to power, opportunity, and life chances. Citizens in advanced industrialized nations have long enjoyed the opportunity of consuming cultural commodities produced in colonized "hinterlands" both inside and outside of their national boundaries. Modernist literature, art, and music in Western countries has consistently spectacularized difference, titillating "respectable" audiences with sensational portrayals of "primitive," "exotic," and "oriental" outsiders. The cross-cultural communication carried on within today's contemporary popular music retains residual contradictions of centuries of colonialism, class domination, and racism.[44]

This is certainly the position from which Taylor speaks about Peter Gabriel's use of non-Western musics (although he does not mention the striking *visual* image of Gabriel with N'Dour—one that remains very much in the "mainstream" of public consumption in the video to the song "In Your Eyes," still regularly played on music television).[45] It is the rock star who gets the billing and whom the audience comes to hear; the other musician or musicians are there to "support" him. It is *his* music that is being performed, enhanced with various forms of "decoration." *He* is to be credited with discovery of the exotic; he is to be celebrated for "finding" these new sounds and incorporating them into his own work. Because of this, the other comes to be on display for the pleasure of the Western performers and audience: "[T]he Orient is *for* the European observer," Said writes.[46]

But at least in the case of Page and Plant's *No Quarter* project, this is much too easy a summary of the politics involved. First, the structure of the piece as it is found in the studio recording has been altered so that instead of beginning with the riff, it begins, as noted earlier, with what could be considered an abbreviated *taqsim*. The melody and lyrics of the opening verse are recognizable, although Plant embellishes the third line with a long ornamental melisma inspired by Arabic/Indian vocal practice (it is rhetorically significant that this melisma should come on the words "To sit with elders of a gentle race," I think, the shift in musical style suddenly placing Plant within that group of elders, as belonging to them much more forcefully than on the Led Zeppelin studio album). There is also the prominence of the nay in this opening section, the use of a drone by the string players, and Page's exploration of the mode on his Les Paul Trans Performance, heavily affected with wah-wah—the unmistakable sound of the electric guitar coming through the "foreign" scale pattern.

Second, there is the violin solo, which I would argue is the emotional center of the performance. There is the visual spectacle that accompanies this solo, Wael Abu Bakr emerging from his anonymity within the Egyptian ensemble, standing and becoming the subject of a close-up camera shot that lasts throughout the whole solo. Musically, this is a jarring moment, the regularity of the groove having been suspended, the noise of the large ensemble being replaced by the intimate, delicate, intricately ornamented violin melody. The violinist circles his melody around particularly pungent notes of the mode, creating enormous tension; the melody could certainly not be mistaken for a Western one. It is also placed in a rhetorically significant position with respect to the text. Just prior to the beginning of the violin solo, Plant has admitted to the confusion into which he has been thrown by his strange surroundings. He has shifted from a narrative that seems to embrace his encounter with the other to a less sure description of it: the wilting heat of the dessert, the blowing sand that fills his eyes, the wasted look of the place, and he ends this description with the line "trying to find where I've been," which leads directly into the violin solo.

Third, there is the end of the piece, in which "Kashmir" gives way entirely to a jam that ends up, as mentioned in chapter 1, with a quotation from "Black Dog." The jam begins with the band laying down a heavy riff, with guitar, bass, and drums in sync, over the delicate sounds of the Egyptians' violins playing a high drone figure accompanied by finger cymbals. The riff keeps intruding into the drone texture until finally the latter is obliterated by the power of the rock quartet's music. This is, again, a site for contested identity. What is interesting about this contestation is that despite the enormous display of power by the rock band, despite the whole "Eastern" journey being momentarily overtaken by the basest rock and roll sentiments (the lyrics to "Black Dog"), this intrusion just peters out. The great blast by the rock quartet just ends, and what is left are the droning Egyptian violins and percussion, which in fact bring the whole concert to a conclusion themselves, the "stars" having left the stage. How should this ending be interpreted? Have the Egyptian musicians finally captured the spotlight for themselves completely, been given the final musical word? Or is this concluding scenario part of their role as handmaidens to the stars, accompanying them, supporting them as they leave the stage, waving to the crowds?

Beyond the dynamics of the performance, it was made clear in an interview in *Q Magazine* that at least some of the Egyptian musicians saw their work with Page and Plant as an opportunity for greater exposure in the West: "Ali [Abdel Salem, one of the percussionists] and the Egyptians are on a mission, he cheerfully admits, a crusade to make Egyptian music . . . a commercial crossover. Neither naive nor unambitious, Ali has a solo album planned on the back of this tour. (As do several of the other Egyptians, apparently.) . . . 'I'm quite famous in London and in Egypt,' Ali assures us, 'but Led Zeppelin [*sic*] is a big project for me. And I'm looking now to build a career worldwide.'"[47] It should be noted that this interview with Ali Abdel Salem is exceptional in the press coverage of the Page/Plant project (the article also generously prints a picture of the Egyptian ensemble along with the rest of the backing musicians); almost all of the attention and acclaim was given to the rock stars, press coverage nearly always referencing Page and Plant's long fascination with and use of Eastern musics but rarely even mentioning any of the Egyptian musicians by name.

RAP ARTIST Puff Daddy's reworking of "Kashmir" in 1998 throws an interesting curve into this discussion of cultural appropriation. In his hands, the song was retitled "Come with Me" and was used in the soundtrack to the movie *Godzilla*. Musically, Puffy changed the form of the original song so that the A section, dominated by the riff, and the transition are the main focus. He retains the grand orchestration of the original, using large string and brass sections, as well as a core band. The B section of the piece is also kept intact, but the C sections are omitted. Jimmy Page sanctioned this arrangement of the song, saying in an interview aired on *Much Music* at the time of its release that he liked very much what Puff Daddy had done with it. In fact, Page was part of the project, playing the guitar parts in the recording, appearing in the video and in a live performance of the song on the television show *Saturday Night Live*, on May 9, 1998. A new section added to the piece after the first two verses features Page playing alone, not a blistering rock solo but gentle arpeggiations that use no distortion and have a thin timbre. Nothing about Page's playing here could be considered virtuosic, nothing indicating his status as one of the great guitar heroes. His role is to accompany Puff Daddy. Over repetitions of the main riff of the song, Puff Daddy raps his own angry lyric about betrayal and misunderstanding. Even though the B section with its glissando octave fall in the strings is retained, it is doubtful that this reference to Arabic music is heard as such in the context of the new arrangement. Any other overt reference to the East—musical or lyrical—has been erased. The riff, the grand transition, and the orchestration have become a powerful vehicle for a new message, far removed from the exoticism of the original.

"Come with Me" is credited to "Puff Daddy (featuring Jimmy Page)," and this billing—complete with parentheses—is indicative in part of the way in which Page, in fact, is the one to have been colonized in this performance (although he was undoubtedly paid handsomely for this privilege!). His song has been renamed, although one of the most important elements of the original, the riff, which sits at the core of the song, shapes the new rendition almost entirely. Aside from his ownership of the riff, Page is kept very much in the background of the performance. As in the Led Zeppelin studio recording, his guitar really cannot be heard as distinctive from the rest of the orchestra and his "solo" can hardly be considered as such. It is Puff Daddy who is clearly in control: in this case, he is the "discoverer," the one who has searched to find "new" sonic resources, the one whose concern has not been to preserve an "original" or to try to embrace the rock aesthetic that created it but to take from it what interested him in the creation of his own work. The riff and other elements appropriated from "Kashmir" here serve as a foundation on which something new is built, although in this case the original musical gestures are largely preserved—that is, they are not molded into a new rhythmic or metric framework the way non-Western materials taken over by rock music often are. The riff is, in fact, much more dominant than it is in the original, since the C section of the piece in which the riff is not heard is omitted from "Come with Me."

Nonmusical representations in the video performance of the piece are also important to take into account. In the video, Puff Daddy is the central focus of attention, acting out a narrative in which he takes on Godzilla (one of the purposes of the video is to serve as an advertisement for the movie, but it also valorizes Puff Daddy as an action hero in his own right). Page appears in the video fleetingly. He does not appear at all until halfway through and then not "in the flesh," as Puff Daddy does, but on the video screen that stands in the middle of Times Square in New York City, the site of the second half of the video performance. The camera catches his image only a few times—playing an electric guitar—and then only partially, incompletely, and very quickly. For those who know this as Puff Daddy's song, who do not generally listen to Led Zeppelin, Page's appearances in this video are probably largely meaningless. But for me, and perhaps also for other fans of Led Zeppelin, the way in which Page is represented here can be taken in at least two ways. We might complain that his role has been unfairly diminished, his contribution to the song and his status, in general, as a "rock god" belittled. Or we might have the response, as I did, that Page is being further mythologized. He is once removed from the reality of the other musicians, who are actually playing in Times Square; he towers above them on the screen a bit like the Wizard of Oz. His image is never really clearly captured, creating the impression of an elusiveness, a mysteriousness, that for those Led Zeppelin fans who are already well acquainted with and impressed by the Page mythology serves to reaffirm and deepen these considerably.

Page's agreement to participate in this venture was an important gesture. Led Zeppelin has for a long time been reviled for stealing from blues musicians, using their music and not giving them due credit, a situation that led to the successful suing of the band by Willie Dixon over their use of his "You Need Love," which became Zeppelin's "Whole Lotta Love." Interestingly, no outrage has been expressed at Zeppelin's appropriation of Eastern musics, perhaps because it was quite limited, perhaps because those journalists who wrote about it have not known those musics well enough to pinpoint the references, or, most probably, because Eastern musicians do not necessarily have access to our legal system or, for that matter, to Led Zeppelin recordings.[48] In the act of his collaboration with Puff Daddy, Page signaled a willingness to give back as well as take; in his role as background or accompanying musician, he allows Puff Daddy to claim the song as his own. But even here, Page's "willingness" and "permission" are key. Puff Daddy had to ask permission to use the song, and Page may well have insisted on his name being included in the credits. He undoubtedly was paid, not only royalties but probably also for his part in making the new recording. So while Page is on the periphery, he is certainly not being taken advantage of economically or even artistically.

Page's participation in this reworking of "Kashmir" is important for another reason. The backlash against rap has been enormous, especially from white rock musicians who have questioned whether it can actually be considered music. By not only giving permission for "Kashmir" to be reworked by a rap artist but also participating in this reworking, Page indicated his interest in the genre and his acknowledgment of its artistic worth. This is not to say that rap needs to be sanctioned by Page or any other white rock musician, only that it is encouraging and hopeful to see it happen after so much intolerance and ignorance. But although someone like Page has enormous credibility with fans and the power to persuade them to think about things in new ways, this does not seem to have happened to any appreciable degree with this collaboration. I began collecting data from my fan questionnaire shortly after "Come with Me" was released, and although I asked nothing about the collaboration specifically, more than a dozen fans volunteered their views anyway. All but two of these were negative, ranging from relatively benign condemnations ("a disgrace," "a shame," "too bad") to charges that Puff Daddy "ruined" the song, to a couple of violent outbursts: "['Kashmir'] A great song that was recently raped by Puff Daddy"; "Obviously great until Page reworked it with that piece of shit Puff Daddy." One fan conceded that "it was quite nice to hear Zeppelin blasting out of cars in the ghetto." The only really enthusiastic comment was "['Kashmir' is] Awesome!!! From the symphonicness when Led performed it, to the rap version that Page performed with Puff Daddy, it doesn't get any better!" Much of the original song remains intact in Puff Daddy's version—the riff, the orchestration, sections A and B of the form—and Page himself plays on it, so it must be the rap itself that so offends these fans. It is difficult, therefore, to read the negative comments as anything other than a general condemnation of rap music, one that has large-scale overtones of racism.

STEVEN FELD HAS written that "[m]usical appropriation sings a double line with one voice. It is a melody of admiration, even homage and respect, a fundamental source of connectedness, creativity, and innovation. . . . Yet this voice is harmonized by a countermelody of power, even control and domination, a fundamental source of asymmetry in ownership and commodification of musical works."[49] What Feld articulates here is something of the *tension* that inheres in these cultural borrowings, a tension that Baz Kershaw has theorized in terms of paradox: while there may be a desire to position oneself on one side of this argument or the other, either the borrowings are a form of homage or simply musically interesting (and innocent) or they are exploitative—the reality is that they are both simultaneously. With this realization, the difficulty shifts from determining *which* position holds the truth to holding the tension, the paradox, in the mind.[50] Part of Kershaw's argument is based on Homi Bhabha's notion of the *ambivalence* of "hybrid cultural forms . . . [which Bhabha identifies] as a product of the interdependence of binary opposite, whether 'black' and 'white' or 'oppressed' and 'oppressor,' because neither can exist without some recognition of the difference in the other—so ambivalence serves to break down the binary and to usher in greater complexity, a potential multi-vocality, in the power relations fostered by colonialism."[51] But it seems to me insufficient to comprehend this as a general principle; each hybrid cultural form holds this paradox in a particular balance, a balance that will make sense in different ways to different listeners. Arguments need to be constructed, then, on the basis of individual works or, at the very least, individual artists, on how appropriated musical references have been contextualized (this is really the point of Hisama's critique of Bowie), and certainly on the person who is doing the listening.[52]

FOUR

The Wanton Song

The Riff and the Body

Anterior to its status as a sign, music is an action on and of the body.
—David Lidov, "Mind and Body in Music"

[I]f you find out by feeling for it how Debussy might have held his hands and body when he played the piano, you might get a better feeling for his music.
—John Blacking, *How Musical Is Man?*

On the faster numbers Jimmy Page was practising duck walks across the stage and on the slower ones he arches over so far backwards that it was only the weight of the music coming from the guitar that kept him from falling over. At one point he was even conducting the band during a spirited rendition of "Nobody's Fault But Mine."
—Jon Carlsson, *Melody Maker*

The lights go up in Madison Square Garden, July 27, 1973, and Jimmy Page is in motion. This concert, from which most of the video for *The Song Remains the Same* was taken, begins with "Rock and Roll," and Page, as usual, enacts the song using his full body, pressing into service most of the catalog of stylized physical gestures he normally uses in performance. As he plays the riff at the beginning of the song, he stands in place for a moment, stomping the ground with one foot, then his heel, the same foot again, then the other, and back again to articulate the quarter-note beat. When he changes the riff slightly, he assumes his most frequently used stationary position, with his left leg extended forward, torso bent slightly back (fig. 6). He brings his right hand and forearm over the guitar strings, mostly at the end of musical gestures (fig. 14). And there are three quite spectacular gestural moments that help to articulate the form of the piece in this particular performance. The first of these comes at the beginning of the guitar solo, which Page marks by throwing his right hand up in the air to mark an empty beat and sliding to center stage from his more usual position at stage left (see fig. 16 for a similar hand and arm gesture). The second comes near the end of the verse sung after the solo, following the line "Baby where I come from";[1] Page jumps up, does the splits in midair, and again throws his right arm up above his head and then out to the rhythm section, articulating the cymbal crash (a similar gesture was captured by photographer Marty Perez, shown in fig. 5). The third comes at the end of the song, where Page stands erect, his right arm straight in the air over his head, while Plant sings "lonely, lonely, lonely time" a cappella, Page's tensed, poised body anticipating the cadential chords. He then throws his arm toward Bonham, instructing him (it would seem) to play the short drum solo that occurs before the final cadence of the piece.

The way in which rock musicians use their bodies in performance is critically important to an understanding of the music. I first came to know Led Zeppelin's music through the studio recordings, and when I eventually saw them in performance I came not only to a richer understanding of the music, generally speaking, but also to a decidedly different understanding of it and of the people making it. Through their embodied performances band members create identities, and they reveal much about the politics and power relations of the group. Through the construction of a fictional body, each performer creates a discourse of power or the lack thereof around him.[2] In addition, band members model physical behavior for the fans watching. How should it look to play a guitar solo? How should a body respond to this kind of music? What physical gestures, stances, facial expressions do our heroes assume?

However members of the band let their bodies speak the music, it is in the first instance the kinetic qualities of this music that urge these gestures on. As Neil Nehring makes clear, there are those who would argue against this assertion, preferring to understand language and music as symbolic systems that are separate from the body and to deal with them analytically as such. Nehring's is a good summary of these arguments, and so I will not restate them here;[3] it is my intention, in any case, to proceed directly from the assumption that all music is kinetic and to explore the ideas of those writers who have tried to articulate how this is so. This includes recorded music, which some writers have argued is "disembodied" because the performer is physically absent. But in my view, the performer's body is very much present, in the particular sonoric gestures shaped and played, in the first instance by him or her (they are human gestures, after all) through his or her body in such a way that they connect with the bodies of those listening.

While all music is kinetic, perhaps always beginning, as John Blacking so eloquently states it, with a "stirring of the body,"[4] in rock music, and Led Zeppelin's music in particular, the kinetic qualities are almost always *foregrounded*. David Lidov theorizes that the more foregrounded the rate of pulse, the more overtly somatic the music. Subordinated rates of pulse, conversely, suggest a "contained or introverted factor of the somatic state." He argues that it is not only the gross articulation of the beat but also the particular way in which musical gestures are distributed across beats that "indexes" such states as "inner, contained excitement," for example.[5] In Led Zeppelin's music (and in other rock music as well), the rate of pulse is foregrounded and musical gestures are distributed along the beat in such a way as to overtly make reference to the body. One kind of musical gesture that is of central importance for the analysis of this phenomenon is riffs, which structure the vast majority of Led Zeppelin's songs. Generally speaking, a riff is a short instrumental pattern that is repeated throughout a song or section of a song, acting as a structuring device over which the vocal line or instrumental solos occur (a riff's composition and use within songs, however, is significantly more complex than this definition suggests—see "The Riff"). Led Zeppelin's riffs have often been mentioned for some of their striking features but never discussed in any detail. Fans understand both the importance of riffs in Zeppelin's songs, many calling them "[t]he backbone of the world's greatest tunes," and the connection between riff and body:

[The] riffs always had that propulsive quality to them.

Uncanny sense of timing, economy and percussive power.

Short, sharp and to the point, no fluff, no wank.

[N]asty swagger.

One thing I really like about Page's riffs [is] how they push and pull against the straight $\frac{4}{4}$.

Great. Gutty [*sic*], gets things moving—kicks you in the ass.

They are really bone-crunching.

[Page] taps into our heartbeats and life rhythms to draw us into his journey.

It seems like the guitar is part of his body.

Not only has little been said about the riffs themselves, but there also has not been any exploration of how they work within various songs. There has been no discussion of their kinetic qualities, perhaps because it has been difficult to know how such an analysis might be undertaken. And there has been little attempt made to analyze in detail the embodied live performance, the particular gestures made, and what these might mean in relationship to the music. What I hope to accomplish here is to instigate a discussion of these issues. Of course some of what I have to say with respect to this particular repertory applies to the music of other artists as well, some of it, indeed, to rock music in general. Some characteristics of particular riffs, the way in which these are used within songs, and the way music and body are related in performance are by no means unique to Led Zeppelin; they stem rather, from cultural influences such as the blues and the idiosyncrasies of, especially, the electric guitar. Still, the details have been left untouched for too long and there is certainly enough that is unique to warrant the kind of attention I have given the music and perform-ances here. Ideally, such analyses should be made for a number of rock artists and comparisons drawn, work that I hope this study might encourage.

The Riff

In his discussion of syntactic musical analysis, Richard Middleton explores the pros and cons of segmentation, that is, borrowing from structural linguistics the idea of breaking a piece into "pertinent units . . . those which are functional in respect of semantic communication."[6] He points to the difficulties that may inhere in determining what constitutes a meaningful segment in music and suggests that along with pitch and temporally based units (a note, a series of notes, a phrase, and so forth) parameters such as timbre should also be consid-ered, making in the process the useful argument that both "[p]arameters and units can be considered as bundles of *features*" on which analytical attention might profitably be focused.[7] While segmentation may indeed be problematic for much music, it seems quite a good way to think of the riff. The riff is usually clearly defined as a unit that carries meaning—in the case of many Led Zep-pelin songs, it is at least one of the primary units of musical meaning. And it is a particularly useful way of knowing something about a song not only to try to define the characteristics of the riff but also to determine how this riff is used throughout a song (to what extent it is used and where in relation to other sonic events, for example). And Middleton's concept of the unit/parameter combina-tion as a bundle of features is a particularly good way of thinking about the riff. There may be a tendency to think of riffs as repeated rhythmic patterns, but they are much more complex than this. Riffs comprise rhythm, melodic shape, harmony, and timbres that are related to one another in specific ways.[8] Led Zep-pelin's riffs (and those of many others) often include different instruments playing different melodic and rhythmic patterns—some may be considered polyrhythmic, or at least as participating in a kind of rhythmic heterophony, different instruments all playing slightly different versions of the same rhyth-mic or melodic pattern.[9] The riff may also vary over time, melodic, rhythmic, and, especially, timbral elements being added, deleted, or otherwise altered in repetitions. What might the semiotic significance of these variations be?

There is so much variety in Led Zeppelin's riff-based songs—and there are so many of them—that it is difficult to know where to begin giving examples. One fan commented on the variety of riffs by saying: "Unlike [some] bands, you won't hear the same riff used twice in Led Zeppelin's catalog." I have no desire to attempt to categorize or otherwise reduce, in its entirety, this rich body of work, but it does seem necessary to offer here some preliminary description on which further analysis can be based. Furthermore, there are some important generalizations that can be made concerning the riffs and their use within songs, generalizations that may help us to understand why they impact on the body in certain ways. I will begin, then, with a descriptive analysis of some of the riffs and proceed to a richer kind of interpretation, which takes into consideration the bodily implications of the way in which these riffs are structured.

One can begin to make some sense out of the repertory by moving from *structurally* simpler riffs to those that are more complex (I emphasize the word "structurally" because this kind of simplicity has nothing to do with semiotic complexity) and then perhaps further refining this by examining those riffs that include the octave as a prominent feature,[10] since this melodic gesture occurs with great frequency as a defining element *in electric songs* (as opposed to acoustic songs) and needs to be problematized as an important gestural element.[11] A close look at four such riffs that move from structural simplicity to greater complexity will serve as my beginning point for analysis, that is, the riffs in "The Wanton Song," "Immigrant Song," "Celebration Day," and "Black Dog." I might easily have chosen other riffs that demonstrate similar principles in other ways.

In this scheme, then, the riff to "The Wanton Song" (ex. 4.1) is probably a good place to begin. Segmentation is problematic with this riff, since the pattern can be defined in three ways: 1) a recognizable repeated pattern that is one measure long, 2) the threefold repetition of the pattern followed by a cadence, and 3) an eight-measure pattern that consists of two four-measure units, each with a different cadential pattern:

The one-measure pattern is what would probably be considered the riff proper for many people. It consists of guitar and bass doubling a melodic and rhythmic pattern that contains three especially noteworthy features: 1) a flurry of rhythmic activity at the front end of the measure, followed by silence, 2) near melodic stasis during this rhythmic activity, with the exception of the octave leap, which is rhythmically syncopated, and 3) the overall low pitch. On the bass and snare drums, Bonham articulates the riff in a slightly different way, keeping the sixteenth-note feel by swinging the eighth notes and mirroring the octave jump in his articulation of the backbeat on the snare (this is probably not a conscious mirroring, since playing the backbeat on the snare is very common in rock drumming, but it works in a particularly synchronistic way with the rest of the riff in this case).

The octave leap as a defining melodic gesture occurs also in "Immigrant Song" (ex. 4.2). This riff, as I argued in chapter 1, is so similar to that of "The Wanton Song" that the two were effectively merged on Page/Plant's 1995 tour. The smallest unit of meaning in this riff is probably the guitar pattern that lasts for two beats, repeated twice within each measure. The bass guitar does *not* simply double the guitar but plays a pattern that does not include the sixteenth-

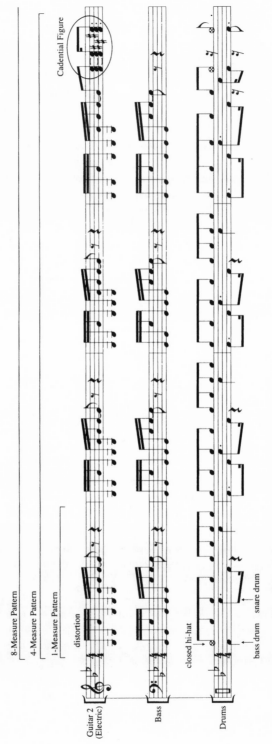

Example 4.1. "The Wanton Song" riff, indicating three possible sementations

Cadential Figure

Gtr. 2

Bs.

Dr.

Example 4.1. (continued)

Example 4.2. "Immigrant Song" riff

note repetitions on the second half of beats 1 and 3. The bass guitar does not play the octave leap, either. Instead, a rest occurs where this melodic gesture appears in the guitar, highlighting the octave leap—the bottom end drops out, and the guitar leaps up an octave simultaneously. The drums mirror the guitar pattern more closely, only eliminating the sixteenth-note pickups from snare and bass drum, although on the closed high-hat cymbal a rhythmically straighter version of the riff is played, which does include the sixteenth notes—an eighth, followed by two sixteenths on every beat (and so a more contracted version as well, reducing the riff to one beat from two). There is one further variation on the riff that occurs, which is that during the outro the bass guitar doubles the guitar riff exactly, only an octave lower.

The riff to "Celebration Day" is considerably more complex than either of these two. In the first instance, it consists of two different gestural elements: the first, which I am calling an "Introduction," consists of chords played by guitar and a melodic line played by Jones on six-string slide bass and doubled on guitar (concerning this part of the riff Jones commented to me, "I had converted a Danelectro longhorn guitar to a six-string bass and then put a nut extender on it to turn it into a lap steel," which accounts for the unusual timbre heard). These elements of the riff are marked "A" and "B" in example 4.3. The piece opens with Page strumming a series of chords over a tonic drone (A), a cadential progression that moves from the lowered seventh scale degree, G^7, chromatically to the leading tone, $G^{\sharp 7}$, finally arriving at the tonic A^7. These chords are voiced in an interesting way: they are in second inversion, but the root is not present, leaving only the diminished triad, inverted so that the third of the chord is the uppermost pitch. Jones's melodic line begins two octaves plus a third down from Page's guitar—and this enormous drop in pitch is an important characteristic of the riff, which I will discuss in more detail later. The melodic line itself is characterized by another octave leap, from the A up an octave, which is then filled in using descending motion from A down to C, alternating these pitches of the scale with a constant return to the lower A—continual descending motion, in other words. The large leaps are not made cleanly, but Jones slides in and out of them (down and up from them), emphasizing their largeness by materializing the gap between the pitches. At the end of this pattern, the rising octave from A to A is heard again, as well as the jump up in pitch back to the C♯ an octave and third above the A. For the riff proper (ex. 4.4), the melodic line is reduced to an octave leap down from A to A, then up to G, descending to F and E, and then dropping back down to A, which moves back

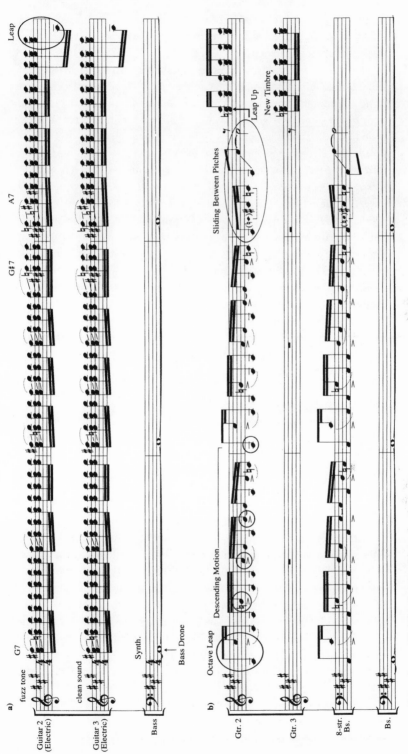

Example 4.3. "Celebration Day" introduction

up quickly to an octave A. During the riff used in the verses, the regular four-string bass guitar is melodically static, focused on the tonic A, but articulating a rhythmic pattern different from that of the riff.

All this is made considerably more complex through Page's characteristic guitar overdubbings. A second guitar doubles the A^7 chord whenever it returns, using a clean sound as opposed to the fuzz tone of the first guitar, making the sound fuller—and thereby making this part of the riff more prominent than the melodic line—as well as adding a different timbral quality to it. When the drums and electric bass enter, another guitar part is overdubbed, cutting through the rest of the texture, playing only the octave leap A's (with a C♯ pickup) in the first measure of the riff and the same C♯ pickup back down to the lower A of the octave in the second measure (see ex. 4.4).

Finally, I have chosen to look at one of the most complex (and celebrated) of Zeppelin's riffs, that of "Black Dog," which was written by John Paul Jones.[12] The element of this riff frequently commented upon is its metric irregularity, which hinges on the displacement of the beat by guitar and bass in relation to the drums at various points. Aside from the musicians having to negotiate these rhythmic/metric complexities, though, it is also a virtuosic riff in terms of the melodic line, the continuous stream of eighth notes moving at a fast tempo requiring considerable technical facility to play. Both of these elements of the riff are important to consider in terms of how it works on the body of the listener, but there are others factors as well.

This riff works on the element of continuous movement (mostly straight eighth notes, elaborated at one point with a triplet turn) interrupted twice by an accented quarter on the lowered third scale degree (C, bending upward to C♯), which falls to the tonic, A. It begins with a three-note pickup, leading in ascending motion to the tonic, which falls on the downbeat of the first measure. The weight of this downbeat is obscured by the fact that Bonham chooses to articulate the next beat—the weak second beat of the measure—with the crash cymbal as opposed to the downbeat; in fact, he does this every time the riff occurs, ensuring that it is a deliberate gesture. Bonham's act summarizes much of what this riff is about: metric displacement that takes the listener off guard, destroying expectations. The riff constantly comes back to the tonic, which is invariably given the longer value of a quarter note, lending it some weight, but this return is always at different points within the meter, thwarting the impact of the return—it sounds either too early or too late. The riff ends with a winding downward cadential gesture that lands on a power chord an octave below the tonic A heard throughout the riff—again, the octave plays a significant role in the shape of the riff. The only elaboration of this riff occurs during the fourth verse—near the end of the song—when Page doubles it at the interval of a third higher, increasing its intensity and prominence.

I will discuss the use of riffs within entire songs later, but it is important to note here that "Black Dog" is comprised almost entirely of riffs that are variations of this opening one; the a cappella section is the only exception. There are three of these variations, the first coming as a kind of extension to the main riff (what Jones calls the B section of the riff—see ex. 4.5). It appears directly after the main riff is heard for the third time and consists of a transposed rendering of the opening gesture of the main riff (a fourth lower), that is, the three pickup notes and the gesture of the first three beats of the first full bar. This variation consists of four and one-half beats repeated three and one-half times, distributed evenly over measures of 4/4, which causes a metrical displacement, making the accented pitch G–G♯ (accented through articulation, through the fact that it is dissonant, and also because it leaps upward by a sixth) constantly fall on a different part of the beat. Jones conceived the meter of this section to work in the following way: "When I wrote it, the 'B' section of the riff was actually phrased as three 6/8 bars and one 5/8 bar over the straight 4/4 but nobody else could play it!" The metric irregularity of this riff is accented by hearing it against the steadiness of the drum pattern, which continues to mark beats 1 and 3 on the bass drum, the backbeat on the snare. Drums and riff reunite on the downbeat when the main riff returns.

This leads into the second variation of the riff (ex. 4.6), which is related to the triplet figure heard in the main riff and also the descending drop down to the octave A heard at the end of the main riff. It consists of a sixteenth-note turn pattern (turning around the tonic A), which then leaps down to a power chord on A. The bass guitar plays only the power chord, not the turn figure, accentuating the weight of that power chord.

The third variation of the riff (ex. 4.7), occurs after the a cappella section, beginning with the words "Hey baby." This motive is drawn from the gesture of the main riff that occurs directly after the opening pickup notes, which includes the rhythmically accented, dissonant C/C♯–A figure.

It is interesting to note that in two songs with highly complex riffs, this one and "The Ocean," there appear sections in which all movement is suspended while Plant sings a cappella (or nearly so in "Black Dog"), vocalizing on simple vowels ("ah ah" or "la la") as if to compensate in some way for the radical complexity of the riffs. Given that this interjection of simplicity and calm comes via the human voice while the complexity comes via electric instruments, there is a tendency on my part to hear the binary between nature and technology being enacted in these songs and perhaps also the binary between masculine (if one hears the virtuosity, distortion, and volume of these riffs as signfiers of masculine power) and feminine. As I argue elsewhere in this book, I do not think it was particularly unusual for Plant to be cast in the role of feminine other to the masculine-coded power of rock instrumentalists.

Music and the Body

While Richard Middleton admits that there may be some usefulness to understanding music in terms borrowed from linguistics, including the idea of seg-

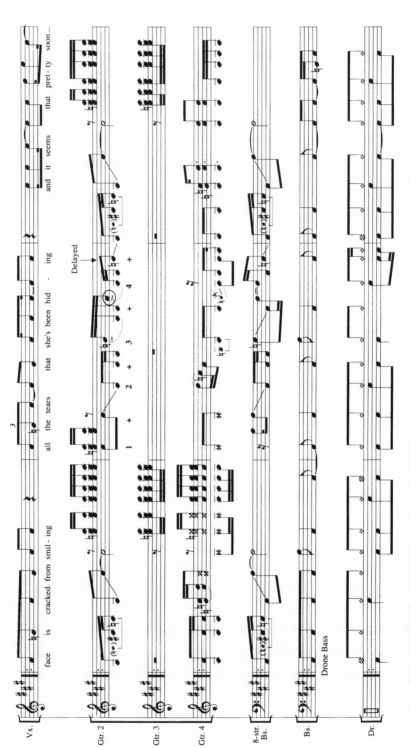

Example 4.4. "Celebration Day" riff, including guitar doubling

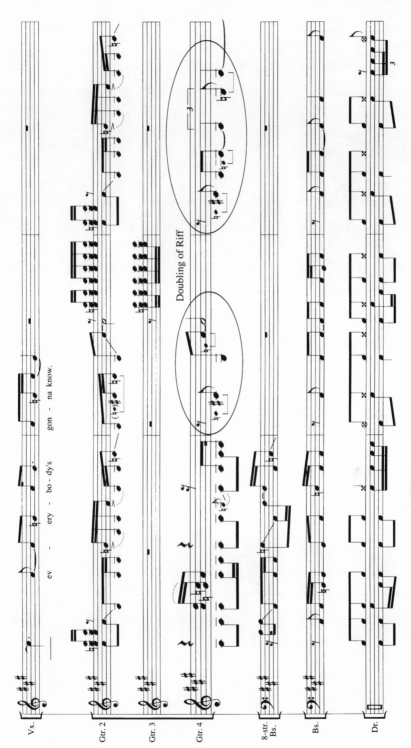

Example 4.4. (*continued*)

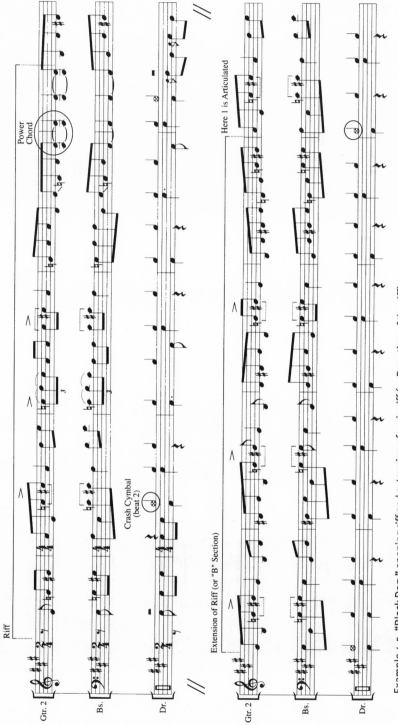

Example 4.5. "Black Dog," opening riff and extension of main riff (or B section of the riff)

Example 4.6. "Black Dog," second variation on the main riff

Example 4.7. "Black Dog," third variation of the main riff

mentation, he ultimately thinks that this approach may fall seriously short of the mark. This is because there is evidence to suggest that our musical understanding may be "prelinguistic." A prelinguistic level of understanding for music suggests "the possibility of a specifically musical 'thought' derived from the operations of sensorimotor intelligence; they also imply a 'language of feeling' connected with symbolisms of the unconscious and movement patterns of the body."[13] Although he does not mention Lacanian psychoanalysis, Middleton's comments here also suggest that music belongs to Lacan's Imaginary Order, rather than his Symbolic Order, the latter of which is governed by language.[14]

Allowing that musical understanding may be prelinguistic or part of the Imaginary Order makes it possible to theorize it in terms of both the body and the mind, rather than the mind exclusively. Bringing the body into the discussion of music is critically important—crucial, in fact, in dealing with Led Zeppelin's riffs, whose kinetic qualities are at the heart of what makes us understand and respond to them. How we proceed with such an analysis is a matter of some debate: the desire to maintain the mind/body split in Western culture and to focus analytical attention on music that *seems* to have less to do with the body than the mind has hindered scholars from developing a way of talking about the somatic qualities of music.[15] Nonetheless, there are those who have at least acknowledged the importance of the body in understanding music, if they have not developed full-blown theoretical models through which music can be analyzed in this way. Jacques Attali makes the bold assertion that music "is rooted in a comprehensive conception of knowledge about the body."[16] John Shepherd and Peter Wicke begin to get at how sound impacts on our bodies through their idea that sound, unlike vision, "lifts off the surface of its material source" and "encompasses and touches the listener in a cocoon-like fashion" and because sounds quickly decay and new sounds replace them this is not a static physical engagement with sound but one that is "in process and dynamic."[17] Shepherd and Wicke suggest that this cocoon creates a world unto itself in which the listener is enveloped.[18] To this we can add the physical impact of the organization of time on the body. John Blacking and Claude Lévi-Strauss have both suggested (separately) that the organization of time in music takes the body out of ordinary or everyday time into what Blacking calls "virtual time,"[19] what Lévi-Strauss characterizes as the "obliteration of time" leading to "a kind of immortality."[20] An analogy can be made with what anthropologist Victor Turner, theorizing the use of time in ritual and theater, calls the "subjunctive." Ritual or theater removes one from the "indicative," the world of "actual fact," to a world of "as if."[21] The effect that these authors suggest this has on the body is to release it from the everyday and open up the possibility of a different reality, a liberatory experience, which, as John Blacking puts it, may lead to states

in which people become keenly aware of the true nature of their being, of the "other self" within themselves and other human beings, and of their relationship with the world around them. Old age, death, grief, thirst, hunger, and the other afflictions of this world are seen as transitory events. There is freedom from the restrictions of actual time and complete absorption in the "Timeless Now of the Divine Spirit," the loss of self in being. We often experience greater intensity of living when our normal time values are upset, and appreciate the quality rather than the length of time spent doing something. The virtual time of music may help to generate such experiences.[22]

In *The Anthropology of the Body*, Blacking broaches this subject again, suggesting that coming out of everyday time and into musical time may bring us back to our bodies in a significant way, making us once again conscious of them, reconnecting us with somatic experience.[23] The consequences of this for Blacking are profound: "[Music] can make people more aware of feelings they have experienced, or partly experienced, and so restore the conditions of fellow-feeling, a body awareness, educability and plasticity that are basic to the survival of the species."[24] Jacques Attali would agree in as much as he considers music to be "a dialectical confrontation with the course of time";[25] he would also agree with Blacking that music is "liberating" but suggests that this liberation is connected with catharsis, "[i]n pursuit of exorcism through noise and dance."[26] Like Lévi-Strauss with his concept of myth as "overcoming the contradiction between historical, enacted time and a permanent constant,"[27] Attali views music as "past time to be produced, heard, and exchanged."[28]

In *The Phenomenology of Perception*, Maurice Merleau-Ponty links language inextricably to the body, arguing that the only kind of language that exists is spoken, that there is no such thing as "abstract" thought at all, hence he dissolves the mind/body split: "The word or speech must somehow cease to be a way of designating things or thoughts, and become the presence of that thought in the phenomenal world."[29] Further, this (spoken) language has to do with bodies communicating: "What I communicate with, primarily, is not 'representations' or thought, but a speaking subject, with a certain style of being and with the 'world' at which he [*sic*] directs his aim."[30] Even when language exists in one's head, for most people it is there as a result of having been previously heard, words thus have textures, timbres, intonations associated with them; that is, they are embodied gestures: "The gesture does not make me think of anger, it is anger itself. . . . [I]t is as if the other person's intention inhabited my body and mine his."[31] This final point has critical implications for understanding not only how language works but also how music works (something that the fan who said: "[Page] taps into our heartbeats and life rhythms to draw us into his journey" understands completely). Merleau-Ponty argues that hearing words spoken by another human being transforms our bodies: "[T]aking up of this intention is not a process of thinking on my part, but a synchronizing change of my own existence, a transformation of my being."[32] Hence, "[i]t is through my body that I understand other people, just as it is through my body that I perceive things. The meaning of a gesture thus 'understood' is not behind it, it is inter-mingled with the structure of the world outlined by the gesture."[33] "[T]he body must in the last analysis become the thought or intention that it signifies for us. It is the body which points out, and which speaks."[34] These ideas about the materiality of language, its embodied nature, are also found, of course, in Mikhail Bakhtin's writings, where he speaks of "utterances" in the same way as Merleau-Ponty talks about "gestures" of language and stresses the multifaceted or "heteroglossic" nature of these utterances and their continual "dialogic inter-action with other utterances."[35] This is a particularly useful and important way in which to think about musical utterances as well, especially in music that is composed and performed by the same people and for which a score is nonexist-ent (or where one might be made much after the fact and generally not used by listeners to the music). There are of course various ways in which to hear recorded music, but once one knows who the people making that music are—that is, has a visual representation of them—it is difficult indeed to separate their musical utterances from the bodies that make them. When I hear a Led Zeppelin recording, I hear—and so interact with—the bodies of the four indi-viduals who created this music. I am always aware, perhaps sometimes subcon-sciously, of who it is making this music, of the body in the utterance.

These ideas take us a considerable leap forward in trying to theorize in a gen-eral way how sound, language, and music act on the body. Sound touches us, physically. It connects us with the body from which it is coming. It is an intimate form of human contact. This may well be one reason that music is so powerful: it engages us physically with the bodies of the musicians who are making it. This may have important implications for the study of sexuality and music, as well of other forms of bonding that occur while playing or listening to music: I am in your rhythm and therefore in your body—we are one, perhaps first through sharing an "extradaily"[36] time and second through the particular rhythmic, melodic, harmonic, and timbral gestures, which impact on our bodies in a par-ticular way. One can see a highly visible manifestation of the former (the cre-ation and sharing of an extradaily time) at rock concerts, when thousands of people articulate the meter through clapping, sometimes at the request of the performer. Further, all sound may envelop us to some degree, but music, with various elements that are, as Shepherd and Wicke suggest, coming and going, several instruments, parts, and so forth, that are all around us, accomplishes this in a deliberate and calculated way. Musical sounds are special because they are out of the ordinary: they represent an organizing of sound different from the everyday. And if they are louder than everyday sounds for a sustained period of time, they command our attention completely and may completely envelop us physically. This may be why volume is such a critical element of rock music and why it is so powerful. Extreme volume is not only transgressive, but it is also a way of creating a cocoon of sound. Other sounds are blocked out—the rest of the world is blocked out. The physical impact of sound may also be the reason for the importance of the bottom end in rock music (and also rap, as Tricia Rose has pointed out):[37] it is largely the bass guitar and bass drum that one feels directly moving through the body. Shepherd and Wicke imply but do not go so far as to say through their use of the word "cocoon" that this envelopment is in fact a safe place, eked out in the act of listening. Further, it is not only the tactile nature of this sound that surrounds us with its warmth but also the suspension of everyday time that is comforting and that allows us to reconnect with the physical in a mode outside the everyday. Middleton gives a few concrete examples of how this might work in music, suggesting that "the 'even four' of mainstream jazz and the 'pogo four' of punk rock are attempts to point beyond the possible, to an undifferentiated flow of time."[38]

How, though, do we take these powerful arguments and find a way in which to use them to analyze sound in a more detailed way? Middleton tries to get at how bodily movement might work in music by discussing levels of structure, "the deepest level" of which "is, so to speak, pre-musical: it describes a movement from an initial motif to a terminal motif, a semantic form or gesture."[39] Middleton also suggests that musical space works as a *metaphor* for physical space, in terms of not only melody or rhythm but also harmony. He argues, for example, that harmonic motion from I to V covers "more distance" than that from I to IV, nuancing this theory by adding that our sense of this greater distance has to do partly with the notion of difference, since the tonic note is present in both the tonic and subdominant chords but not in the dominant.[40] In addition, "deep structures" in music, such as the underlying harmonic movement or melodic structure (as derived from Schenkerian analysis, for example), are "forms [that] can be thought of as 'gestures:' 'cognitive shapes' (with affective and motoric connections)."[41]

Although he does not mention it, with these arguments Middleton begins to move toward Mark Johnson's theory of image schemata, which offers perhaps the best hope (at this point) for a practical application of how body and music are linked. Johnson's image schema "consists of a small number of parts and relations, by virtue of which it can structure indefinitely many perceptions, images, and events." Schemata are "recurrent pattern[s] ... [which] emerge as meaningful structures for us chiefly at the level of bodily movements through space, our manipulation of objects, and our perceptual interactions."[42] The following example is offered by Johnson to help clarify: "[T]he body can take up the role of the 'thing contained' or the 'container.' But in either case, we seem to develop our sense of in-out orientation through a host of bodily movements, manipulations, and experiences."[43] In other words, we project metaphorically from the basic image schema outward: from understanding our bodies as containers to understanding "[s]queezing out the toothpaste" as the movement of something out of a container, much in the way that fluid moves out of our bodies, to what may seem at first to be a distantly related concept, such as "I'm getting out of the race," where the race is seen as a container (our bodies, in this instance, as the things contained). Johnson posits that the "act of metaphorically extending a schema from the physical to the non-physical" in this way is pervasive[44] and that, importantly, this is a way of understanding that is not "part of our self-reflexive awareness"; that is, the image schemata "do not require deliberation on the perceiver's part."[45] Johnson calls the image schemata structures of understanding because "they are patterns in terms of which we 'have a world,' which is what is meant by 'understanding' in its broadest sense."[46] This idea is, in fact, similar to Merleau-Ponty's concept of language as the expression of the body that allows us to "[sing] the world," to create our world through our bodies.[47]

Johnson does not offer a comprehensive list of image schemata, but the ones that he does formulate in some detail all have application to music and are especially useful in coming to understand the ways in which Led Zeppelin's riffs are meaningful as gestures that act on the body. These include the schemata of force, balance, path, link, cycle, scale, and center-periphery. Robert Walser has theorized the use of distortion in heavy metal in terms of Johnson's force schemata.[48] He links distortion to the excessive use of force, first generally, as in the distortion produced when one screams (signaling that the capacity of the vocal cords has been exceeded) or when the circuitry of electronic equipment is overdriven (as in the distortion heard when "a small radio is turned on full blast"), and then linking this specifically to the use of distortion in metal singing and guitar playing as a desirable characteristic of the sound that links force with "extreme power and intense expression."[49]

We could also use Johnson's force schema in a more localized or specific way to understand the details of a musical gesture such as a riff in terms of the way it impacts on or is otherwise connected to the body. For example, Johnson argues that forces act on our bodies or that we can through our bodies exert force on something else. Forces are characterized by having "directionality," and "a single path of motion," and "degrees of power or intensity" and are "always experienced through interaction." "The Wanton Song," riff again because it is structurally simple, is probably a good place to begin trying to apply the concept of force to the analysis of Zeppelin's riffs. This riff has always suggested a very direct physicality to me. There are two elements in the one-measure pattern: sound and (near) silence. The sound at the front end of the riff is extremely forceful, hitting the body like a blast and then quickly pulling back into silence. The force can also be analyzed more specifically than this: the blast of sound consists of a number of reiterations of the same pitch, and each of these reiterations strikes the body with renewed force.

We could also theorize this riff in terms of Johnson's balance schema. Balance is a central part of our understanding of our bodies, in that they are balanced when we are upright (Johnson offers the example of a baby learning to walk, who struggles to acquire bodily balance, balancing in this instance representing stability[50]), and we also experience balance in terms of equilibrium: we lose this equilibrium when our stomachs are too full and become distended or when our hands are too cold, for example. We stop eating or apply warmth to our hands to restore balance or equilibrium.[51] Johnson spends considerable time articulating the metaphorical projection of the balance schema onto visual phenomena, using the example of the position of a circle within the enclosed space of a square to be "off balance" when it is not directly in the center or how this "off-balance" circle might be balanced by the addition of another circle at an appropriate place within the square. Johnson goes on to abstract painting for a further example of the metaphorical projection of balance, concluding that "the balance in the painting can be made sense of only by interpreting 'weight,' 'force,' 'location,' and 'value,' metaphorically, based on a schema whose structure specifies forces or weights distributed relative to some point or axis."[52]

We can project this onto music by thinking of balanced phrases (the two phrases of a period, for example), movements, instrumentation, and a whole host of other aspects (including how these may work together to create a larger sense of balance or lack thereof in a piece), but again we might also use this schema to understand the riff. In "The Wanton Song" riff, there are extremes that might give us the illusion of balance: sound followed by silence, for example. This might also be experienced in terms of heaviness (a feeling of being weighted down by that opening blast of sound, which again relates to the concept of force) moving to lightness (the weight shed with the coming of silence). There is also intense movement followed by no movement (or almost none)— our bodies put into motion and then left in suspension—another physical extreme. So in terms of balance, we might experience this riff as initially taking our bodies out of balance and then having balance restored with the silence. The notion of extremes in terms of force and balance is very important in having a bodily understanding of this riff. We might also understand it in terms of the idea of force as a kind of interaction; there is physical communication, followed by a pulling back from this communication. Johnson theorizes the balance schema as "a point or axis around which forces or weights must be distributed so that they 'counteract' or 'balance off' one another."[53] In the case of music, axes might be melodic (in terms of range) or rhythmic/metric; indeed, I think it is the balancing of ideas around the rhythmic/metric axis as affecting us physically that David Lidov is getting at in his statements about containing or expressing overtly various somatic states. In "The Wanton Song" I would argue that one important axis is metric and that we might think of the balance around this axis as being rather skewed in favor of the opening beats of the measure. The axis is also particularly foregrounded when the snare drum articulates the backbeat (the fourth beat of the measure), on which no other instrument plays.

Yet another way of understanding the physical basis of this riff is through the path schema, "a linear spatialization of time," such as walking from point A to point B, or in terms of metaphorical projections, of setting and realizing goals. Because of the abrupt silence in the riff, it appears momentarily that the path has been interrupted, that we've been stopped dead in our tracks after a flurry of activity, suspended in our motion, only to be pushed forward on the path but at a different rate (the articulation of the backbeat), at a different rhythm.

Having used Johnson's schemata to analyze the physicality of this riff, we might now be able to turn back to some of the more general statements on music and the body made previously and incorporate them into the analysis. For example, the extreme juxtaposition of sound with silence might force us to examine the Shepherd/Wicke idea of the cocoon and, connected to this, the idea of extradaily time more closely. Although it can be argued that we are kept in an extradaily time throughout the entire riff (and throughout the entire song), we might feel as though we are taken in and out of the cocoon of sound with this riff, at one instant completely surrounded, enveloped by, and subjected to the forceful sound and at the next moment released from this cocoon, forced back into the experience of everyday life momentarily. (I know I have heard the phone ring during that silence, for example, where I had not heard it during the initial onslaught of the riff, momentarily bringing the "real" or "indicative" world back into focus. As a teenager I also remember hearing my mother calling me during a moment of silence in a rock song that I was playing at excessive volume and her frustration because she had been calling me for some time without my hearing it.)

It is easy to see how "The Wanton Song" riff differs from the riff to "Immigrant Song," which moves along the horizontal axis of rhythm in a steadier way, rocking the body back and forth evenly between the octave pitches that land directly on the beat. The balance schema may also be used with this riff, however, to get at the impact of that octave leap on the body. Throughout the riff, it is the lower octave that is heard most of the time, the upper octave being heard only for the duration of a single eighth note. This pitch tends, therefore, to be experienced as a breaking out of the container of the lower octave. As I mentioned earlier, the bass guitar rests as the guitar leaps up the octave, creating an opening for this pitch to break free from the container (or giving way to it doing so), also easing the force of the riff on the body for a brief moment. There is no break in the sound as there is with "The Wanton Song" riff, so the cocoon created is continuous, with no opportunity for the real world to interfere (depending, of course, on how loudly the stereo is playing). Depending upon the kind of physical experience one is after, the use of silence in the riff, or the lack thereof, may be regarded as a feature that makes it more or less effective as a musical gesture.

Balance around a melodic axis and, at the beginning of the piece, around a rhythmic axis is of central importance with the riff to "Celebration Day." This riff generally makes one feel off balance because of the rapid movement back and forth between the large leaps in the melody (in some cases more than two octaves). The issue of balance is partly so central because this large musical space is negotiated not by hitting the pitches discretely but by sliding back and forth between them, materializing—having the body travel—these great distances. The sliding between notes happens incredibly quickly as well: these are not leisurely descents and ascents but violent and sudden, a bit like hitting an air pocket while flying in a plane. Before the riff settles into a regular rhythmic pattern, these large, swooping gestures fall unpredictably within the measure. The whole effect of this is unsettling—one's body is dragged up and down forcefully, relentlessly, suddenly, unexpectedly. The riff can also be understood in terms of the path motive, where, again, the journey is short-circuited, the body moving up and out, suspended momentarily by the chordal part of the riff and then pulled back down again. What balances the unsteadiness of this riff is, in the first instance, the drone that is heard underneath it and eventually the (reasonable) steadiness of the bass guitar, which takes over the function of the drone during the verses of the song, when it is statically positioned on the tonic. There is also no harmonic movement during the verses. We can experience the drone, static bass, and lack of harmonic motion as a stable container from which the other elements of the riff—the various timbres, huge melodic leaps, slides—struggle to break free.

So far I have been using Johnson's image schemata to describe elements of rhythm and pitch, but what about timbre? As I pointed out earlier, there is a complex use of timbre in the "Celebration Day" riff that I haven't accounted for at all in my use of the schemata. The two parts of the riff are timbrally very different. At the beginning of the piece, the lower melodic part is heavily distorted and simultaneously muffled-sounding. The high chordal lick is also distorted, but it is much brighter, partly because of the high range, partly because of the way these two elements of the riff have been produced, the higher, chordal part more foregrounded than the low, melodic part. This gives the higher chordal lick prominence. It is also more prominent throughout the song, when the low, melodic part of the riff is almost completely subordinated in the mix, the high chordal lick cutting through the texture on a regular basis, clearly heard. The high chordal lick, then, has greater weight in terms of the balance schema. But there is another element to consider, and that is the doubling (and slight varying) of the low melodic part when the drums and bass enter. The guitar timbre here is also slightly distorted but not in the least muffled: it has a very direct and piercing sound and is heard prominently in the mix. This element of the riff overshadows even the high chordal lick in terms of timbre and position in the mix. One might think of these multiple elements of the "Celebration Day" riff in terms of Johnson's center-periphery schema (and indeed, this schema might be a very good tool for weighing various elements of a recording in terms of where they are positioned in the mix). The most central element of the riff is the doubled guitar part, the other elements acting on the periphery of our aural perception throughout the song. The center-periphery schema, according to Johnson, works because "[t]he fact of our physical embodiment gives a very definite character to our perceptual experience. Our world radiates out from our bodies as perceptual centers from which we hear, touch, taste, and smell our world."[54]

As with "The Wanton Song," the riff to "Black Dog" offers a flurry of activity followed by, not silence in this case, but stasis (in the last power chord of the riff, which is left to ring) over an a cappella vocal line, having a similar physical effect—force, no force—to that in "The Wanton Song." It may be that part of the reason the extension to the riff (Jones's "B" section) has such an impact when it arrives is because we have become used to the force of the riff being lifted during the verses. The extension thwarts that expectation, that momentary relief, and hurls us into even greater metrical tension. Part of the similarity between this riff and that of "The Wanton Song" also arises from the nature of the rhythmic pattern, the relatively even duration of the notes, so that the force is in this way even and sustained. Because this is a longer riff, however, the moment of force is more prolonged, pushing against the body for a longer period of time, and it is intensified at those moments of interruption that I described earlier, where an accented C♮ falls to the tonic. It is not only the increased rhythmic duration of these pitches that creates greater force but also the nature of the pitches themselves: that is, the C is a blue note, a strong dissonance within the scale. It falls, as this kind of blue note so often does, down to the tonic, where the tension is momentarily released. It is interesting that even though the tonic appears several other times throughout this riff, its force is not nearly so great because it is not preceded by the blue note. Dissonance, especially combined with syncopation, works as a strong physical force. Those points push the envelope in terms of force acting on the body, which is already under pressure from the forcefulness of the rest of the riff. The intensification of force at these accented points becomes even greater in the riff's extension, where the use of the blue note–tonic motive, now transposed and constantly displaced across the meter, becomes the guiding principle of the musical gesture. An obvious way to think of this gesture—which must be construed in terms of not only metric displacement but also, indeed, *which* pitches (in terms of function within the scale) are being used—is in terms of Johnson's concept of equilibrium (not balance, in this case). The blue note–tonic pattern is *overcoded*, both musically and culturally; it is a dissonance that appears in syncopation, and it is saturated with its history as a gesture of critical importance in blues music.[55] It therefore works as a kind of distortion in the melodic line, distending it (like that full stomach), the appearance of the tonic and the continuation of the even eighth note pattern bringing the line back into balance.

Riffs do not, of course, appear only one time within a song but repeatedly, and so they can also be conceived of in terms of Johnson's cycle schema. The significance of cycles is that they "constitute temporal boundaries for our activities."[56] While Johnson represents the cycle schema with a circle, he emphasizes that this is an imperfect way of thinking about it, for even though we can point to individual cycles that regulate our bodies and form our conception of the physical world, these cycles overlap, creating a complex interconnected web.[57] And these cycles are also qualitatively different (night and day, for example).[58] Many individual cycles also peak; that is, they "exhibit a character of buildup and release," a woman's menstrual cycle, for example, or the life cycle, from birth through maturity to death. Johnson therefore suggests that a better graphic representation of the nature of the cycle is the sine-wave pattern.[59]

These are important characteristics of cycles to keep in mind when making the metaphorical link to the riff as cycle within Led Zeppelin songs. Along with a foregrounded beat, the riff as cycle also acts to take us out of everyday time, keeping us locked within its musical elements that continually repeat. But the riff is never used statically as an undifferentiated gestural pattern throughout a song. For example, the main riff to "Black Dog" is doubled a third higher by guitar during verse 4, which is the last verse of the song and the last time that riff is used and signifies a peak in the cycle of the riff's use throughout the song (the riff is "thickened," intensified by this doubling). Similarly, the riff in "Babe I'm Gonna Leave You" is heard throughout the song, but it is heard in both acoustic and electric versions, the latter during the chorus. These momentary electric eruptions of the riff might also be construed as "peaks" in the cycle. In "Dancing Days," the riff is played an octave higher at the end of the song, also, in effect, creating a peak right at the end of the cycle, much like the birth cycle. We also have to take into account the fact that in the majority of songs the riff is not heard throughout, so that the cycle is interrupted, the flow broken. I will have more to say about this in "The Riff in the Song."

I elucidated earlier how in "The Wanton Song" there are three different levels on which one might understand the riff; the smaller units can be considered cycles within cycles. In "Celebration Day" this does not occur. Several articulations of the riff are not grouped together in some way—either the riff is being heard or is not being heard in the piece. In "Immigrant Song" iterations of the riff are not grouped together, either, until the end of the piece. There a cadential articulation is made first after four repetitions of the riff and then after two repetitions, so that the cycle is protracted (a common design in many songs by other artists as well).

"Black Dog" is a very different case in terms of cycle, in the first instance because the main riff is used in a stop-time framework: the length and complexity of the riff are highlighted because it is set off by (nearly) a cappella sections of singing (the final power chord of the riff rings through the sung section). Also, because there are three related riffs in this piece, the concept of cycle is much more complicated than in other pieces. It is possible, because the riffs are all structurally related, to hear these as a single cycle with qualitatively different parts to it. Whereas we might understand the use of a short, often-repeated riff as a metaphorical projection of a heartbeat or breathing, this riff might be related to a more complex kind of cycle, such as that of digestion, which consists of a number of stages. Or we might think of the use of riffs in "Black Dog" more in terms of Johnson's link schema than in terms of cycle. Johnson begins his discussion of this schema with the statement "[w]ithout links, we could neither be nor be human,"[60] pointing to that most critical of human links, the umbilical cord, to underscore how fundamental and important this concept is to us. Physical links with other human beings include everything from so intimate an act as sexual intercourse to something that can be as fleeting as a handshake. Further, Johnson reminds us that one metaphorical projection of the link schema is our lineage: we are linked to our parents, brothers, and sisters, and, as Johnson says, our lives are shaped by the "ongoing process of linking, bonding, and connecting that gives us our identity."[61] In music, there are many ways in which the concept of link is metaphorically projected, often acting in the same capacity—as a source of feeling connected and comforted—as physical links with other human beings do. For example, in the case of the riff, this is usually the most distinctive musical gesture of the song (certainly the majority of Led Zeppelin's riffs can be so characterized), and as it returns from a momentary absence, in order, for example, to link two verses of the song together, it is a source of comfort and pleasure to the listener to hear its shape uttered once again.

The Riff in the Song

These considerations lead us into a discussion of how the riff works within a song, where aspects of the cycle and link schemata, as well as notions of force, balance, and path, are as important as the riff itself. For as David Lidov reminds us, the way a musical gesture works within the framework of the entire song is of crucial importance: "If we consider the musical motive in its musical context rather than abstractly, its somatic value is not just a function of its own structure but also of its relations with other patterns."[62] In my analyses I am most concerned with where the riff does and does not occur within the song, but I try to take into account other factors that may lead to the particular physical way we have of understanding the use of that riff. In Led Zeppelin's repertory the riff is used in a vast number of different ways to structure a song. Far from simply being a device over which lyrics are sung or guitar solos played, the riff functions differently from song to song. As one fan keenly observed, "[Zeppelin] really integrates [the riff] into the music really well, unlike other musicians where the riffs stand apart from the rest of the song." Some of the important questions to ask with respect to how the riff works in these songs are: Does the riff begin the song? Is it used as an introductory musical gesture, thereby foregrounding it, calling attention to its importance? In songs with verse/chorus structure (by no means a majority in Led Zeppelin), is the riff heard during the verses or not? During the chorus? In between verses? Is it heard during the outro (the end of the song, including the fade-out), if there is one? How many songs with a twelve-bar blues structure also employ a riff? Is the riff used during the guitar solo if there is one? Is the entire riff heard during each of its repetitions, or is only part of it employed? If there is more than one riff in a song, how are these deployed? The answers to these questions could move us further toward understanding how the riff acts on the body in terms of Johnson's image schemata and also in terms of the general impact of sound on the body, the "extradaily" use of time, and the physical aspects of communication as outlined by Merleau-Ponty and Bakhtin.

Indeed, very few generalizations can be made on these questions with respect to Zeppelin's music.[63] It is true that in several songs with verse/chorus structure, the riff is generally heard at the beginning of the song, as an introduction, and in the verses, but often not in the chorus ("Good Times, Bad Times," "Your Time Is Gonna Come," "Celebration Day," and "All My Love," to name a few). The chorus, therefore, acts as a rupture of the cycle, a disjunction, which might act as a release from the extradaily time world of the riff (and possibly into another—a second—extradaily time world). In "Celebration Day," this is especially dramatic, since movement to the chorus is marked by a change in key to the relative major, which brightens the piece considerably, as well as a change from the harmonic stasis of the riff to a regular rate of harmonic change. In other words, the harmonic container, the image schema I used to analyze this riff earlier, dissolves in the chorus. In addition, all but one guitar part, which consists of strummed power chords, drop out of the texture and the electric bass assumes the main melodic role (the bass is positioned at the front of the mix during the chorus in order to bring out its importance; the guitar remains in the back). There is, then, a significant shift in the main (instrumental) speaker, a new body with which to interact, one who is "singing his world" in a dramatically different way than Page has been. Jones's bass line, while still encompassing a wide range, moves in stepwise motion or outlines the pitches of a chord, generally engaging in a stable tonal discourse. Interestingly, the characteristic "swoops" of the riff are not entirely gone but appear, greatly tempered, on the last beat of each measure of the chorus, played by the six-string bass, providing a remnant of the cycle—some continuity with it—for the listener.

While some songs, like "Celebration Day," make a clear distinction between verse and chorus in terms of where the riff is heard, there are also more complex uses of the riff in verse/chorus songs. For example, "Misty Mountain Hop" does not employ the riff for the first four measures of the verse, at which point it returns; it also returns in between lines of the melody during the chorus. A similar use of the riff occurs in "For Your Life" (it is not heard for the first two measures of each verse, and then it returns). And while there is no chorus in "Immigrant Song," a similar use of the riff is made here—it is suspended for the first two measures of the verse and then returns.[64] There are (at least) two ways of hearing this "suspension" in terms of force. On one hand, it may be heard or felt as an absence of force, as a kind of vacuum between articulations of force. On the other, the suspension of the riff might create enormous force (or tension) in anticipation of the riff's return, this force being released when the riff returns for the second half of the verse (in these cases tonic harmony accompanies the return of the riff, which also accounts for the sense that force or tension has been released).

It is much more unusual that the riff appears only in the chorus and not in the introduction to the song and in the verses: one example of this is "No Quarter," in which a distinctive riff is heard only at the beginning of the refrain. Another example is "Ramble On." In both cases, the chorus or refrain and the introduction of a riff occur at a climactic point in the song. These are places of culmination, peaks that are sustained for some time through the introduction of the riff cycle. Especially in "No Quarter," it is at this point that the body is finally drawn into the steady articulation of the beat by drums as well as the introduction of the riff, swept away into a powerful extradaily time. Both of these songs are primary examples of what Page called "light and shade" within a piece—a blending of acoustic and electric elements into a single piece. In both cases, the electric section forms the chorus, while the acoustic sections correspond to verses. In these songs "electric" and "riff" seem to be connected, and in these riff-based sections there is more force acting on the body, both through the electric guitar and through the working of the riff cycle on the body. But we can immediately come up with an exception to this idea: "Babe I'm Gonna Leave You" is also structured around an acoustic verse and electric chorus idea, but as mentioned earlier, both sections employ the same riff.[65]

Another way of employing the riff is to use it only as an introduction and in between verses, never during them. This occurs in "Dancing Days" and "Houses of the Holy," to name two examples. Neither of these songs contains a chorus, so the structure consists of verses (one or two at time, with no consistency about number) separated by iterations of the riff and, in the case of "Dancing Days," an instrumental section (not really a solo) that does not use the riff (in "Houses of the Holy," a guitar solo is heard over the riff during the outro, a fairly common feature of Zeppelin songs, which I discuss in more detail later). As mentioned earlier, one way in which this structure can be construed is through Johnson's link schema, where the riff, the familiar musical gesture that opens the piece, reappears between verses, to join them together and to provide continuity among them: a reminder of the source of the song—its history and parentage.

It seems to me particularly noteworthy to take account of whether or not the guitar solo is played over the riff, because when a solo occurs—and they are not a requisite feature of Zeppelin songs—it is a moment of singular importance. This is the point at which "the virtuoso" steps forward, asserting his subjectivity in a profound way. Does he choose to do this within the riff cycle or outside it, and what is the effect in either case? There are a number of songs in which Page does not play his solo over the riff, which ensures that the primary focus of attention is on the solo ("Ozone Baby," "Darlene," the first part of the solo in "Walter's Walk," "Celebration Day," "Living Loving Maid," "Ramble On," "The Wanton Song," "Heartbreaker," "Lemon Song" "Dazed and Confused," the second solo at the end of "The Ocean," "How Many More Times"). In fact, in the last five instances mentioned, the solo is set off from the rest of the song through a dramatic shift in meter (in all cases) and tempo (in all cases but "How Many More Times"). In all these examples save "The Ocean," these shifts in tempo and meter are preceded by silence. While in all of these cases the tempo shifts dramatically upward for the solo, "In the Evening" and "Carouselambra" offer examples in which there is a significant slowing of the tempo for the solo (or, in the case of "In the Evening," for part of the solo). In "The Ocean" the metrically complex riff is straightened out to an even four bars during the solo, but in all of these songs the accompanying music used during the solo is much simpler than that of the riff.

This distancing of the solo from the riff, through silence, dramatic shifts in tempo, or straightening out the rhythm of the accompaniment ensures that the solo is understood as a significant event. But further than this, if the solo lies outside of the riff cycle, it lies outside the extradaily time created by that cycle, moving the body out of that cycle, sometimes abruptly. It asserts its radical otherness from the cycle, its defiance of this "order" through which the song moves. It represents discontinuity and, in the case of a piece such as "Heartbreaker," where the solo is marked off by silence, rupture. Again, one can hardly hear these moments of rupture without focusing on the body behind them—Page's body—and this assertion (insertion) of his subjectivity into the flow of the song. We might think of these as moments of metanarrative, during which the narrative of the song is subordinated to Page's subjectivity.

One might think that the more complex the riff or the more soloistic it is, the less likely that Page would choose to solo over it, since it is more likely that such a riff would detract attention from the solo. This is the case with "The Crunge," for example, where the riff is constructed out of two different parts—the first used as an introduction and during the opening part of each verse, the second during the latter part of verses (in the first verse beginning with the lyric "I ain't disclosin' no names"), both of them metrically and rhythmically complex. There is no guitar solo in this song, which is largely "about" the strangeness of the riff, from which the body is never drawn away. But "Black Dog," "The Ocean," and "Hots On for Nowhere" all include solos over complex riffs with which Page has to compete mightily. In these solos, Page works much more within the confines of the riff, so that the solos are tied to the overall narrative. Page's own subjectivity is more engulfed within the extradaily time of the riff cycle: he is "part of" rather than the other. Yet there are still signs of his transgression. In "Black Dog," for example, Page's solo is very much derived from the main riff, developing, at the beginning, the triplet figure. But this figure is also a prominent sign of rhythmic deviation (transgression) in the main riff, and so Page negotiates uneasily between conforming to the riff and identifying with that part of it that is transgressive. Again, the appearance of a guitar solo over the riff can certainly be viewed as a peak in the cycle. In "Black Dog" this peak comes at the end of the song (continuing ad infinitum, since it fades out).

In only a few cases is a single riff used in an uninterrupted way for an extended section of a piece: "Whole Lotta Love," "When the Levee Breaks," "Fool in the Rain," "Trampled Underfoot," and "Carouselambra" are among the only examples of this technique (and in "Whole Lotta Love" there are several sections in which the riff does not appear—see chapter 5). In "Trampled Underfoot" the riff is replaced every eight measures by a cadential pattern (which is doubled in length, from one measure to two, at the end of every twenty-four measures).

"Fool in the Rain" offers perhaps the best example of the constant use of a riff, which in this case is articulated primarily on keyboards: the illusion of change is created through two rhythmic variations on the riff, the first a simple emphasizing of its pitches through a change of rhythm from quarter notes in $\frac{12}{8}$ meter (creating syncopation) to triplets and the second eventually changing the meter to $\frac{3}{2}$ and dividing the riff up between left and right hands. It is much more usual, especially in songs that are not verse/chorus-structured, for the first riff to be replaced by another or several others, which may or may not be variations of the main riff. "Over the Hills and Far Away" is a particularly rich example of this. It begins with a metrically complex riff played on acoustic guitar; a new electric riff, doubled by bass and guitar, is used for the verses, but this riff is comprised of two parts. For the first four measures, during Plant's couplet, one musical gesture is used, and during the following instrumental four measures a different, complementary gesture is used. A new riff (with a change of harmony) is used for the guitar solo, and yet another riff is introduced for the outro. This last feature (introducing a new riff for the outro) is not all that unusual. Other examples include "That's the Way," and "Out on the Tiles." "Hots On for Nowhere" also uses the main riff in both verse and chorus, and the solo occurs over this riff as well. In fact, every song on *Presence* save for the blues-based "Tea for One" is built on a riff and all include guitar solos built over the riff. In each song the riff is heard in all the verses as well. In fact, songs on this album are either constructed out of a series of different riffs ("Achilles Last Stand" and "Nobody's Fault but Mine"), built on a main riff with variations ("For Your Life" and "Candy Store Rock"), or built around a single riff but including short breaks (for example, between verses) during which the riff is not heard ("Royal Orleans" and "Hots On for Nowhere"). *Presence* stands out among the band's output as being the only completely electric album. According to Page, the album was "a reflection of the total anxiety and emotion at the period of time during which it was recorded," referring to the fragile state of the band's existence after Robert Plant and his family had been in a near-fatal car accident.[66] The structure of the songs seem to provide further evidence of this single-minded intensity.

Songs based on a twelve-bar blues pattern often do not incorporate a riff (examples include "I Can't Quit You," "You Shook Me," "Since I've Been Loving You," "Tea for One," and "I'm Gonna Crawl"), but several of them do ("Lemon Song," "Moby Dick," "Heartbreaker," "Black Country Woman," "Rock and Roll"; the last three use a modified twelve-bar form). What is significant for the discussion here is that where a riff is used in twelve-bar blues songs, two parallel (if you will) cycles occur, the harmonic cycle and the melodic/rhythmic/timbral cycle of the riff. The riff is "transposed," heard over different harmonies, something that is quite strikingly different from other songs, where there is harmonic stasis or where harmonic change forms part of the "bundle of features" that makes up the riff. The harmonic progression of the twelve-bar blues is in itself physically powerful, comprising long periods of stasis on the tonic (relaxed), juxtaposed with forceful, but only momentary, excursions away from it. The riff is pulled into this powerful cycle, sometimes heard throughout the entire harmonic pattern, sometimes not. In "Black Country Woman," the harmonic cycle is modified so that it becomes twenty-eight measures long. The pattern begins with eight measures on the tonic, four on the subdominant, and four again on the tonic. The last eight measures are repeated before moving to the dominant, that lasts for one measure, as does the subdominant that follows it, closing with two final measures on the tonic. The riff is two measures long and is heard throughout the entire harmonic pattern. At the dominant, the point of greatest harmonic difference, the riff is split in two as its first half is heard over this harmony, its second half over the subdominant. This is avoided in "Heartbreaker," where the riff is also two measures long, because the harmonic pattern avoids movement to the dominant. In cases where the riff does change over the course of the pattern, it inevitably changes at V ("Lemon Song" and "Moby Dick"), rupturing its identity as it comes into contact with the extreme point of harmonic otherness.

"Rock and Roll" actually consists of two different articulations of the harmonic pattern, one twelve measures long, with two measures on the dominant and no fall to the subdominant after this, during which the main riff is heard (a section that I will call A). The other is twenty-four measures long, a simple doubling of the standard twelve-bar pattern, over which the verse/refrain is sung and the guitar solo played and during which Page plays power chords that mark each downbeat (this could possibly be called a second riff—B):

> drum intro/A/B (verse/refrain)/B (verse/refrain)/A (with vocalizations)/B (solo)/B (verse; add piano)/B (varied: vocalizations as in A, no verse lyric; riff appears)

I would not want to suggest that simple modifications of the twelve-bar pattern are exceptional, since they occur so frequently in rock music, nor that the twelve-bar pattern is a standard or "norm" from which these modifications "deviate." But in this particular song it is interesting that the "absent" subdominant in the twelve-bar pattern with which the piece begins is "accounted for" in a spectacular way during the longer verse/refrain/solo section: the subdominant chord is articulated on the downbeat of the measure and is followed by two measures of stop time, thereby pointing to it in a particularly prominent way.

The Body in Performance

In his book *The Sight of Sound*, Richard Leppert argues for the importance of watching how music is made—"how the performers look and gesture, how they are costumed, how they interact with their instruments and with one another, how they regard the audience, how other listeners heed the performers"[67]—in order to understand more fully how musical sounds that can seem so "abstract, intangible and ethereal" may in fact "locat[e] and communicat[e] the place of music and musical sound within society."[68] Leppert suggests that "the agency of human sight" may in fact mediate the gap between the ethereal nature of musical sounds and the physicality required to produce them.[69] At the beginning of this chapter I noted how my experience of Led Zeppelin's music changed after I saw the band in performance, so while I have tried to argue earlier for the physicality of musical sounds in and of themselves, I agree with Leppert that *seeing* how the sounds are being made does bring a further level of understanding. In fact, David McNeil argues something similar with respect to language when he states that the gestures used when people speak make the listener understand the discourse as "instantaneous, nonlinear, holistic and imagistic," not simply as "a linear progression of segments, sounds and words."[70] Blacking, in fact, goes much further in stating the significance of watching a performer as suggested in his epigraph at the beginning of this chapter: if one comes to understand how the musician holds his or her body or certain parts of his or her body during performance, one will be able to "feel" the music much more deeply.[71] Merleau-Ponty offers the same theory with respect to language: "And as, in a foreign country, I begin to understand the meaning of words through their place in a context of action, and by taking part in a communal life . . . I begin to understand a philosophy by feeling my way into its existential manner, by reproducing the tone and accent of the philosopher."[72] Perhaps this accounts for so many fans of guitar-based rock bands picking up the instrument themselves, in order to "feel" the way certain licks or songs came into being through the hands of Jimmy Page, Eddie Van Halen, or Sheryl Crow, or perhaps it is what makes people want to sing along with recordings, to feel the vocal cords resonate the way, say, Lauryn Hill's do when she sings the hook to "Doo Wop (That Thing)." In any event, the "sight" of music has been grossly neglected until very recently and deserves more serious attention, especially in rock music, where "look," movement, and spectacle are such important elements. Again, I would stress the importance of studying the gestures of individual performers and those performers within their groups, if applicable, for while it can be said that, especially, grand gesture is important in much rock music, performers have developed these differently, using their bodies in significantly different ways from one another. I think of the very different ways in which Keith Richards and Jimmy Page, two rock guitarists from the same time period, geographical location, and musical tradition, each with a well-developed catalog of physical gestures, use their bodies in performance, for example. Here I hope to describe and underscore how important the body was in Led Zeppelin performances, mostly with respect to the struggle for power and what the nature of this power was.

In focusing my attention on Page during the 1973 Madison Square Garden performance of "Rock and Roll" at the beginning of this chapter, I meant to point up the fact that in Led Zeppelin shows Page made himself the focus of attention—and authority—not only through his guitar playing, through his ability as an instrumentalist, but also through the use of his body. In this and, especially, other up-tempo rock songs, Page is constantly moving and gesturing in extravagant ways that urge a viewer to look at him. It may be that he is "naturally" inclined to move to music, but many of his gestures are clearly calculated for their effect, consciously developed, and used in certain ways.[73] Jones confirmed to me that band members were aware of the importance of visual spectacle: "[Page's spectacular movements onstage] were an integral part of his and Led Zeppelin's style. His and Robert's movements onstage were the principal visual interest of the band, leaving the rhythm section to give it a solid dynamic (and harmonic) base" (more on this momentarily). It is possible (and important) to isolate Page's gestures and study them because they have remained much the same throughout his career. Indeed, the idea of writing about the physical gestures Page makes in performance occurred to me when I saw him play in Toronto in 1995; I had not seen him perform since his days with Led Zeppelin and was struck by how his gestures had remained essentially the same and by the thrill I got from watching him use his body to such great effect. I think that part of this thrill had to do with seeing the same fictional body—the body of Led Zeppelin mythology, immortalized in *The Song Remains the Same*—re-created twenty-odd years later. His physicality is also exaggerated by how little other members of the band move (Catherine Graham suggested to me that by comparison to Page they are "stage decor"[74]). One would think, for example, that the eye would fall mostly on Robert Plant, because of his central position onstage, because of his stature (he's over six feet tall), and because he is the singer, the one who is communicating with words. But in looking at shots that include the whole band in *The Song Remains the Same* and the August 11, 1979, Knebworth performance and when I have seen Page and Plant in concert, I am struck by how often my attention is pulled away from Plant and toward Page, because Page creates such a spectacular fictional body onstage and because Plant so often yields his physical power to Page. This is not to say that the others do not create fictional bodies but rather that they do not command the viewer's attention, nor, I would argue, are they as elaborate, stylized, and consciously developed as Page's.

I have already used Eugenio Barba's concept of the extradaily to describe the way in which music can pull us out of ordinary, everyday time into a virtual, mythological, or subjunctive time (depending on which writer's term one wishes to use). But Barba meant this term to describe the way in which the body is used in theatrical performance as opposed to the way it is used in everyday life, what he called the creation of a "fictional body." Barba believes that an actor (or in this case a musician) creates theatrical "presence" by changing the way in which the body is balanced (shifting body weight), thereby creating "tensions" that "generate an extra-daily energy quality which renders the body theatrically decided, 'alive,' 'believable.'"[75] Barba stresses that these extradaily techniques are based "on the wasting of energy" and that, unlike the everyday use of the body, where minimum effort is expended in order to convey maximum information, the opposite is true of extradaily uses of the body.[76] He differentiates, of course, among theatrical techniques that are more and less codified through a conscious tradition but makes it clear that no matter how unconscious, all actors who are effective on the stage are using their bodies in extradaily ways.

These are important considerations for an understanding of how the members of Led Zeppelin used their bodies in performance. First, we can say that there are, indeed, codified traditions of extradaily body technique that are used in rock music performances. Page's choosing to move his body incessantly is a decision to follow not only, in the early days, his contemporaries like Jeff Beck but also black blues performers such as Howlin' Wolf and, of course, the example of Elvis Presley—a white performer who adopted the overtly embodied performance techniques from his black idols. Some important gestures that Page makes also tap into more particular traditions, such as his modified duck-walk appropriated from Chuck Berry. I will return to a discussion of Page's gestures in more detail in a moment, but I want first to discuss those of the other band members, so that Page may be set in relief to them.

Plant generally confined himself to standing in the same place and moving to the music, walking around onstage (importantly this frequently occurred to get out of Page's way, as when Page would move to center stage—Plant's usual location—in order to play a solo, as he does in "Rock and Roll"; see front cover photo for an example), and occasionally striking poses. Plant taps into the codified tradition of using a wide-legged stance, his body squarely in front of the audience, which signifies confidence and power, because the body is so firmly grounded, with weight evenly distributed, balanced, and in control (see Wendy Annibell's photograph of Plant for an example, fig. 18). One of the most important extradaily uses of his body is how he thrust forward his chest, which until 1979 was always nearly bare. This thrusting forward had the effect of increasing his stature, of making him larger than life and seemingly self-assured, of asserting his sexuality, of, in short, giving him "presence" even when he was not singing (a characteristic that Barba calls pre-expressivity[77]). Even so, other of Plant's physical gestures counteract these confident poses. Most of the dance-like movements that he makes to the music belie a certain awkwardness with his body, awkwardness that is not unusual in white heterosexual men and which signifies their discomfort with dance movements and bodily spectacle. Unchoreographed movement to the music suggests a willingness to break out of the confines of the bourgeois denial of the body (one of my students once pointed out how much Plant seems to enjoy his body in *The Song Remains the Same*), but this attempt at physical liberation is tentative. I suspect that the very awkwardness of Plant's gestures may have been comforting to other white heterosexual males who were watching him, a trace of his "masculinity" and hence sameness (safeness) in the face of many other signals that suggest his gender otherness (see earlier and, especially, chapters 1 and 5). But dancing and other kinds of physical spectacle were also to be kept to a minimum because, as Plant explains in a 1977 interview with *Melody Maker*'s Ray Coleman:

> If any of my movements appear sexual, then they are really just accessories to the music at that point in time. I get quite heatedly involved with what's going on musically, and invariably I'm right in front of John Paul's equipment or Jimmy's. I'm concentrating on what I'm listening to and I move accordingly. There are movements I do all the time, regularly, but if I was going to start thinking about how I was going to appear, I might take myself a little too seriously in the wrong direction.[78]

In other words, it is the music that should always remain the central focus of attention, not the performer's body, and it is the music that determines, supposedly in an unpremeditated way, how the body should respond. In a way, this taps into an idea about authenticity in music that goes back to the nineteenth century, namely, that the further removed music was from the social and physical, the purer (and better) it was. Coleman's comment to Plant during the interview suggests as much: "I put it to him that he did not sell sex on stage as did some of his contemporaries in hard rock singing, but that he relied largely on the music instead of posing."[79]

Plant occasionally allowed the music to take his body completely away, as in the extravagant gesture that involved tensing the chest to an extreme degree (to the point of shaking his whole upper body) while stretching the microphone cord between his hands (see fig. 13). He makes this gesture during the performance of "Rock and Roll" in *The Song Remains the Same*, during the stop time at the end of the guitar solo, when Page is playing fast repeated triplets. Plant's gesture materializes the musical tension created by the suspension of the beat on the dominant, the required resolution of this chord delayed so that Page can finish his solo with a virtuosic flourish of notes. But Plant makes the same gesture again later, during the performance of "Dazed and Confused," when there is nothing in the music to suggest this kind of extreme tension, thereby creating a wonderful counterpoint between body and music. Again, this gesture involves his chest, that part of his body that clearly serves as the main signifier of his disjuncture with dominant culture. This physical gesture is spectacular in and of itself but is particularly so in light of most of Plant's other gestures in terms of energy: while he often moves in time to the music, the gestures he makes are not crisp and focused in the way that Page's are but, rather, shuffling, contained, and uncommitted.

Bootleg video of the Danish television special (March 19, 1969) on which Led Zeppelin appeared illustrates that at that early time John Paul Jones had a physical presence onstage that subsequently changed quite dramatically. In that video, Jones can be seen moving vigorously, his whole upper body keeping the beat, but in *The Song Remains the Same*, for example, filmed four years later, he is at the extreme opposite of Page's kinetic stage presence, hardly moving at all and, in fact, often positioning himself behind his keyboards when he was playing bass, in effect materially isolating himself behind a barrier of technology. In the August 11, 1979, Knebworth video he is not behind the keyboards, but his movement is still extremely restricted, and in contrast to the image of Page with his guitar slung low around his hips, Jones holds the bass guitar statically at chest level, undoubtedly so that he can maintain optimal control over his technique (see cover photo for an example of this stance). About his relative lack of movement onstage, Jones commented to me: "I hadn't really noticed but it might have had something to do with hearing the bass properly onstage and maybe having to stay in one place. Bass is actually a harder instrument to move around with especially if you are playing intricate finger-style lines." This is undoubtedly true, but Jones's control with respect to physical movement and his position of the bass guitar onstage is also a powerful signifier of his seriousness as a musician and his professionalism, and it probably is part of the reason that so many fans characterized him as being a steady and reliable presence in the band, exhibiting none of the surface showmanship of Page and Plant, just "solid" musicianship (see chapter 5 for fan comments concerning this issue, as well as that of the male distaste for spectacle). What is interesting to consider is that despite Jones's physical control and its significance for the appearance of professionalism and serious musicianship, the lack of this control on Page's part does not make him less serious or professional in the eyes of fans. Many critics and fans have noted Page's "sloppy" playing, (a majority of fans who commented on Page's solos on the fan questionnaire made reference to his "sloppiness"), but this is rarely expressed as a real criticism. Fans forgive the "mistakes" because "when you work without a net, sometimes things work and sometimes things don't," or, "Jimmy Page's solos have the ability to touch my heart and to make it skip a few beats. Instead of technical brilliance, the *solos* feature what is truly important in rock music—guts and heart." In other words, Page's ability to express emotion in his playing (bodily based) and his penchant for experimentation are more important to many fans than technical perfection. It should be pointed out, however, that they are undoubtedly willing to forgive his sloppiness because at some point he has proven to them that he can, indeed, achieve a level of technical brilliance on the guitar that he is willing to *sacrifice* in the name of emotional expression or musical experimentation.[80] Jones, however, is seen by fans as "the most talented" member of the band, "knows the most about music," and is "solid"; "he's a perfectionist," "a true musician," not at all interested in showmanship.

Although John Bonham's body was mostly hidden behind the drum kit, his physicality was of tremendous importance in shaping the idea of this band as powerful. Rock drummers materialize the concept of music making as manual labor to a greater extent than most musicians through the kind of physical gestures they make: repeated blows to the instrument (this might also be equated with a kind of primitiveness or naturalness of the instrument and its players, applicable, certainly, in Bonham's case). Their gestures, however, can vary enormously in terms of extravagance: think of the staid physical presence of Charlie Watts compared to the exuberant physicality of Keith Moon, for example. Bonham was a physical drummer, but he did not make the kinds of extravagant gestures of Moon. Bonham's power came from his large physical stature, which allowed him to play hard and loud but with physical *control* that was exhibited in live performance. A mythology that surrounds Bonham's playing has to do with physical power. One of the details of his technique that is often mentioned is that he achieved his enormous bass drum sound using only *one* bass drum and one bass drum pedal, the implication being that he had such a powerful touch that he didn't need elaborate equipment. That Bonham was also capable of great subtlety as a drummer is rarely mentioned (one need only listen to "In My Time of Dying" to get a sense of the subtlety of which he was capable). I would argue that Bonham's mythology is, then, largely bound up with his physical strength. Further, I would suggest that for fans who know the band's biography, Bonham's physical stature and strength in performance are mapped onto his rural way of life: he owned and ran a farm when he wasn't working with the band. In *The Song Remains the Same*, Bonham is depicted on his farm in one scene of his fantasy sequence, standing in a field alongside an enormous bull. Bonham's legendary temper, which manifested itself in acts of physical violence when he was under the influence of alcohol, must certainly also contribute to his mythological physical stature.

Put into the context of the way in which other members of the band use their bodies in performance then, Page's gestures seem especially spectacular and can be interpreted in light of his public role as "guitar hero," virtuoso. In an essay that problematizes the way in which nineteenth-century virtuoso pianist Franz Liszt used his body during performance, Richard Leppert comments that "Liszt's entire body reads the music to the audience at the same time as his fingers, so to speak, realize the notes";[81] and so for Jimmy Page. Examining particular gestures that Page makes repeatedly in performance, as well as the general physical relationship that he has with his instrument, can move us closer to an understanding of how this happens and to the social and musical significance of these gestures.

Ray L. Birdwhistell reminds us that "'gestures' not only do not stand alone as behavioral isolates but they also do not have explicit and invariable meanings."[82] Although photographs and illustrations isolate gestures artificially from the larger context of movement in which they are made, they offer a starting point for the discussion of several of Page's most frequently made gestures; they are also important media for the analysis of his physical gestures because photographs in books and magazines are the medium through which his image is widely distributed and understood. For example, figures 2, 3, 4, 5, 6, and 9 give some indication of how Page often related physically to his instrument. Figures 3 and 6 illustrate the way in which Page often holds his guitar and body when he stands still and plays. An important feature of this pose is that while he strikes the wide-legged stance associated with many rock guitar players and singers,

Page almost always positions his left leg forward from his right, which has several effects. First, it suggests forward motion, readiness for action, even when his body is standing still, as opposed to the stasis of having both legs spread apart and equidistant from each other. Page's preferred stance is also weaker than having both legs firmly planted and wide apart. With one leg forward, the balance is skewed, the weight no longer evenly distributed; it is, in fact, as if he has to brace himself—perhaps against the (metaphorical) force of the music, which tends to make him bend his torso back, as in figure 6. (It is interesting that the *Melody Maker* journalist quoted in one of the epigraphs at the beginning of this chapter would understand the force of the music to be holding Page up, rather than being the very thing bending his body back.) Having the left leg forward allows his upper body to hold his torso in this position without bending his knees; it also allows him to rock his torso back and forth, a motion that he frequently makes when in this position.

Earlier and in chapter 5 I mention how low Page always wore the guitar—around his hips—which some commentators have indicated reduced the amount of control he had over his playing and compromised him in terms of precision. The photographs I have pointed to here demonstrate not only how low-slung the guitar was but also how excessively Page liked to move the instrument around. Figures 4, 5, and 8 show a particularly common placement of the guitar in relation to Page's body, which was over his right hip. He often moves it there from the conventional position, centered at the front of the body, or, in fact, moves it back and forth, from center to right hip, while he is playing. The right leg may or may not be raised when the guitar is over on the right hip, or Page may raise it in the midst of playing while the guitar is so positioned.

It is not only the transgressive act of moving the instrument around so much that is striking (especially with Jones there, illustrating how an instrument like that *should* be held and treated), although this is certainly noteworthy, but also the way in which Page goes about making these gestures. They are not made "cleanly," with crisp movements, but with a sense of abandon—the guitar is treated athletically, the way in which Page moves it on and around his body something like the way a twirler moves the baton: fluid and virtuosic, the guitar at one moment above his head, the next behind the back, out to one side, then the other, or otherwise pulled away from his body (see especially fig. 17). Page's virtuosity as a guitarist is metaphorically projected onto his relationship with the instrument; he literally "struggl[es] with his instrument, taming it, making it obey," visually, even as this is what he does aurally with sound.[83] While all this movement of the instrument (and body) may indeed have compromised the precision with which Page played, this is hardly the point. Moving the instrument around so deftly and with such confidence gave the visual impression of his complete mastery of this piece of technology.

Furthermore, it gives the impression that this instrument has life in and of itself—that it is a force, a presence. Moving it points up its materiality—it is not just a static piece of technology but also a body with which the player has a physical relationship, a body that is above all *on display*, as Page showcases it by balancing it on his hip, holding it over his head (as if it is a sacrificial object) or out to the audience (again, see fig. 17, which presents a characteristic way of Page holding the instrument during solos).

Playing the instrument on the hip is an important way in which Page creates his fictional body as well. A fictional body is created in the first instance when the instrument is strapped onto the body and the body must learn to negotiate stance and movement in relation to it. But again, this can be done in various ways, downplaying the new way in which the body must be balanced in order to play the instrument (as Jones does), for example, either limiting the shift of balance to the upper body alone or overtly pointing to the new balance, the new body. Although there are many variations on the way in which Page holds his body when he plays the guitar on his hip, two general comments about this gesture can be made. Holding the instrument to the right puts an emphasis on this side of his body, whether this occurs simply through his moving his arms and the instrument over to that side or involves a complete shift of balance by bringing up the right leg as well. In the latter case, Page's weight is actually shifted over to the left side, which is steady, while the right side becomes ungrounded and distorted (by jutting outward). This extradaily use of his body, this movement into "the subjunctive," is unstable, precarious. It points to Page as being physically decentered, what Leppert construes as the body being out of rational control, and so, therefore, "[t]he center does not hold; rational gravity gives way to sensual chaos. . . . The experience of decentering is made visible in the body of the artist."[84] The way in which Page moves the guitar over to the side is a metaphor for this decenteredness: the right side of his body and the hip on which the instrument rests in particular form a zone of psychological difference; it signals that now Page has moved further into the subjunctive, further into his otherness, further into the music. Raising his leg deepens the movement further, creating even greater instability. Raising the leg also points more directly to the materiality of the instrument: "Look; this is the vehicle through which I have become other."

In order to further understand this leg raising and other gestures that Page uses, it might be profitable to turn to David McNeil's study of the way in which gesture and language interact. McNeil groups gestures into four different kinds: iconic, metaphoric, deictic (pointing), and beat gestures,[85] all of which are used by speakers in a dialectical way with language.[86] Briefly, a gesture is iconic "if it bears a close formal relationship to the semantic content of speech"—for example, a reference is made to someone climbing a ladder and the hand moves upward—it is metaphoric if it is intended to represent an abstract concept, such as knowledge. Deictic gestures point to something, often something abstract, and beats are movements of the hand or arm that simply seem to mark a word or phrase. Beat gestures can easily be transferred to music—we can mark each beat of a musical meter with a hand/arm gesture, or we might mark certain beats that we want to stress with such a gesture. This becomes especially interesting when watching a performer such as Page, who may choose to mark beats that are otherwise not accented, adding a layer of kinetic complexity to the music that is otherwise not there or that is minimal when one listens to the recording. This occurs in an especially dramatic way, for example, during the performance of "Rock and Roll" when Page jumps up into the air during the last verse (this gesture is much more than a simple beat, of course, but it is a good example to use here to get the point across). He makes this gesture in the middle of a verse—not at the beginning or end, which we might think would be to better dramatic effect—and on the second half of the downbeat, on a part of the beat generally considered weak. In the studio recording, Bonham articulates this part of the downbeat at precisely this point with the crash cymbal and so it has already been marked, set off as a point of particular emphasis in the verse, but Page's leap into the air at this point suddenly makes it the single most important sonic event in the piece: a cathartic moment, a moment of intense release in this song that is, through the physical gesture, sustained in its energy (and hence physical force). After seeing Page mark this point in the song with his body, I have never been able to listen to the studio recording without hearing this moment as incredibly significant, and perhaps it is the same for Page: when he performed the song in Toronto in 1998, he made the same leaping gesture at precisely the same moment in the song as he had in 1973.

The gesture that Page makes in figure 9 could be called iconic. This gesture is often made when he is playing high notes, especially in an extreme range (a particularly striking example can be found in the August 11, 1979, Knebworth video performance of the solo to "Black Dog," which Page at one point centers around a few very high pitches); raising the guitar materializes the highness of the range and at the same time suggests that it requires physical effort to produce these notes. But Page uses this gesture at other times as well, to point to the instrument in a dramatic way. In chapter 2, I discuss this gesture as Page regularly made it during the fanfare that introduces the guitar solo in "Stairway to Heaven," in which Page valorizes the instrument, displaying it as if it were a sacred object.

Deitic gestures of both the concrete and abstract kind are also very important to Page. In figure 5 his right hand and arm are raised in the air, perhaps poised as they often were to point to the rhythm section. I indicated this kind of pointing gesture in my description of Page's performance during "Rock and Roll" at the beginning of the chapter. There, at the end of the song, he throws his arm out toward Bonham as if to signal him to begin playing. There is another dramatic example of Page using his right arm to give signals to the rhythm section during the performance of "How Many More Times" on the 1969 Danish television show, where directly before the drums enter he counts off four beats using his entire forearm, again throwing it toward the rhythm section on each beat. This gesture increases the climactic effect of the moment: this is the last song on the show. The band has been vamping on the song's riff for a few minutes while Plant introduced each member to the audience. Page's conducting gesture comes at the end of this lengthy introduction, signaling the real beginning of the piece. With these gestures Page is in effect *conducting* the rhythm section and by doing so is demonstrating to the audience his authority (his role as decision maker). As Jones explains, these gestures were unnecessary (hence pointing again to Barba's principle of maximum effort for minimum result): "Cues were given either by Bonzo [Bonham], Page or myself as appropriate, although not many were necessary as we used to watch and listen to each other closely at all times, another strength of the band. Page's gestures were usually for show." They confirmed for the audience Page's control over the musical events and so served as another way in which he demonstrated his virtuosity. This virtuosity has to do with the ability to play and conduct simultaneously, thereby having control over both the instrument (the local) and the band and general musical design (the global) at the same time.

The gestures that Page makes with his right hand and arm, however, are mostly of the abstract kind, in which he is not pointing at someone or something specific but rather interpreting something about the music or indicating what effect the music is having on his body. As McNeil puts it, these gestures tell us "[h]ow the speaker is construing the discourse structure as he or she proceeds through the narrative."[87] McNeil discusses at length how hand and arm gestures are used in discourse, emphasizing that they frequently are made to mark important junctures within a multilevel narrative.[88] Because Page's hands are occupied much of the time with playing the guitar, it would be difficult for him to follow this pattern of gesturing as consistently as it is used in spoken discourse; still, he frees up his right hand very often in order to make a deitic gesture, as described earlier, or some other kind of iconic or metaphoric gesture, which either serves to mark the musical structure in some way, which illustrates something about the nature of the musical idea that has just been presented, or serves to "push the communication forward," what McNeil calls communicative dynamism.[89] Figures 14, 15, and 16 capture three of the ways in which Page gestures with his right hand and arm; he uses all of these gestures in the performance of "Rock and Roll" in *The Song Remains the Same*. The small gesture shown in figure 15 can be seen during the riff of some of the verses (especially toward the end of the song), where Page brings his hand up and juts his elbow back after strumming the two chords as the last of these continues to ring. The delicacy of his hand and its closeness to his upper body suggest that he is holding the sound close to him and also signal his readiness to play again—whatever he has just played is not final; there is more to come. The gesture in figure 14 is a frequently made one that involves moving the hand across the guitar strings to play a chord and then continuing movement outward from the instrument, providing a visual flourish to the musical gesture, somewhat like Page's pointing of the violin bow toward the audience during "Dazed and Confused" (fig. 12); this gesture seems to throw the sound out to the crowd. It is a much more final and forceful gesture than that shown in figure 15 and one that exudes confidence, rather than the tentativeness of the former gesture. It is particularly interesting, then, that Page should use both of them to play the same musical idea, indicating once again that using different physical gestures can help alter the meaning of musical ideas. Both these gestures also point to the effort it has taken to make the musical sound ("look what I have just played"), asking the observer to recognize it as having taken effort and that that effort has now been released; in addition, I would suggest that both gestures, especially the second, are intended to indicate that the musical gesture was brilliant, a way of ensuring that it is recognized as such.

Figures 3, 4, and 16 illustrate another important kind of physical gesture that Page often makes, which is holding his head to the side, turning away from the source of the sound, indicating concentration or perhaps that the mind is somewhere other than the body, transported by his muse. In live performance or video, this gesture is often extended to involve Page shaking his head from side to side, not necessarily "in time" to the music, thereby creating an interesting polykinesis between his physical gesture and the musical rhythm, his eyes usually closed but not necessarily (one example of this occurs during the solo in "Stairway to Heaven" in *The Song Remains the Same*). While Richard Leppert suggests, based on reading nineteenth-century critiques of Franz Liszt's performances, that any overtly dramatic physical gestures made by a musician code inspiration,[90] I would argue that it is, in particular, gestures such as these that Page makes with his head that materialize the idea of inspiration very strongly. Page seems to be in touch with another world at these moments, pulling musical ideas from his source, in full concentration while he is doing so. They are also gestures that are associated with sexual pleasure.

Related to this is the way in which Page demonstrated the draining physical effect that performance had on him through even grander gestures: for example, in *The Song Remains the Same*, at the end of "The Rain Song," he moves his incredibly sweaty body very slowly, removing the guitar pick from his mouth as sweat drips from his face, his upper body slightly collapsed—or, better, crippled—to further demonstrate his exhaustion and frailty, stumbling slightly, only acknowledging the cheering crowd by faintly nodding his head toward them, while he seems to be catching his breath. In all, he strikes one as having just run a marathon, determined to keep the aching body moving as it cools down. The way in which Page demonstrates his exhaustion at this moment also suggests him as a feminine other: "In the instant of his collapse, the hyper-phallic [guitarist] is literally transformed into his extreme opposite, the fainting woman."[91] Leppert discusses how this display of the virtuoso's body in performance, the simultaneous "physical stamina and . . . apparent exhaustion," was interpreted in the nineteenth century with respect to Liszt. Leppert quotes a review of one of Liszt's concerts, which commented that Liszt "performed with a power and stamina that would have been a source of astonishment in any other player, but not in Liszt who, when carried away by his own inspiration, *appears to forget all physical suffering and not to notice any weariness until the final chord has died away beneath his hands*."[92] A performer like Page plays into this model of virtuosity exactly, using his body—fictionally, since it requires very little movement of the body to play the guitar—to enact his virtuosity in the guise of both the stamina it seemingly requires to produce the sounds and the brutality his body must suffer in order to create them.

While it is important to examine all these gestures on the micro level to try to tease out how they might be meaningful individually, it is also important to step back once again and examine the larger picture. For this I return to Leppert's essay "Desiring Difference." There, he discusses how it is not only Liszt's ability as a pianist that inscribes his otherness from the audience but also his grand gestures. "Restrained emotion was the word of the day for bourgeois audiences in the nineteenth century";[93] by putting his body on display, Liszt went against the prescribed norms of decorum and—Leppert's point—this transgression of norms was indeed something the bourgeois, especially men, desired for themselves but could not have because they were not musicians: in other words, they looked at Liszt desiring the freedom with which he could express himself through his body: "Virtuosity's visibility served as evidence to prove the radical otherness of art."[94]

This kind of audience decorum is certainly not required at rock concerts; we can dance around freely, clap to the music, shake our heads, perhaps even imitate Page in some of his movements—bending our torsos back as we hear a particularly high or fast passage he plays on the guitar as he makes the same gesture, for example—demonstrating physically, overtly, that we comprehend the nature of Page's musical idea and sharing with him his physical manifestation of the gesture. But most of us would still not gesture to the music consistently in the grand way that Page does—there remain unspoken rules of bodily behavior that would make it look very weird indeed for an audience member to be duck-walking around an arena—not to mention that in the confines of a large crowd overt gesturing is nearly impossible. And, perhaps more important, in making any of these gestures we are in any event *responding* to what Page is doing—physically and musically—rather than *creating* the music and the body that go with it ourselves. Page is the one creating and demonstrating "inspiration" "virtuosity," "freedom," "power," and "unbridled emotion" for us; his overt gestures still make him considerably other to most people in the audience. These overt physical gestures not only are signs of "freedom" from the constraints of polite society, but, as Leppert points out, also represent "genius," in its association with "the untamed—the unmeasurable, the sublime."[95]

Finally, there is a crucially important point to be made with respect to my analysis of the band members' physical gestures and especially my privileging of Page in this analysis. Despite his constant pointing to himself in performance through his physical gestures, there are those in the audience who look past this or who may not even really see it at all because their attention is focused, for whatever reason, on someone else in the band. I think of my own infatuation with Robert Plant when I was younger and how all I saw when I watched *The Song Remains the Same* was him. Jimmy Page could have turned cartwheels onstage and I would have thought it a momentary distraction from my focus on Plant; it made absolutely no difference to me. Further, there has to be allowance made for the fluidity of movement in performance—there were moments when Page stood quite still and one's focus of attention was drawn elsewhere, especially when Jones played a keyboard solo, for example, and moments when Page was not on the stage, such as during Bonham's drum solo. Nevertheless, Page's elaborate extradaily technique worked to underscore his central importance, his power and, as mentioned earlier, his otherness. This effort to point to himself begs the question "whose story is being told" in these performances, as well as "who is telling the story." In the first instance, the answer to these questions must be Jimmy Page.[96]

FIVE

Whole Lotta Love
Performing Gender

Several times during the performance of "Since I've Been Loving You" in Led Zeppelin's documentary film *The Song Remains the Same*, the camera turns its focus away from the stage and out into the crowd in an attempt to document the audience members' reception of the event. Among the people shown is a woman in a white hooded jacket who appears near the end of the song. Even though her appearance is brief, she has always been a source of intrigue for me, a focal point not only of this song, but, in fact, of the whole film. She is sitting still, her chin resting on her folded hands. For some time her expression is unchanging, riveted as her attention is toward the stage, until she finally breaks into a smile, then laughs and slowly shakes her head in what seems pleasurable wonder mixed with a bit of disbelief. The performance of this song is certainly a highlight of the film—Jimmy Page has played a blistering solo; Robert Plant has ridden an emotional roller coaster, from his trademark banshee wails to near-whispered moans, all of the performance cradled in the weighty (read: authenticating) tradition of the blues—it is a "heavy" song and it has been a "heavy" performance. The woman's incredulous look coming near the end of it may serve as the filmmaker's way of confirming this: the audience was transfixed, mesmerized, blown away. But two aspects of this image give one pause: First, a majority of the audience for Led Zeppelin was (and still is) male, and the discourse that surrounds not only Zeppelin's music but also hard rock in general has coded it as "male," so why on earth would the filmmakers choose a *woman* to affirm these traits of the performance (especially in the mid-1970s)? And second, given the popular image of women fans of rock music as hysterical, how do we account for her composure, her controlled (controlling?) gaze?

Her appearance in the film could easily be dismissed, fleeting as it is, but I think that by doing so we would miss an opportunity to problematize a host of what have become commonplace assumptions about Led Zeppelin's image, music, and reception thereof in terms of sexuality and gender. To erase her from the narrative of this film is to continue to distort or erase women's experience of this music and to allow a narrowly and rigidly construed view of masculinity to continue to dominate the discourse about it. Women have been part of the audience for Zeppelin and other hard rock music since the late 1960s; many women who came to love the music then (including myself) remain avid fans, and because of the band's enduring popularity new women fans are continuously drawn to the music. A discussion of gender and sexuality with respect to the band, then, not only is historical but also engages with the current and ongoing reception of the music. Was/is Zeppelin's audience primarily male and what difference does this make? Were/are the women who made/make up part of the audience primarily part of the groupie scene or just there because their boyfriends were/are? Should the expression of sexuality in the band's visual image, lyrics, and music be defined exclusively in terms of the concept of cock rock? Is there something inherently male about the music itself (and how is "male" defined)? Is it, in fact, misogynistic? In what has been written about the band thus far in other works, these queries have been overwhelmingly answered in the affirmative. Where, then, does this leave the filmmakers' decision to focus on the anonymous woman (and she isn't the only woman in the audience who is captured by their cameras) and her pleasurable gaze on Plant, Page, Jones, and Bonham in *The Song Remains the Same*? Where does it leave *me* as an avid fan of this music since I first stumbled upon my brother-in-law's copy of *Led Zeppelin III* in 1972 at the age of fourteen and played "Immigrant Song" over and over again until I wore out the vinyl? Where, indeed, does it leave millions of fans, both male and female, who engage in a sophisticated and complex way with this music in terms of gender (and everything else), or the musicians, whose main objective was to create a repertory marked by eclecticism and diversity?

Part of the problem is that women who know and love Led Zeppelin's music have not been very engaged in constructing the published discourse around it or, for that matter, around male-made rock in general. Journalists, academics, and others who write about the band have been for the most part men, who have claimed, derided, or otherwise defined the music as male. The few women who have written about the music do not seem to be themselves actively engaged in its consumption. I have come across only one academic who discloses that she listens to it (and her discomfort with doing so—see later). Their interest, too, has been in delineating and interpreting the characteristics of the culture that seem to make it male. Either, then, they are, as Robert Walser has already pointed out with respect to Deena Weinstein's book on heavy metal, erasing themselves from the discussion of the music culture in the pursuit of "objectivity" (a claim I would also make for many of the male academics who write about the music, who rarely position themselves within the matrix of desire with respect to it),[1] or they are really not very engaged with the music and have no personal stake in the characterizations of it that they are making. The issue of representation, then—"[W]ho speaks for whom, why, how and when," as Elspeth Probyn has summarized it[2]—has been especially problematic for this music where issues of gender and sexuality are concerned.

My own gendered experience with the music and visual imagery, as well as responses to the fan questionnaire, point to the enormous gap that exists between how enthusiastic consumers of the music respond to issues of gender and sexuality and how disengaged academics and journalists do. I will begin this chapter by reviewing the latter—the commonly held notions concerning gender and sexuality in Zeppelin and, by extension, hard rock and metal—and then I will set these in relief to what the fans have to say on the subject. I will then turn to a detailed discussion of Zeppelin's image and music in order to offer a critique of and alternative to how certain images and sounds have been interpreted in the past. Since my aim is to challenge the rigidity of gender constructions with respect to this music, I do not wish to replace one fixed way of looking at it with another, and so I want to acknowledge that I come to this discussion and analysis as a white heterosexual woman and that I deal here mostly with heterosexual points of view. I do not wish to suggest that this is a normative or compulsory way in which the music is or should be consumed.

> Led Zeppelin's music is young men's music—and forever will be.
> —David Cavanagh, "The Rovers Return"

In a fascinating study that charts what they call the women's sexual revolution (as opposed to *the* sexual revolution) Barbara Ehrenreich, Elizabeth Hess, and Gloria Jacobs cite Beatlemania (circa 1964) as an important turning point for young white women's expression of their sexuality.[3] These authors explain that, in the wake of a growing disenchantment with the prospect of marriage and life in the suburbs, young white girls saw in the Beatles or, previously, Elvis several things. Elvis "stood for a dangerous principle of masculinity,"[4] a "hood" who was "visibly lower class and symbolically black (as the bearer of black music to white youth)";[5] the Beatles, "while not exactly effeminate, [were] at least not easily classifiable in the rigid gender distinctions of middle-class American life."[6] Further, these were not men with whom the girls would marry and "settle down"; the "romance would never end in the tedium of marriage.... Adulation of the male star was a way to express sexual yearnings that would normally be pressed into the service of popularity or simply repressed. The star could be loved ... with complete abandon."[7] In other words, the Beatles and Elvis offered both alternative constructions of gender to these young women and a safe way to explore and express their own sexuality. Idolizing these performers was an empowering act.

It is remarkable how little the discourse that has emerged around hard rock has taken this into account. Perhaps this is because writers perceived the kind of sexuality being enacted in hard rock music that began in the late sixties as being distinct from what had come before, although Simon Frith and Angela McRobbie, the first to explore the issue of sexuality in rock music, run Elvis, at least, together with later male rockers. Their 1978 article "Rock and Sexuality" claims that "[i]t is boys who form the core of the rock audience, who are intellectually interested in rock, who become rock critics and collectors."[8] Based on the readership of the British magazines *Melody Maker, Sounds*, and *New Musical Express* and the viewing audience of the BBC television show *Old Grey Whistle Test*, Frith and McRobbie concluded that two-thirds of the audience for rock music were at that time male and that at rock concerts "the general atmosphere is sexually exclusive, its euphoria depends on the absence of women."[9] They offer no further data to corroborate these claims (a persistent problem in generalizations such as these that are made about rock music). The results that I obtained from my fan survey (247 men to 76 women) show a slightly lower proportion of women to men respondents than Frith and McRobbie report. The question is, do we dismiss such a significantly large minority, especially when it includes women who are very intellectually interested in rock, who are collectors, and who—via the new medium of the Internet and, like me, through published writing—are becoming critics?

"Rock and Sexuality" took an important first step in opening up discussion of this issue in academic writing about popular music, and it has been (and continues to be) so central a document in the discussion of masculine codes in this music that it is worth reviewing here in some detail. Frith and McRobbie characterized the music as "cock rock," meaning "music making in which performance is an explicit, crude, and often aggressive expression of male sexuality—it's the style of rock presentation that links a rock and roller like Elvis Presley to rock stars like Mick Jagger, Roger Daltrey, and Robert Plant."[10] In his book *Sound Effects*, Frith links Page and Plant more specifically with this style: "[T]he approach is most obvious in the singing style that derives from Led Zeppelin's Robert Plant, in the guitar hero style that derives from Led Zeppelin's Jimmy Page."[11] The Frith and McRobbie article goes on to characterize cock rock performances in some detail, offering answers to many of the questions I raised earlier about Led Zeppelin and which continue to dominate discussions of this music:

> Cock rock performers are aggressive, dominating, and boastful, and they constantly seek to remind the audience of their prowess, their control. Their stance is obvious in live shows; male bodies on display, plunging shirts and tight trousers, a visual emphasis on chest hair and genitals.... Cock rock shows are explicitly about male sexual performance (which may explain why so few girls go to them—the musicians are acting out a sexual iconography which in many ways is unfamiliar, frightening, and distasteful to girls who are educated into understanding sex as something nice, soft, loving, and private). In these performances mikes and guitars are phallic symbols; the music is loud, rhythmically insistent, built around techniques

of arousal and climax; the lyrics are assertive and arrogant, though the exact words are less significant than the vocal styles involved, the shouting and screaming.[12]

Frith and McRobbie contrast this with what they call "teeny bop" music, "a blend of pop ballad and soft rock," which draws lyrically on such themes as the boy "being let down and stood up, about loneliness and frustration" (hardly characteristics exclusive to that genre of pop or rock music) and which "is consumed almost exclusively by girls."[13]

Critiques about the essentialism of these definitions and the static nature of the binary split between the two "genres" have been offered, including that by Frith himself.[14] This criticism recognizes that far from being static, the way in which popular music is consumed/interpreted is dynamic, ever-changing, dependent on the individual doing the consuming and interpreting. But despite the acknowledgment that this is so, no one has really challenged the definition or reception of cock rock. Jennifer Taylor and Dave Laing, who were the first to critique the article, simply reinterpreted Frith and McRobbie, arguing that

[t]hey account for the small proportion of girls in a "cock-rock" audience by the fact that girls' notion of sexuality is soft and gentle, while here they are confronted with the iconography of "male sexual performance." In the alternative perspective we have sketched in, this situation [taken as a given] can be explained in terms of the narcissistic celebration of male power which structurally excludes the female spectator and produces the ecstatic male response to Thin Lizzy and other bands.[15]

Frith wrote (in 1985) that while he is embarrassed by the fact that the "Rock and Sexuality" article is still frequently cited, he believes that "[i]n terms of who controls and consumes music, our points still seem valid ... pop still plays much the same part in the organization of adolescent gender roles."[16] Again there is an affirmation of the definitions given in his original article: "Teeny bop culture, for example, is as much made by the girls who buy the records and magazines as by the boys who play the music and pose for the pinups."[17] But it is the definitions themselves that have to be more critically examined—the interpretation that what is being produced at a performance by a male rock band is solely "male sexual performance," that who is doing the consuming are males, and that both males and females perceive sexuality and gender in the way that Frith and others suggest.

In so much of what has been written about hard rock music, old gender dualities and notions of sexuality remain intact. Deena Weinstein (1991) characterizes heavy metal culture as masculinist and argues that it is largely about male bonding.[18] On the subject of sexuality in metal, she asserts that "sex, in heavy metal's discourse, is sweaty, fun, and without commitments. ... W.A.S.P.'s infamous 'Animal (F**k Like a Beast)' ... and the Scorpions' 'Animal Magnetism' stress the carnality and underscore the absence of a spiritual element in sexual activity." She mentions Led Zeppelin's "You Shook Me" as an example of such physicality and calls this kind of sex "an emblem of youthful male power."[19] John Shepherd's discussion of vocal timbre and gender in popular music (first published in 1987; reprinted in 1991) is based on the Frith/McRobbie division between cock rock and sweeter-sounding genres, which Shepherd classifies as the "woman as nurturer" sound (a detailed discussion of Shepherd's categories appears later as part of my musical analysis).[20] Jon Savage (1988) cites an article from the 1956 *New Musical Express Annual* asserting: "The excitement of young women was devalued in face of male preoccupations like 'technique,' 'artistry,' and 'authenticity'—a division which still persists today,"[21] but gives no evidence that this is in fact the case. Will Straw writes (1997) from the premise that collecting records is predominantly a male preoccupation and attempts to account for why this might be so.[22] His analysis per se is certainly valid and interesting, but his premise perpetuates the idea that women have no interest in collecting records, bootlegs, and other memorabilia, which is simply untrue.

A particularly troubling perspective to me is taken by Norma Coates (1997), who writes that the sound of the Rolling Stones and, by extension, "male" rock music "is coded as unmistakably phallic"[23] and that "[r]ock masculinity, at least the stereotype which, I assert, is still very much in play discursively and psychically, is one in which any trace of the 'feminine' is expunged, incorporated or appropriated," without giving any evidence, in the form of analysis, of how this might be the case. Given her view, it is no wonder that Coates feels discomfort at her desire to "dance around and get crazy" to this music, which, she says, makes her "complicit in [her] own submission to that [phallic] power."[24] In reading these words I felt enormous sorrow that her pleasure is compromised by an essentialist view of how gender might work in music. She also discusses the Frith/McRobbie binary split between rock and pop, reiterating again the division of these musics along gender lines—rock as masculine, pop as feminine.

A number of other accounts stress similar points of view,[25] but none is as harsh as that by Simon Reynolds and Joy Press in their book *The Sex Revolts* (1995).[26] I would argue that to anyone who knows Zeppelin's music, Reynolds and Press's analysis is generally so off the mark that it deserves little comment; I include discussion of it here because it appears in a book published by a highly reputable academic press (Harvard University Press) and because it is, as Robert Walser points out in his review, the first to make gender and sexuality in popular music the focus of a study—to provide a "broad analysis of popular music from this perspective."[27] I worry that for these reasons their fanciful analyses will likely garner serious attention and further entrench the discourse that surrounds Led Zeppelin's music. Reynolds and Press refer to "[t]he hypermacho, misogynistic white blues of the '60s"[28] and, with specific reference to Zeppelin, their "hyper-phallic bombast"[29] and twice to their "penile dementia."[30] About "Black Dog" Reynolds and Press write that "[t]he devil in disguise motif recurs in 'Black Dog'. . . . Plant is wracked with desire, shivering and shuddering like he's going through cold turkey: the turgid, gruelling riff incarnates sex as agony and toil." And in a truly remarkable exegesis on the song "When the Levee Breaks" they say that "women often loom as a demonic threat in Led Zeppelin's songs ("Dazed and Confused," "Black Dog," etc.). Is 'When the Levee Breaks' a sort of allegory of this fear of feminine engulfment, elevated to a histrionic pitch of cosmic dread?"[31]

In terms of lyrics, these readings cannot be very easily upheld and point to the persistence of the idea that Zeppelin's music was somehow influenced by the occult; in fact, Reynolds and Press's descriptions have clearly been affected by their reading of Stephen Davis's sensationalistic biography of the band (cited in their bibliography), which begins with the story that the members sold their soul to the devil in exchange for their success, which Davis then ties neatly into the long history of this myth in blues culture.[32] In fact, there is no "devil in disguise motif" in "Black Dog," a lyric that is a raw description of, in the first instance, the singer's lust for a woman and, in the second, how he feels he has been "taken" by her. Plant's tone, which sounds like the whine of a spoiled child, partly because of the high range but partly also because his voice drops in pitch at the end of every line, makes it fairly clear that his perceived victimization is intended as a parody: the poor, rich rock star, whose symbols of wealth and privilege—money, car, and fame—might be appropriated by a woman. The lyrics to "Levee," a blues song that Zeppelin knew via the recording by Memphis Minnie, refer to a person desperate about having to leave home to find work elsewhere. The only references to this person's partner (the sex of either is not identified) speak of anguish at having to leave a "happy home" and "baby," about not being able to take "baby" with him or her. If anything, the lyric relates the person's perceived impotency in the face of economic hardship—at the prospect of losing his or her entire sense of place and culture in order to go to Chicago to find work because of hard times. Reynolds and Press do not tell us, specifically, where or how the "fear of feminine engulfment" occurs in the song: what one *could* accuse Zeppelin of is appropriating a lyrical scenario utterly removed from their own experience (and Reynolds and Press rightly question why Zeppelin might identify with such a scenario[33]).

The authors come closest to the mark in their description of "Dazed and Confused":

Love is disorientation, debility and paralysis. Led Zeppelin's "Dazed and Confused" . . . is the definitive take on this scenario. Doom-laden glissandos of blues guitar and a scabrous, burdened bassline conjure a sepulchre of sound for Robert Plant's languishing moans and tortured shrieks. Plant is prostrated on the "killing floor," a standard blues metaphor that originally referred to an abattoir. His mind is poisoned and befogged by the noxious fumes of her feminine miasma. He's at death's door, flaccid and enfeebled, until he and the music rally for one last attempt to claw their way out of this aural slough of despond. But to no avail: the riff-mania subsides again into a dank decay, with Plant emitting his final death-rattle moans and whimpers.[34]

There is, in fact, no reference to the "killing floor" in this lyric, which appears, rather, in "The Lemon Song" (persistent factual errors of this kind hardly help the credibility of academic writing on popular music); aside from that, the portrayal of love as debilitating and paralyzing in this song is believable—but must this necessarily be interpreted as negative? The more serious difficulty is that this description forms part of a chapter in *The Sex Revolts* called "She's Hit: Songs of Fear and Loathing," which juxtaposes "Dazed and Confused" with a hyperbolic description of The Rolling Stones as "one of the most misogynistic groups ever";[35] Jimi Hendrix's "Hey Joe" (about the murder of an unfaithful woman); and Nick Cave's songs that deal with murdering women, discussed in a disproportionately long section.[36] "Dazed and Confused" hardly belongs in this company. Although a few female fans of Led Zeppelin's music have difficulty with the lyrics to "Dazed and Confused" (calling them "misogynistic," based mostly on the line "soul of a woman was created below"), most like the song's "darkness," understanding the lyrics as "a statement from a young man who feels so overwhelmed or intimidated by some quality of his woman (her sensuality, her intelligence, her beauty, her confidence, etc.) that she is evil: 'soul of a woman was created below,'" or simply as "a great classic blues song about the woman who done him wrong." What is particularly interesting about Reynolds and Press's interpretation is how heavily it relies on the music, which is rare indeed. I suspect that when they speak of "feminine engulfment" in "When the Levee Breaks" they might have been referring to the musical engulfment of Plant's voice in this piece, where lyrics hardly matter; but if this is so, they do not make it explicit and, in any case, it is not clear how this might work metaphorically to signify engulfment by a feminine subject. It is a shame, in fact, that they do not point more specifically to the way in which music helps shape the narrative they have in mind for "Dazed and Confused," either; the way it stands, the sounds that they do point to—the "doom-laden" blues guitar and "scabrous, burdened" bass—could be interpreted in a plethora of ways that have nothing to do with gender or sexuality.

> I'm 38, attractive, wife, mother, high-level executive and educated.
> I usually blow the hair back on people when they discover not only
> my taste in music but [my] knowledge of [Led Zeppelin's] history.
> —Female respondent to fan survey

I was careful earlier in my narrative to point out the dates on which the statements I quoted were made, because it is important not only to comprehend the volume and nature of the criticism but also to historicize it. The literature on rock and sexuality begins in 1978, fourteen years after Beatlemania began, and it continues to the time of this writing. Throughout a time when women's sexuality has been openly expressed and explored to a greater degree than before in Western culture and when women have consistently used rock music as a means by which to express and explore their sexuality, the discourse about it has remained static and exclusionary. The persistent masculinist discourse has resulted in a particularly ugly view of Zeppelin's music and, by extension, male-made rock music with respect to gender and sexuality—that of both the performers and the audience. Part of what makes the anonymous woman audience member in *The Song Remains the Same* worthy of attention is that her image and actions force us to reconsider this discourse. First, she is there, making up part of the audience in 1973. Second, she is not only gazing at what she considers to be a pleasurable spectacle, but she is also sitting still and *listening*; she is composed, analytical, playfully engaged with what she is watching. She is not hysterical—in fact, this distinction is left to the male fan shown right after the song has ended, who bellows cathartically (also a wonderful image). This opposes the perception of the female fan that has been propagated since television audiences received those powerful images of female fans of rock music weeping and fainting over Elvis and the Beatles in the 1950s and 1960s, respectively. This is not to say that hysteria over rock stars—whether by men or women—is in some way a wrong response, invalid, or unworthy of further critical examination, only that our conclusion cannot continue to be that it is the only response *even by the same man or woman during the entirety of the same concert.*

In her article "Sexing Elvis," Sue Wise asks why male rock music has been so uncritically accepted as "phallic" and why women's responses and uses of this music have not been more seriously examined.[37] Steve Waksman's article on Led Zeppelin and cock rock takes two important steps forward in this respect: first, he considers the musical sounds in his discussion of gender to a greater extent than anyone previously (see later), and second, while he generally offers evidence and interpretations that work to reinforce the idea that Zeppelin's music, image, and actions were sexist and generally for and about males (he validates Frith and McRobbie's observation one more time), he opens a small window by suggesting "it would be a mistake to conclude that . . . rock sexuality offers no satisfying outlet for female heterosexual desires."[38] In this context he cites Pamela Des Barres, the infamous 1970s groupie who was often in the company of, among others, Jimmy Page, as a woman who "was clearly coveted as a prize by male rock stars, yet who in having sex with those rock stars also enacted her own version of sexual fantasy" (and, we might add, power).[39] It is somewhat troubling that Des Barres's experience as a groupie would count as Waksman's primary example of heterosexual women's experience with rock music, since her mode of engagement is exceptional and has little to do with the music. Fortunately, he also quotes two women journalists who argue, respectively, that the music is a source of erotic pleasure and a source of phallic power, both of which can be appropriated by women.[40] Waksman still concludes, however, that "Zeppelin's brand of phallic display was indeed male-oriented, and the band's antics sometimes had violent effects that were not merely imaginary.[41] But neither of these points foreclosed the possibility of active female desires within which the boys figured as coveted objects."[42]

Robert Walser's discussion of gender in hard rock and metal begins to depart more significantly from essentialist descriptions, moving closer to the problematizing of gender that Wise calls for, challenging accepted notions of rock iconography as statically phallic and the consumers of the music as exclusively male—and heterosexual male. While acknowledging the traditional view of these music cultures as sometimes overt and crude celebrations of machismo and as perpetuating patriarchal values (with which I would certainly agree), Walser recognizes that "images of masculine display are available to be construed [by fans] in a variety of ways."[43] He points specifically to the way in which some gay male fans of the music view videos as erotic fantasies[44] and reports that he has observed women fans engaging with the visual images and music in the same way as their male counterparts. He problematizes the appropriation of feminine attributes (makeup, clothes, hairstyles), especially by glam metal bands, in terms of not only the performers who are doing the appropriating but also women fans who consume these images.[45] Most important for my discussion, Walser asserts that "an analysis of metal that understands it only as a reproduction of male hegemony runs the risk of duplicating the exscription it describes."[46] While Walser is talking here specifically about glam metal and androgyny, his comment has broad significance for discussions of gender with respect to hard rock and metal. In fact, I would go so far as to say that for Led Zeppelin the duplication of this exscription already exists: the positions cited earlier have become *the* way in which Zeppelin is discussed by journalists and academics in terms of gender and sexuality.

Walser's position owes something to cultural critic Judith Butler (and she in turn to Foucault); it was Butler who wrote that "[t]he power of language to work on bodies is both the cause of sexual oppression and the way beyond that oppression. . . . Language assumes and alters its power to act upon the real through locutionary acts, which, repeated, become entrenched practices and, ultimately, institutions."[47] It is not so much that those who write about the performance of masculinity in Zeppelin or hard rock music are wrong (although in some cases they are) as it is a question of the proportion to which this aspect of the music receives attention. In case there should be any question, I want to stress that I do not wish to apologize for or erase from the equation the critically important issues that have been raised concerning sexist or misogynistic behavior in hard rock and metal. Rather, I want to suggest that this is not the only behavior and these not the only gender/sexuality issues that need examining and that they are far from the only way in which both male and female fans receive the music. How else can the visual iconography be construed? How else the music experienced? How are the iconography and music consumed by fans rather than critics? How large a role does the analysis of masculinity now normative in journalistic and academic criticism play to fans, both male and female, of the music?

Walser and Waksman tread lightly in their comments about women's participation in and reception of metal, and I suspect this is out of an understanding of the politics of representation—they are men trying to define something about women's experience. But from my own experience as a fan and from the information I have gathered from other fans, I can say confidently that Walser is right to say women engage with this music in the same way as their male counterparts and that both men and women engage with it in a variety of ways with respect to gender and sexuality. I can begin with my own experience.

When I first became attached to "Immigrant Song," at the age of fourteen, it had nothing to do with the band members (I didn't know who they were, let alone what they looked like; in fact, I recall that the lack of information about the band on the album covers intimidated me somewhat) but rather the sound of the music. My siblings were substantially older, and so I felt a certain isolation from the rest of the family. I was a bit of a loner outside the home as well. The only social/academic circles I belonged to involved theater and music, and those of us interested in "artsy" things were marked as other by those who fit more happily into the mainstream. My retreat from all of this was often the rec room down in our basement: the home of the stereo and my burgeoning record collection. Listening to the energy and strength of "Immigrant Song" was an empowering experience. I had no idea what the lyrics were—I could understand only snatches of them—but that riff, with its crisp octave snap that repeated at about the same rhythm as an energized heartbeat, its timbre so insistent and confident, the bass guitar pounding that rhythm into every part of my body, and Plant's majestic if incomprehensible proclamations, made that song where I wanted to live. Later I began collecting all of Zeppelin's albums, books on them, and bootleg recordings. I came to identify with Robert Plant partly because I was in awe of his abilities as a singer (as an aspiring singer myself) and partly because I was sexually attracted to him. I am not sure that the two can be separated. Importantly, when I fantasized about knowing Plant and the rest of the band there were always two elements included that were inextricably bound together: I was a musician of equal stature to them—as talented and commercially successful—and I was also beautiful and sexy and loved by them for that reason as well. In other words, my fantasy involved being powerful *and* attractive and respected for both characteristics. I did not quite want to *be* Robert Plant; rather, I wanted to be *just like* him in terms of his ability to sing and his success in practicing his art. This is similar to those responses Ehrenreich, Hess, and Jacobs reported from women fans of the Beatles in the midsixties. Appropriating the power of those performers for oneself was as important for some as was the sexual freedom they suggested (although the two are not inextricably linked in that study).[48] And for some reason I thought that this was in the realm of possibilities, certainly not that it would be impossible because I was a woman. Perhaps this is because there were at least a few women who had already occupied such positions—Janis Joplin, Grace Slick, a little later Ann and Nancy Wilson of Heart and Stevie Nicks, for example—although I did not gravitate toward these women performers myself. For about six years I absorbed every drop of information I could about Led Zeppelin and listened to their music with pathological exclusivity because it was such a powerful, liberating, intellectual, sexual, and spiritual experience for me.

Most of the fans—male and female—who answered the questions on my survey relate similarly powerful experiences with the music, and the thirty-eight-year-old woman I quoted earlier is typical of many women whose knowledge of the music and band is on par with that of their male counterparts. The majority of the women who responded own all of the studio albums (seventeen do not, some of these being very young and perhaps not financially able to collect), and some pointed out that they own both vinyl and CD versions or pressings from various countries—details of collecting that are usually associated with men. About a third of the women collect bootleg recordings—a significant number. Some of the fans who responded to the survey have been avid Led Zeppelin fans since the 1970s; others have come to the band much more recently. Except for those who saw the band live and so were able to recount their experiences, there was no distinction between the two groups in terms of the answers I received. It should be noted, however, that the answers I received concerning gender and sexuality may well have been different (or differently expressed) thirty years ago, especially by women, who might well have been less explicit.

On the version of the questionnaire sent to *Proximity* readers, I asked the question: "Do you think you relate to the music in a specific way because of your sex/gender?" The questions were construed a bit differently to those on FBO and were sent separately from the rest of the survey, as a follow-up:

Is Zep's music "sexual" to you (I mean the music, not the guys . . . but maybe it's impossible to distinguish between the two for some of you, which is fine); if so, how? Any tunes in particular? Do you think that you relate/respond to the music in a specific way because of your sex/gender? According to many writers, Zeppelin is supposed to be "guy" music. Why? If this is so, why, Lady Badgeholders, do you listen to it? Any further reflections around this subject welcome.

I did not ask a specific question about gender on the version of the survey that went to zoso.net: it only occurred to me to ask the question overtly as I began to receive responses to the survey. Furthermore, only twelve people on "For Badgeholders Only" responded to my questions about gender, so the total number of responses I received on the specific question was quite small (sixty-six); nevertheless, much information on the issue came from several other questions I posed on the survey.

Answers to several questions related to gender and sexuality reflect the complexity and depth of experience most avid fans have with the music and visual iconography. Responses generally reflect fans' knowledge of the entire repertory, not just a few songs (this is one of the problems with so many journalists and academics who write about the band), a variety of visual images of the band members, and what is known of the band's biography. While the majority of women acknowledge that as women they are sexually attracted to band members and find the music "sexy," they tend to want to point out that there is more to their attachment than this or that questions of gender and sexuality cannot be separated from the rest of the experience of the band, from the "power" and "emotion" of the music (which is in some cases equated with something they describe as elemental or "primal" that operates at a "deeper" level than the sexual), from the energy it gives them, and from how they can experience the songs on various levels (and from my own experience, as noted earlier, I would say that these levels can be experienced simultaneously). These women wrote:

I'm not sure if I relate to it differently [because of gender]. The band as a whole is so powerful, the music so potent.

I don't think I do. I'm a die-hard music fan and that is how I listen to all music. I'm very critical and I listen very carefully.

Yes, as a woman I found them and their music quite sexy; however the songs had interesting content, unlike some heavy metal/hard rock groups, whose songs were *only* about sex and pretty misogynistic sex, at that!

Part of it is sexual . . . the band I mean. . . . Robert Plant makes me have involuntary—non chemically induced—dreams of every fantasy I have ever had in my life . . . from sexual to religious. BUT—the music itself . . . I don't know how to describe it. . . . [T]he music makes the knots in my back muscles disappear. Moby Dick at full blast—or [the 1998 Page/Plant single] MOST HIGH!!—or No Quarter with or without John Paul Jones and/or Egyptians, at full volume on my car CD on the way home from work gives me strength to face the "second shift" of washing, cooking and cleaning. And I am not Zombieing through being the "Mom" and Hausfrau, daydreaming of "Going to California." . . . Zeppelin is a better mood altering drug than any chemical! . . . To steal a line from a preeminent baby boomer politician ("It's the economy, stupid. . . . "), IT'S THE MUSIC, STUPID!!!!!! (. . . not meant to be ugly . . . just emphatic) . . . [T]he difference between Zep and all the others is the RAW EMOTION in their music.

I don't believe gender has anything to do with the pure response at the "primal" level which I believe Zeppelin taps into (I know of plenty of males who get "horny" listening to Zeppelin). Yes, as a female, I am sexually attracted to men I consider to be "hot" (in this case, Robert Plant does give me the tingles), but I am an intelligent, mature adult, and I can (and do) separate the music from the man. I also find that Mozart's music touches me deeply, but I have no great liking for the man behind the music.

I do not feel anything resembling a "fuck off" attitude in Zeppelin's music—it isn't anything even approaching an anti-female attitude—that's more in the style of The Sex Pistols, or any other 70s punk band, or many of the 80s–90s rap groups. Sure, Zep had a hard, driving beat, but that's the nature of rock music. And yes, they sang a lot of "my woman is evil" songs, but that is the nature of the blues. Zeppelin's music is raw power, much like (to me) Mozart's music—it hits you on an elemental, primal level—and it doesn't matter what your gender or sexual persuasion is.

Back in the 70's Zeppelin wasn't just music it was a ZONE.

As far as the whole gender issue goes, when it comes to music, I am a set of ears connected to a mind first, and a female second. By the way, if the gender issue was valid, I ought to love [the ballad] "Thank You"—I don't. I find the lyrics way too sappy for my tastes—I also don't care much for Byron, for the same reason.

Eighteen women who responded to the survey saw the band live in the 1970s. Most of them provide quite a lot of detail about their experience of being at the concerts. One woman wrote:

I've seen Led Zeppelin and Page/Plant live many times. My first concert experience was the 7/27/73 LZ show at Madison Square Garden in New York City, still the most exhilarating concert I've ever attended. Twenty-five years later I'm still hooked—to the music and to rock photography. It was to that 1973 concert that I'd carried my first camera—a 126 Instamatic, a gift from my grandmother—and . . . I shot some of my most memorable photos from my front-row view of the show. A few days later, 7/30/73, I captured LZ on film as the band left the Drake Hotel the day after the robbery, the only existing photographic record of this event in LZ's history (no reporters or anyone else was there at the time and RP and JP were in a ham-it-up kinda mood). My photo collection has grown considerably since then, and my equipment is far more sophisticated, but it was these LZ photo opportunities that inspired me to continue. Today, a concert without the accompanying photos is for me only half complete.

I was especially intrigued by this answer, whose author is Wendy Annibell, first because I thought I might be able to obtain some of her photographs for use in this book but second because the answer poses such a challenge to commonly held notions about how women consume hard rock and metal. I am pleased not only that I was able to use one of her photos—the shot of Robert Plant at Madison Square Garden in 1973—but also that she was generous enough to answer my follow-up questions and allow me to reveal her identity. Wendy speaks about going to *multiple* Zeppelin shows. She does not talk about socializing at the concert at all but is completely consumed by the experience of seeing and hearing the band and the importance of her being able to capture a photographic record of it. I was curious to know whether she was taken to Zeppelin concerts by a boyfriend and asked her this in a follow-up question. Her response was:

> I attended the 7/27/73 MSG concert with two girlfriends (one of whom is still a friend). I also saw Zep on 2/7/75. Pretty sure I caught a '77 show as well, but there's no saved ticket stub to stir my memory for certain. I went to the concerts because I wanted to see the band. Period. I never had any boyfriends who shared my interest in Led Zep music. Not much has changed in that respect either: my husband *hates* Led Zep (and rock music in general).

She claims not to be concerned with the image of the band "in whatever way it may be interpreted by different people. [This] seems unrelated to my enjoyment of the band's music." She was there because *she* wanted to be there to see the band and experience the music. She took photographs because she had recently been given a camera and had it with her—it was her interest in photography that led her to take the pictures, not her infatuation with the men in the band. In fact, when I asked her whether she might have a "sexy" picture of Plant that I could use in the book, she offered the one reprinted here but said that she did not think that it was particularly sexy herself—that she was not particularly taken with this kind of image.

I was also curious how she came to know the band's music—whether this had occurred through boys she knew or in some other way; in her answer she mentions another aspect of her involvement with the band that is supposedly uncharacteristic of women, collecting and preserving albums: "Yeah, I guess you could say I discovered the music on my own. No one in particular turned me on to the band, but Led Zep was extremely popular among my friends at the time. . . . I bought all the Zep albums way back then and made a big deal out of keeping them in like-new condition. They remain so today."

It is very difficult to determine what percentage of women attended Led Zeppelin concerts: such statistics were, obviously, not kept, and people who attended the shows may not have been particularly aware of or interested in such information. The assumption frequently made (by Frith and McRobbie certainly) is that not many women attended rock concerts in the 1970s, and accounts such as that given by Stephen Davis in the biography *Hammer of the Gods* reinforce the notion that it was predominantly very young men who attended Led Zeppelin concerts, drawing analytical attention exclusively toward this segment of the fan population.[49] On this subject John Paul Jones says that "from what I can remember our audiences were pretty mixed, there wasn't the male 'mosh-pit' of today's gigs. Couples were the norm at the shows [and] there was no sense (for me) of 'directing' playing to either sex. It seemed in those days that everyone was into (and had an opinion on) the music the show, etc." One woman who responded to the survey commented that she stopped going to shows not because she wasn't connecting with the music but because of the dangerous environment: "I wouldn't go to any more live shows because I was literally afraid of the crowd scene; the firecrackers and drunks." Hers was the only comment of this sort. Clearly much more research needs to be undertaken to determine the audience makeup for these concerts in terms of gender distribution, but it is clear from the survey responses, from my own experience, from casual conversations I have had with people who attended shows, and from the audience scenes shown in *The Song Remains the Same* that women did attend the concerts.

Men responded to the question that concerned gender and sexuality similarly, often stating that gender did not make any difference (thirteen categorically stated that it made no difference, and three of these continued with comments unrelated to the question, a sign, perhaps, that they were uncomfortable with answering it or just indifferent to it). Others went on to say that the music was for "people," not one sex or the other, that it was "tantric" or sexually spiritual in some other way (contrary to what Deena Weinstein has to say about sex in metal only having to do with sweaty fun, many Zeppelin fans link sex with spirituality in their experience of the music), or that it was deeply meaningful to them for reasons that had nothing to do with sex or gender:

I think that Plant and Page (to a lesser degree) possessed a spiritual androgyny that's appealing to both sexes.

I guess guys like more out front, in your face intense music. I think some of the subtlety is lost on them, where women will notice the subtle nuance of a piece more rapidly. Plus there's the fact that the guitar is a very guy (phallic) instrument. Perhaps subliminally it has to do with manifesting biological urges and being virile, even masturbation.

Yes [I respond to it differently because of gender], it is animus-oriented music, but transcends cock rock.

Some of their music has a strong sexual energy to it which I can relate to; also they write songs about women which I can relate to.

I don't know, can't answer that. I think people, no matter what sex, recognize great music and great music will always stand the test of time.

The attitude of "no nonsense, here we are and we're gonna rock you" is kind of macho.

Not really. I relate to it because it's great music. Great to drive to, make love to, or just hang out and relax to.

Not at all, I like many artists not just male ones, a favorite now is Sheryl Crow.

Hard question. Zeppelin is a grass roots people's band for rock 'n' roll. They are for anybody, not male or female, but both sexes. I don't know why women like Zeppelin music. Everyone hears music differently.

No, there is something instinctively tantric about Led Zeppelin. Perhaps some of their accusations of women in their songs was due to being instinctively tantric Western men in a non-tantric Western world.

No, but I think it's great that Robert can very poetically describe love as easily as he describes graphic lust. A brilliant person, I'd bet. Great observations on the emotional and physical aspects of love and sexuality.

Yes, I believe Led Zep is very male oriented at least as I initially related [to it]— via the riffs and the lusty sounds.

My take on it is—you have to progress from the physical response to the mental response and then the emotional response and then that all blends in with environment and past experiences, etc.

As a gay male, I can't think of an apt way to answer this question, sorry! (I've commented more with "Dazed and Confused" [where he says]: Having had disastrous relationships with women, the lyrics—mysogynistic tho' they are— do have a perverse appeal.)

This last fan was the only one to acknowledge a gay or lesbian orientation, and I wanted to follow up with him, hopeful that he would be interested in providing more information about the reception of Led Zeppelin in the gay community. Here are his further thoughts on the issue:

[L]ike a lot of hard-rock bands, Zep drew its share of white male homophobes. Odd, considering the fact that the band was fronted by two foppish, somewhat androgynous intellectuals! I was always aware of that contradiction, and as I've learned from some other gay and bisexual males in their thirties, I wasn't the only one so aware. Certainly the fact that the band happily frequented gay clubs for the pleasure of simply being left alone and had their adventures [dressing] in drag (such as their infamous dinner with George Harrison and Stevie Wonder) made an impression. I would guess that the sexual nature of so much blues-based music (this of course including both Led Zeppelin and the Rolling Stones) couldn't help but appeal to horny people of whatever orientation. Robert and Jimmy always struck me as a more dangerous and more androgynous "version" of Mick and Keith, anyway.

I'm not sure of how good an answer to your question this is. Amongst my straight friends with secret bi urges, Zep and Aerosmith have a listening appeal that other hard rock bands simply don't. Maybe it's because Jimmy was so damned beautiful! (and I say this as a devotedly platonic Plant-o-phile!). I have a couple of gay friends in their early twenties who hate all hard rock (punk and metal included) . . . except Led Zeppelin. Maybe this stems from Frankie Goes To Hollywood's sampling of John Bonham from beyond the grave? My guess is that also, despite the machismo of the music, they were a band that women could love as well as guys; and that being so, they were a band that could appeal to gay and bi guys as well as straights. There just wasn't a prejudicial vibe about them.

For some men, the question that concerned gender evoked a response that had nothing to do with the sexuality of the lyrics or music but rather with perceiving band members as important role models:

I'm male. My parents divorced when I was 8 and I never saw much of my father before the divorce. Aside from other male relatives, Plant was the first male figure I came "to know" and I grew up with Zeppelin.

Or:

Look at Jimmy Page's head shot on the back of the first (and at the time only) Zeppelin album. Imagine that you are a 16 year old teenage boy facing the very real possibility of being drafted in two years to go to Vietnam. Every night on the six o'clock news there is a body count. All your cultural values are totally at odds with everyone over thirty, which at the time seemed very, very old. No one understands you. Look at the attitude and measured arrogance in Jimmy's face. Listen to the incredible screaming, psychedelic, crunching, brain twisting, quantum leap forward guitar work and production values on the album. I thought, "Wow, this Jimmy Page is exactly what I want to be." . . . Part of it was timing. Part of it was the way times were. Part of it is that young men look for role models. Led Zeppelin and Jimmy Page were always there when I needed inspiration, comfort, or escape. . . . I don't remember the gender question, but I don't think I found it important to me. My love for Led Zeppelin had little or nothing to do with sex.

Many men said: "If I relate to [Zep] in a specific way, I think it would be because many of their songs were written from a man's point of view." I would disagree that this makes much difference. On the one hand, women listeners are able to jump this hurdle quite easily, identifying themselves as the objects of desire, pain, frustration, and so forth, about which Plant sings. But I think more probably they understand themselves as *subjects*, the emotions Plant describes as ones *they themselves have felt*, the pronouns used making no difference to their ability to understand or relate to the experience. I hear no particular "man's point of view" in Plant's lyrics, something I will discuss in more detail later. In fact, the lyrics might well be dismissed altogether, making little difference to the reception of the song (as in my initial experience with "Immigrant Song"). In Led Zeppelin's music, this is an especially important point to keep in mind. Although some of Plant's lyrics are very good and significant (and many fans said that they were very important), some, especially those that are borrowed or paraphrased from blues tunes, are less so, and some get completely lost in the mix or because of Plant's pronunciation. Their lexical meaning is hardly relevant; it is his delivery that matters. On this matter one female fan said that "[f]or me, the words are there to make sounds, and certain words sing particularly well. As for the meaning of the words, well, I'll put it this way. If a song has particularly idiotic lyrics, I'm not all that likely to care. If they are wonderful, I will like the song that much more." Another woman commented: "I sometimes wonder if Plant didn't just press the "quick pick" button on the Webster's Dictionary." Another point of considerable importance with respect to lyrics in songs is that it is possible and, I would suggest, common to listen to lyrics selectively—to pick out certain words or phrases that are intelligible and dismiss the rest or to dismiss those that are not particularly meaningful to the listener and become attached to those that are.[50]

Plenty of fan responses went into explicit detail about the sexuality of the music and visual images. Many women readily admitted their physical attraction to band members and their bodily/sexual response to the musical sounds and described these in great detail. The following responses all come from women:

Yeah, I do [think that I relate to the music in a specific way because of gender]. Specifically, the music feels like it's pulsing through you.

Yes . . . come on what's not to love. Every little girl then and now squeals to Robert's sexy sex sounds. I swear that man has a hard on at every concert. Orgasmic. And Jimmy's foreplay strumming accelerating into ecstasy. Yes! Very basic, animalistic sounds — hormonal, you know.

[People] assume that chicks would be offended by how blatantly Percy [Plant's nickname] & Pagey seemed to strut their obviously lustful-yet-nonchalant attitude towards everything. They don't get the fact that is what attracts chicks to the music.

As I mentioned earlier, many comments that concerned sexuality were made in response to questions other than the one that asked about gender/sexuality specifically. For example, in response to my query "Your comments on Jimmy Page's solos," several women remarked:

Better than sex.

He's having sex with his guitar and the audience.

Electric prolonged orgasms.

But these responses need to be balanced by the many that talked about the soulful or emotional quality of Pages's solos:

Page's solos are definitely from the heart.

Can be sloppy if he's not up to it, but when he's hot he's on fire! So emotional—baring his soul.

A part of his soul.

Very soulful.

LIVE, IF HE'S ON, UNEARTHLY, MAJICKAL [sic], SOUL STEALING.

When asked to comment on the song "Whole Lotta Love," some women remarked on its overt sexuality and indicated that this was a "turn-on" to them. As opposed to being fearful or ignorant of the raw sexuality depicted in this song, they identified with it completely. This is one example of how easily women can relate to a song that is, supposedly, sung from a male point of view:

[I]t is not only a song about sex, but the combination of Page's wizardry and Plant's vocalizations makes you feel as if you are either witnessing or involved in the love-act (depending upon how vivid of an imagination you have).

Lusty "way down inside" makes you think of . . . Robert's "size." Ouch!

I'd like to get me some of that! How shocking!

The blatant come on of the lyrics has made me shriek more than once.

I'd give a million dollars to be the one to cause Robert to emit those moans. . . . Every inch of Robert's love and he's going to give it to me. C'mon baby! It's been years and I'm still waiting. A lot of cheeky innuendo that I'm only now understanding and enjoying. When I was smaller I just thought it was a kick-ass rocking song.

I want to grab my man and be a slut.

It is definitely a turn-on. Raunchy, rude, and very forward. Plant tells you that you need love; not suggests, TELLS—declares, if you will. You need it, and I'm here to make sure you get it. The rest of the band seem to agree, as they pound the song into your soul.

And about seeing the band live, several women commented as follows:

Orgasmic.

Euphoria. Pure enlightenment. Supernatural. Orgasmic.

Robert is incredibly gorgeous and has all sorts of little tricks up his sleeve to entice the females in the audience. This is of course in addition to the fabulous performance he gives.

In answer to the question "Which band member(s) do you identify with most closely and why?" thirty women said they identify most closely with Plant, twenty-four with Page, and fifteen said they do not identify with any band member. The near-even split between women who identify with Plant and those who identify with Page is interesting: one might have thought that the singer—the front man—would have been the overwhelming draw for women, but this is not the case (it might have been different in the 1970s).

Comments that concern why women fans identify with a certain band member are also revealing. In the case of Plant, only a handful of women mentioned his looks or sexiness as the reason for their identification. Many, however, pointed to a range of other traits: his perceived sensitivity, energy, charisma, aura, mysticism, and search for the unattainable and the difficulties in his personal life (the loss of his five-year-old son and his near-fatal car accident), knowledge of which not only makes him more human but also gives him "depth" and suggests a vulnerable man who might need gentle nurturing:

> I love Robert Plant the best. Because he is a really awesome singer and he seems so cool and a really cool, nice person to be around.

> Robert Plant. Because, like me, he always had a lot of responsibility. He was the leader, the decision maker, yet his life was so tragic.

Those who identified most closely with Page cited his interest in the occult or mysticism, his outstanding musicianship (several of these women are guitar players themselves—again, this was probably not the case when the band was together), or his leadership in the band. Several combined comments about his musicianship with those that spoke about his sexiness or the fact that they had a "crush" on him:

> Jimmy Page. He is just amazing, I have never seen or heard a guitar player that is so universally talented on the guitar. But the fact that he had the best rhythm section in the business helped. . . . I also play guitar and can relate as to how difficult what he plays really is.

> Jimmy Page. Why? Because he's an explorer. He's a searcher of the truth.

> I wish to identify most closely with Jimmy because I very much admire his skills, abilities, and his body (even being older than my dad).

It is also interesting that fifteen women do not feel they identify with any band member. These women included some who said: "I identify with the music, not with the band members," or who said that they identify with all four members, pointing to the importance of the unit—indeed the institution of Led Zeppelin—more than the individuals.

In answer to the question "What is it you like about the band's image, lyrics, etc.?" some women combined a comment about sexuality with those that concerned the band's mystical or spiritual side, again making a link between these two realms. Five responses from women fell into the following category:

> Besides the fact that they were really, really sexy, they had this aura that emanated and a chemistry that worked so well when they were together.

Five responses commented solely on physical appearance, among these:

> They're all gorgeous.

> Plant is very sexual, long hair, tight nut huggers.

> ROBERT PLANT'S CHEST.

A sample of other responses from women include:

> I love the whole flower child, black country look the four of them went for. Robert and Jimmy were just such beautiful men and had this whole enchanted aura onstage.

> Image: The hammer of the gods. And Zep look like it too. Damn sexy guys, in my not so humble opinion. All the rumors of trashing hotel rooms, escapades with underage groupies, and black magic all add to the mystery and aura of Zep. Yeah, it's great when someone like Donny Osmond comes along and the little girls love him, but he's too squeaky clean for me. A little bit of naughtiness or mystery appeals to me. The pictures from that era also show that there's something else there—not just your rock band playing their newest hits for their fans. Case in point—CCR [Credence Clearwater Revival]. Nice group, like their music, but nothing really *behind* them, you know? Nothing that looks like it's driving them. Zep had the look in their eyes, that they needed to do something and were going to do it their way, whether the public liked it or not. Plus, Rob's tight pants never hurt my opinion of their image.

Men were more hesitant to talk about the band's image, many dismissing it as irrelevant to their engagement with the music. This is not surprising, since the consideration of "image" is antithetical to ideas about rock authenticity: it suggests that there might be something constructed (artificial) about the band, that they might have commercial interests in mind—as if any rock or pop artist did not. Ten men continued to talk about how great the music was, not commenting on the lyrics or image at all. Nineteen made comments such as:

> Not into the image thing.

> Nothing. For me, it is strictly the music.

Their image is interesting but it's the music that always gets me.

Twelve men responded by saying that what was important was that the band was not commercially driven, this in spite of the fact that from the outset Led Zeppelin was one of the most commercially successful bands ever: "They just made music . . . not to follow trends or anything like that," and, "The way they did it their way, never sold out." Thirty-three men pointed to the "mysterious, magical image that they portray. All the stuff about Jimmy Page and the black magic stuff. It just fascinates me," or simply the "power, mystery, emotion." Twelve said: "Cool Band . . . I love EVERYTHING about them!!"

Also not surprising was that only a couple of men included the band members' sexiness as an important attribute, undoubtedly not wishing to suggest, as, presumably, heterosexual men, that they themselves found the band members sexy. Some male responses to the question of sexuality in Zeppelin's music pointed to aggression and rhythmic urgency as being "male" characteristics (a few women made this comment as well). But some took a much more detailed and holistic approach, seeing in Zeppelin's music a wide range of sexual or sensual characteristics. Here are two of the most detailed such answers:

Zeppelin music is definitely sexual, sometimes bluntly (e.g., "The Lemon Song" or "Whole Lotta Love"), but more usually it's in the flow of the song, in the light and shade, the change of tempo, the increasing buildup of the music itself . . . Zep III has the slow, sensual blues of SIBLY [Since I've Been Loving You], along with the aggression and intensity of "The Immigrant Song" and the sad comforting feel of "Tangerine," and the fun rollicking of "Bron-Yr-Aur Stomp." The fourth album has the slow to fast of BoE [Battle of Evermore] and "Stairway." Both have that sometimes urgent, sometimes relaxed feel, the epitome of light and shade. "When The Levee Breaks" is pounding, desperate, and sad all in one, which just hits you with the emotional charge that is sex. Houses [of the Holy] has "The Rain Song," more light and shade, with "The Ocean" and "D'yer Ma'ker" as the great 50's feel rocker and silly love song respectively. PG [Physical Graffiti] of course has "Kashmir." That driving, pushing feel of the music is all sex. "Let me take you there!" But "In The Light," "Bron-Yr-Aur," "Down By The Seaside," and "Night Flight" are perhaps the best four consecutive songs ever for sex. They all have that emotional high that is essential for any sexual relationship. Along with "Ten Years Gone," they make you want to cry at climax, it hits you so hard. Presence has "Achilles [Last Stand]," another of those driving, epic songs that rise and fall, rise and fall, keeping you charged and going the entire time. And "Tea For One" has that "sexual healing" quality, the need for comfort and love that makes sex the greatest thing humans can do for one another. In Through The Out Door is chock full of sexuality. "In The Evening," "Fool In The Rain," "Carouselambra," "All My Love," and "I'm Gonna Crawl" are all perfect, not just for sex but because they bring about more of that light and shade, slow and fast dichotomy that defines human sexuality.

Susan: You asked: "Is Zep's music 'sexual' to you?" Is this a rhetorical question? I know of no other band/music that is more sexual (well maybe James Brown or Prince). Why? The light and shade ("Kashmir," "In the Light," "10 Yrs Gone," "Babe I'm Gonna Leave You" to name just a FEW), the tension and release ("In My Time of Dying"), Plant's voice (can you say "The Crunge"?), Page's straining, start-stop riffs ("Black Dog," "Heart Breaker," "Hots On for Nowhere," etc....) and Bonham's energetic drumming ("When the Levee Breaks" and hundreds more). I think the reason many women don't like Zep's sexuality is because it's so prevalent with no excuses. Women who are not comfortable with their own sexuality may be intimidated or made uncomfortable with their music (to be honest, I may even get uncomfortable in mixed company if "The Lemon Song" comes on—depends on the "mix"). Their music is very "masculine" (to me), aggressive and at times explicit ("The Lemon Song," "Black Dog," etc....) I think men like it because they often say in their music everything we think and feel about women, sexually speaking. However, as you know, many women love Zep for those reasons. One of my ex's loved Zep for their sexuality. "Led Zeppelin IS sex" she used to say. Besides, they're so good at it!

In response to the question "Which band member(s) do you identify with most closely?" men overwhelmingly chose Page:

Jimmy Page: 116
Robert Plant: 25
John Paul Jones: 24
John Bonham: 25
Identify with more than one member: 28
Don't identify with a member: 16

The majority of comments point to Page's "mastery" of the guitar as the reason for choosing him. Many of these men are guitarists themselves, and Page is their model and idol. Some are also intrigued by Page's interest in the occult or what they perceive to be his spiritual side, and some link this to his quietness off the stage:

Jimmy Page, dark and mysterious, lets his actions do the talking.

Page, because of his quiet introversion and introspective public nature that some have mistaken as aloofness or downright reclusiveness, which then gives way to an explosive extroversion under the right conditions (i.e., live performances.) He is the sage. He knows how to take chances and make it work. He is the producer and ultimate architect of the goods. He is the driving force.

Probably Page because I play guitar and try to imitate his playing and style, which is harder than hell.

Jimmy, because of his intellectualism, interest in the spiritual (although I'm a strong Christian) and his strategic thinking.

I would have to say Page. As a guitarist myself, I find his playing really stands out, and appeals to me aesthetically, not only in the "rock guitar" genre, but across the entire spectrum of guitarist-musicians. In other words, it's not just his guitar playing that appeals to me, but the *music* he makes. And like Page, I also have a keen interest in spirituality/mysticism, though not in the area of the European "Mystery Schools" (Crowley, et al.), as Page did/does.

For his musicianship. I play guitar as well and I understand his musical ideas. I'm not very fond of the things he has done in his private life, but his [way] of thinking musically fascinates me.

An approximately equal number of men chose either Plant, Jones, or Bonham as the member with whom they most closely identified. Again, I had been of the impression that Plant, as front man and also because of his close association with Page, would have been only slightly behind the guitarist in this category. The overwhelming reason for choosing Jones was that he was not interested in being in the limelight, that he was quiet but the backbone of the band—technically proficient and reliable. These were qualities that were highly valued in him by many:

John Paul Jones: He's a quiet, unassuming, talented musician, who arguably has the most versatility and best musicianship out of anyone in the band. His talents don't readily show themselves unless you really LISTEN to the songs. Many of the songs popularized on the radio don't showcase his abilities as well as other Zeppelin titles, but that's fine with me. I know . . .

With both Plant and Bonham, the reasons had to do mainly with their talent. Only one man commented that he identified with Plant because he was a good-looking man; a few commented that they envied the position these rock stars were in terms of having access to women:

Bonzo. Listen to what he can do with a drum set. He never plays the same thing twice. Listen to "In My Time of Dying" or "Achilles Last Stand," not to mention "When the Levee Breaks," which is the most copied drum line ever. "Kashmir" has been done to death, too.

Plant—to me he is the epitome of man. Looks great, always has, his attitude is bold and brash but sensitive and sophisticated. His solo work is phenomenal. His lyrics were always there for whatever mood I'm in.

I just want to say that Led Zeppelin has been a major part of my life, my identity.
—Female fan

Zep makes me laugh, cry, lust and feel . . . all at the same time. Their music is deeply emotional and touches my soul.
—Male fan

Fan responses make it clear that normative gender identities with respect to Led Zeppelin's music—gender identities that have become accepted as "natural"—need to be reevaluated. Under the paradigm heretofore constructed, there is no way to account for these responses, for women who enjoy the machismo images of Plant, know the repertory as well as their male counterparts, and prefer the "heavy" songs over the more acoustically based ones and men whose concept of sexuality in the music encompasses tenderness as well as the crude and "heavy" side and the messy way in which issues of sexuality and gender are entangled with ideas that concern spirituality, soul, and so on. One way of getting beyond rigid definitions of gender is to invoke Judith Butler's concept of gender performativity. Butler writes that "[the gendered body] has no ontological status apart from the various acts which constitute its reality."[51] In other words, we do not operate from a fixed identity with respect to gender (or, I would add, anything else), but rather we perform gender through our actions, actions that may appear contradictory and that may cause us continually to rethink our understanding of what behaviors constitute masculinity and femininity. I wish to explore this idea with respect to Led Zeppelin further—to try to account for fan responses, including my own—by examining in some detail both the visual iconography and the musical sounds of the band.

Visual Iconography

Wendy Annibell's photograph of Robert Plant taken July 27, 1973, at Madison Square Garden captures many of the characteristics associated with the male cock-rocker image (fig. 18). His pose is typical—legs apart, straight, and firmly grounded, bare-chested, pelvis jutting outward, and right hand raised, bent at the elbow, finger pointed, a gesture that underscores his confident pose, the raised and pointed finger especially stressing the importance or urgency of what he has to say ("let me have your attention; listen to me; this is what's important"). The eye is drawn to Plant's genitals because his pelvis is thrust forward, he has on tight jeans that outline his sex, and he has patches sewn onto the crotch area, the material of which is also worn, all provoking the spectator to gaze at his sex. The angle of the photograph points upward, also pulling the eye toward his crotch and making it and the rest of him tower above the spectator as a powerful masculine icon. Similarly, Marty Perez's photograph of Jimmy Page at the Chicago Stadium in April of 1977 captures him in a classic guitar-hero pose, one that he undoubtedly helped invent (fig. 6). This is one of his most usual poses onstage, with the guitar squarely in front, his legs straight and apart, the left leg slightly ahead of the right. As mentioned earlier, a frequent comment made about Page's playing is how low he wears the guitar, slung around his hips so that some guitarists think he compromises his playing in terms of precision and control of the instrument.[52] The guitar is slung directly over Page's penis, serving as a grand visual metaphor for it, drawing attention to and celebrating Page's masculinity in the most overt way. It is not very difficult to see how the pose relates this celebration of masculinity to the power of the band's music and their position in the world as successful celebrities, characteristics that correspond to Frith and McRobbie's conclusion that these shows are about male sexual performance and Weinstein's that this music culture is "masculinist" and that it is about male bonding.[53]

There is no question that on one level these images can be interpreted as representations of machismo and that men might identify with the display of power; but female fan responses to these images, including my own, reveal that they are also a source of erotic pleasure for women. I received no indication at all from those who responded to the survey that this kind of iconography was ever off-putting or frightening to women, even in the 1970s, as Frith and McRobbie claimed, only that it was/is a source of pleasure for them. Women's erotic pleasure at such imagery has not been discussed much. More than ten years ago, Suzanne Moore wrote that "to suggest that women actually look at men's bodies is apparently to stumble into a theoretical minefield which holds sacred the idea that in the dominant media the look is always already structured as male."[54] At least in writing about rock music, not much has changed. It seems, for example, an oversight in Walser's otherwise incisive study that he acknowledges gay men's erotic pleasure at metal imagery but not heterosexual women's—could it really be that women who responded to his fan survey said nothing to suggest that they were physically attracted to the rock musicians they listened to and looked at? While the importance that collecting photographs of favorite rock stars holds to many female fans has been regularly noted,[55] the idea that these photographs are sources of erotic pleasure—rather than "cute" or "handsome" representations of male idols or representations of ideal but unobtainable men (wealthy, talented, famous, and so on)—is not discussed. I would suggest that this is because the idea that women do not generally enjoy sex or that, even if they do, it is not very polite to acknowledge it is still entrenched in our culture, enforced in the discourse on hard rock, perhaps, by men—or women—who are made uncomfortable by the notion of a woman confident in and curious about her sexuality. I wonder how many of those who read the unabashed responses mentioned previously from female fans stereotyped these women as "loose" or "slutty"; or is it finally possible to understand their answers in the context of their lives as professionals, mothers, wives and a whole host of other identities of which their erotic engagement with Led Zeppelin's music and imagery is one integral part?

In fact, the spectacle of male hard rock and metal performance is a powerful reversal of Laura Mulvey's theory of the male gaze.[56] Mulvey argues that in mainstream film the woman is put on display for the visual pleasure of the male viewer; protagonists (heroes) are generally men, with whom male viewers also identify. One critique of Mulvey's now-canonic theory was undertaken in *The Female Gaze*, a collection of essays that discusses various ways in which the woman viewer is catered to in popular culture.[57] Regrettably, popular music is not discussed in any of the essays, but certainly in performances of so much rock music it is the male body that is displayed—as a symbol of masculine strength and power to male *and* female spectators and as an object of erotic desire for female (and probably also male) spectators. The prominence of Plant's penis through his jeans in Wendy Annibell's photograph may be considered a mark of macho arrogance, or it may be received as one of the many pleasurable stimuli, both visual and aural, that were part of attending a Led Zeppelin concert or collecting photographs of the band and listening to their recordings. The position and shape of Page's guitar—low-slung around his hips—may turn the instrument into a phallic symbol, but there are certainly other possibilities for interpretation available. One is that the guitar acts, in fact, as the male musician's "mistress," whom he treats "now tenderly, now tyrannically, devour[ing] her with kisses, lacerat[ing] her with lustful bites, embrac[ing] her, caress[ing] her."[58] B. B. King, after all, named his guitar Lucille, suggesting perhaps that the instrument possessed the same power to seduce him as a lover but, in any case, assigning to the instrument a feminine identity. Further, the way in which Page moves with the guitar, rubbing it up against his pelvic area, his open-legged stance, the instrument in between his legs, makes the visual image of him erotic to watch from a woman's perspective. In fact, the guitar and Page's physical relationship with it need not be perceived strictly as a metaphor for male sex: the very sight of guitar and body rubbing together is sensuous, regardless of whether one construes the guitar as phallic *or Page as a man*. This last point is crucially important. As Butler theorizes, just because Page has a body that is "culturally intelligible" as male does not mean that we must always understand the actions he performs as "male." Actions that are perceived as belonging to a feminine identity or actions that cannot so unproblematically be assigned to male or female identities can be written onto this "male" body.[59] In a concert situation, these visual images may act to momentarily "freeze the flow of action in moments of erotic contemplation" for both women and men as Mulvey suggests that the image of a woman might in a film.[60]

Mulvey writes that "[i]n a world ordered by sexual imbalance, pleasure in looking has been split between active/male and passive/female," a notion that has already been challenged in *The Female Gaze*; but it is worth mentioning, since it is not taken up there, that this is not the case in rock music cultures.[61] In his article "The Enemy Within," John Savage recognizes the reversal of Mulvey's concept in the idolization of male pop and rock stars by women. But his interest is not in the reversal itself, rather in the idea of the "passivity of the adored object," in this case the male rock stars, and the feminization of or androgynous qualities of pop stars such as the Beatles, who he claims were marketed for young women.[62] This misses crucial aspects of the feminine gaze upon male rock stars. At concerts or through photographs, male rock stars, their bodies on display, become objects of female desire—they conform to Mulvey's idea of *to-be-looked-at-ness*, not only those who might be "feminized" or "androgynous" but also those whose image is built around aspects of identity that are characteristically defined as "male." Male rock stars, in one sense, at least, are the passive objects of the female gaze, a controlling gaze that is partly responsible for the man acting as he does. However many different reasons there may have been for Plant to wear tight pants, it must be acknowledged that one was to attract women (meaning to please and excite them); this is so obvious to my nonacademic women friends that they are incredulous when I tell them that the point still needs to be made in academic writing. In fact, the male rock star conflates what Mulvey considers the two structuring aspects of film that attract the attention of the male viewer: the erotic object and the "main controlling figure with whom the spectator can identify."[63] What this means is that simultaneously the woman who is watching the male rock star can desire him sexually and imagine herself *as* him, as I suggested earlier, with all the cultural and financial capital that he owns. In a later essay, Mulvey criticizes this very kind of identification, saying that "[t]he masculine identification, in its phallic aspect, reactivates for [a woman] a fantasy of 'action' that correct femininity demands should be repressed."[64] In other words, it is the male who is allowed to be the star, while the woman must be content to watch him, imagining herself invested with his power as opposed to having (creating) it herself. But is this the case? Although rock music is still a male-dominated profession, there have been, and increasingly are, women rockers who act out onstage in exactly the same way as Page (Melissa Etheridge is a good example); it is entirely possible for a woman to pick up a guitar, learn to play like Page, and engage in the same acts of showmanship as he does, so it is not a matter of these "actions" being unavailable to women. Women fans can, therefore, fantasize with their male counterparts as they watch Page about stepping into his shoes. And just as Mulvey argues that the act of males gazing at female screen stars as erotic objects is empowering, so I would argue that it is empowering for female fans to gaze at male rock stars—that, in fact, the female fans know they exercise control over the way in which rock stars dress and act in order for them to attract women and also that their gaze on these men offers them an opportunity to explore and express something important about their sexuality. Tori Amos has made the latter point several times with respect to her attraction to male rock stars and, in particular, to Robert Plant. In an interview, Amos said that

I'd be five years old, lying on my bed, with the afghan over me, squeezing my legs together and thinking, "Something should go here one day." I wanted to run away with all those guys, with Zeppelin and Jim Morrison and John Lennon. I [recently] told Robert Plant that I really wanted to pack my peanut butter and jelly and my teddy and my trolls and come find him. . . . Actually, Zeppelin didn't happen until I was nine or ten, when I started to bleed, so it was totally perfect; I was all ready for Robert.[65]

Erotic pleasure is, however, only one way in which these images of Page and Plant can be received, and again, it is unlikely that eroticism can be neatly separated out from various other responses. Plant's bare chest, which Frith and McRobbie "masculinize" by focusing on the fact that men can bare the chest in public and on chest hair as a masculine sexual attribute, can signify in quite a different way. In a conversation that took place in one of my graduate seminars, a female student remarked how drawn her eye was to Plant's bare torso as she watched *The Song Remains the Same*, not to his chest but to his belly, which she identified as a locus of maternal comfort.[66] The sweat on his belly may signify warmth, and its soft fleshiness (before the days of ab machines and the objective of creating washboard-hard stomachs) can be associated with the feminine/maternal. And for me, Page's machismo poses are always uneasily negotiated through his slender, lanky frame, the delicacy of his features, the way in which he so often bends his body inward in collapse as he plays, signifying the "frailty" that journalistic writers have commented on,[67] and, especially in early days but even still to some extent, the childlike qualities of his face. Quite aside from the sometimes frilly or glittery clothes that he wore or his curling-ironed long hair, his body, face, and elfin gestures (journalist Chris Welch once called them feline[68]) have an androgynous quality that is difficult to ignore. This is another reason that it is so important to examine individual artists. In what but the most superficial way can Page's visual iconography compare to, say, that of Guns 'N' Roses guitarist Slash, to take an extremely contrasting example? Or how can the performance of gender by Elvis, Mick Jagger, Roger Daltrey, and Plant—the four performers that Frith and McRobbie lump together— be taken as the same in anything but the most superficial of ways? These alternative readings of Page's and Plant's visual iconography offer instances of various gendered identities being written onto the male body (what Butler calls figure to ground), creating "highly complex and structured production[s] of desire."[69]

One other response I have to photographs of Page presented in this book has to do with friendship. Sue Wise accounts for her powerful attachment to Elvis Presley and his music in these terms, saying that "[Elvis] was another human being to whom I could relate and be identified with. When I felt lonely and totally alone in the world, there was always Elvis."[70] "The overwhelming feelings and memories," she writes about sifting through her collection of Elvis memorabilia, "were of warmth and affection for a very dear friend."[71] I, too, have this kind of platonic affection for Page, as do both male and female fans who refer to him by his nickname "Pagey" and, indeed, the band as a whole as "the boys" (also ways in which the fan can feel closer to his or her idols).[72] The friendship comes first through the music, the means by which Page and others in the band have shared their spirit with me. Through the music I feel as though I have come to know Page personally and shared with him an enormous range of feelings and ideas. Clearly the young man quoted earlier, who came from a broken home and identified strongly with Plant as an important male figure in his youth saw him as both friend and teacher, but this feeling is also evident in the enormous number of comments in the fan questionnaire responses that point to the friendly affection in which band members are held.

What is also important to take into account is that the two photographs of Page and Plant that I have just described present only one side of their visual personae, a side that I chose to deal with here because it has been so narrowly interpreted in the past. But several of the other photographs reproduced here offer a variety of iconography: the band seated at the front of the stage for their acoustic set, for example (fig. 1); Page bent over his guitar, head down in concentration (fig. 8); Plant seated, clapping his hands joyously, his head thrown back in ecstasy (fig. 10). For fans who know the band well, the "macho" posturing is consumed in the context of all the other ways in which they know this band, not in isolation from it. At one moment the viewer might be reminded of the overwhelming masculine power of the performer, at the next of his vulnerability to the power of the music. It may not be possible to have this response to other hard rock or metal performers, whose visual iconography may be less polysemous. But I suspect, rather, that most hard rock and metal performers have been much too broadly drawn and that the experience of visual iconography with respect to these performers is much more rich and varied than what has been described so far.

Music

> My vocal style I haven't tried to copy from anyone. It just developed,
> until it became the girlish whine that it is today.
> —Robert Plant, *Musician*, June 1990

One of the most sexually explicit songs in Led Zeppelin's recordings, in terms of both lyrics and music, is "Whole Lotta Love."[73] Lyrically, the song is a cover of Willie Dixon's "You Need Love," which Plant, at least, knew from Muddy Waters's 1963 recording; musically, the two versions share a similar melodic line, but other than this, Zeppelin's version departs significantly from Waters's.[74] In his book *Crosstown Traffic: Jimi Hendrix and Post-War Pop*, critic Charles Shaar Murray compares the two songs, and, characteristically, he is none too kind to Zeppelin:

[Waters's version] is a seduction, and its most heinous crime, even in terms of present-day sexual politics, is that it could be considered mildly condescending and vaguely paternalistic, though "avuncular" is probably a more appropriate adjective. Muddy's tone is warm and solicitous: he suggests that the woman to whom he is singing is both sexually inexperienced and starved of affection, and volunteers to remedy both conditions. The music to which "You Need Love" is set echoes Muddy's warmth with an intricate guitar figure and a Hammond organ that seeps into the tune like a measure of fine brandy; the total effect is intimate, relaxed, utterly sensual.

Led Zeppelin, by contrast, come on like thermonuclear gang rape. The woman—who, in Muddy Waters's song, is evoked as a real person with real emotions in a real situation—is here reduced to a mere receptacle; an entirely passive presence whose sole function is to receive the Great Zeppelin (as depicted on the group's first two album covers: lumbering facetiousness posing as irony) with a suitable degree of veneration and gratitude. Even her response is superfluous: Zeppelin's vocalist Robert Plant virtually has her orgasm for her. After all, the satisfaction of the woman in the case is not intended for her benefit, but for his: it is the validation of his masculine prowess and the price of his admission to the alpha-male society. The stud-strut of heavy metal is a ritual by which men celebrate each other; it is not primarily intended for women, who—at British metal shows, if not at their American counterparts—demonstrate their understanding of the nature of the event by not showing up. The woman is strictly an abstract, faceless presence; she is essential as a part of the intercourse kit, but not as an individual. "Love," in this context, is a euphemism for something measurable with a ruler; when Plant howls "I'm gonna give you every inch of MAH LURVE," the term "imply" is too mild for the intensity he brings to the suggestion that his love is, quite literally, his penis.[75]

In both cases, Murray has been duped by his superficial reading of lyrics and music. Lyrically the two versions are almost identical, although lines have been shuffled around. Perhaps it is the line "Baby you look so sweet and kind" in Waters's version, omitted by Plant, that suggests the woman's "realness" to Murray (as if these adjectives—adjectives that enforce essentialist notions of femininity—could make a woman more real than the expression of her sexual desire). The line seems out of place in the context of a lyric that is blatantly about sexual gratification, which may be why Plant chose to leave it out. Otherwise, there is a relentless insistence in Waters's lyrics on the central idea of the song: you need "love." From a purely lyrical point of view, there is little room for the interpretation of this love as anything but sexual: how the double entendre of "way down inside, woman you need love" can be glossed over here and not in Led Zeppelin's version is baffling. And from what else can this woman need cooling than from her sexual desire? Juxtaposed with "I've got burning," what could "you've got yearning" refer to other than sexual longing? Furthermore, the line "you gotta have some love" is repeated, with some variations that serve to increase the intensity (it is not only repetition but also the manner in which Waters tries every conceivable way of expressing this sentiment), seven times after the opening verse, and then Waters follows these repetitions with "you make me feel so good, you make me feel alright," repeated three times.

In terms of the lyric, then, it is strange indeed that Murray would interpret Waters as sounding paternal or avuncular in this song. The sexual innuendo of the lyrics is overwhelming and cannot possibly be whitewashed to suggest that this is a father figure counseling a little girl in matters of the heart. Murray himself suggests that it is the *quality* of Muddy's voice—"warm and solicitous"— that is of some importance in his interpretation. What makes his voice sound warm is the low range in which Waters sings, the relaxed vocal sound, and the fact that it comes from his chest and has a rich quality (it is not a thin sound by any means). These qualities make Waters sound "mature" and may account for Murray thinking of him as paternal or avuncular. The rich, warm, deep, relaxed timbre of this voice might suggest fatherly patience, or experience, as can the controlled emotional palette, conveyed through the range, the way Waters stays within the boundaries of the melody, and the consistent vocal timbre that uses almost no distortion.

None of these vocal qualities are found in Plant's performance. He sings the verses in a high range, and even though he does not use falsetto (he almost never does), the sound he produces comes mostly from his throat: it is strained and he uses plenty of distortion. John Shepherd has suggested that the production of sound in the throat as opposed to "deeper" within the body and the strained sound of this kind of singing belie "the tension and experiential repression encountered as males engage with the public world" and that because the sound is produced in the throat there is little of the body behind it: "'Macho' vocal sounds are, in a manner of speaking, 'all mouth,' all projection into the public world with little behind them."[76] Following Frith and McRobbie's binary split between cock rock and teeny bop music, Shepherd proposes that the counterpart to the cock-rock timbre is "woman as nurturer," which he defines as a deeper chest voice, without strain. In some instances, there may be some truth to Shepherd's interpretation of these kinds of timbres (I think of Roger Daltrey singing the Who's "Who Are You," his pent-up anger palpable in the choked quality of his vocal timbre—although he doesn't seem to have much trouble expressing this anger in the lyrics), but it is too static an interpretation to account for much hard rock singing and perhaps in particular Robert Plant's, which, as I argue later, is highly varied in terms of timbre. Part of the difficulty with Shepherd's analysis is that he writes solely about the "strain" of the voice, instead of taking into account the concept of distortion (he never uses this word), which so often accompanies "strain" in hard rock and metal singing. Contrary to Shepherd's notion that "strain" signifies repression, Robert Walser suggests that the use of vocal "distortion" "functions as a signal of extreme power and *intense expression* by overflowing its channels and *materializing the exceptional effort that produces it.*"[77] Here Walser points not only to the expressiveness of this kind of singing but also to its corporeality. Walser's metaphor draws on Mark Johnson's theory of the bodily basis for meaning, in this instance our concept of force; that is, our interaction with the physical environment makes us aware that forces act upon us and that we, too, can act with force upon things.[78] In hard rock and metal singing, Walser argues, strain and distortion are created by using great force and force equals power. But this kind of singing can also be seen as a metaphor that relies on Johnson's idea of the body as container and his notion that extreme emotion can be perceived as "hot fluid" rising up and trying to exceed the boundaries of the container;[79] so the "strain" in hard rock singers' voices might also be understood as emotion that is barely contained and that often overflows its boundaries (Daltrey again at the climactic point of "Won't Get Fooled Again") or dissipates (Plant's descending wail at the end of "Whole Lotta Love"). This way of viewing hard rock singing may also provide an answer to Simon Frith, who has wondered why intensity and sincerity in male rock singing have become equated with singing in a higher, strained register. Perhaps drawing on Shepherd, Frith concludes that this higher male voice does not have much of the body in it: "It's as if in rock convention . . . the sexiest male voice is the least bodily."[80] But it is precisely this straining and the use of distortion that put the body *into* the music; it is this through which we hear the body as container, spilling over its boundaries—or about to. Furthermore, this high male voice opens another interesting space for the consideration of gender performance. Robert Plant may joke about his voice becoming a "girlish whine" in the epigraph to this section, but male fans have also commented on this as a desirable attribute of his voice. One man wrote concerning Plant's voice: "Feminine. Sometimes. Gorgeous. Powerful. Perfect." When I was a member of the Led Zeppelin Internet discussion list a few years ago, I was struck by a similar comment made by a male fan, in which he said that he liked Plant's voice best in 1969 because that was when he sounded most like a woman. And another male fan in a response on the questionnaire said: "[His voice is] so raunchy, torrid and dramatic. No wonder women wanted to fuck him! And I'm a straight male writing these things!"[81]

Actually, Shepherd's categories are not completely black-and-white—at least not for that of "woman as nurturer." Here he allows that there is also a male counterpart to this sound, the "boy-next-door" sound of, for example, Paul McCartney singing "Yesterday." And there is also the "woman as sex object" vocal timbre, which involves the "softer, warmer hollower tones of the woman singer as emotional nurturer becom[ing] closed off with a certain edge, a certain vocal sheen that is quite different from the male-appropriated, hard core timbre of typical 'cock' rock."[82] He writes that "cock" rock and "woman as nurturer" timbres are mutually exclusive and that this signifies the cock rockers' inability to "let anyone in for completion. . . . They attempt to complete themselves, and in this sense the masturbatory symbolism of guitar playing is not without significance."[83] I have challenged the idea that the guitar is statically a male and/or masturbatory visual icon in "Visual Iconography"; here I would like to suggest that Shepherd's interpretation does not allow for the variety of strained, distorted, and, yes, pure timbres used by a singer such as Plant, nor for the reasons that such a singer might employ these timbres on any given occasion. Plant's extreme strain in "Whole Lotta Love" needs to be understood in relationship to the text: his vocal timbre in this piece, which never lets up at all, creates a sense of urgency (or near overflowing) that is palpable. Reading this against the text, we might interpret it as conveying the intensity of his sexual longing (or, indeed, the intensity of his sexual encounter [see later], or see fan comments earlier that suggest this song is a metaphor for sexual intercourse). If this were the only timbre that Plant ever used, it would be difficult to sustain a semiotic reading of this kind. But it is not the only timbre he uses. In terms of the intense use of vocal distortion, one can compare the quality achieved in "Whole Lotta Love" with that of "Custard Pie," in which the sound is more nasal and even more constricted and more heavily distorted than that of "Whole Lotta Love" (there is less of the pitch in "Custard Pie" than there is in "Whole Lotta Love"). These examples can be compared to pieces in which Plant used little or no distortion at all, where he achieves very "pure" timbres—songs such as "Achilles Last Stand," "Kashmir," and "Immigrant Song," all of which use different timbres—"Achilles" strained and in the uppermost regions of Plant's chest register, "Kashmir" much more relaxed but still in a high register, and "Immigrant Song" in a very high register for the first part of each verse but reasonably relaxed and in a lower register for the second part of each verse. Plant chooses these timbres and registers to complement the music and to express the text. In between these extremes of "pure" and "distorted" timbres is a range of others—for example, that used in the song "Black Dog," in which distortion is used but with a more open vocal sound than the constriction of "Whole Lotta Love" (partly owing to the production). And of course, because Led Zeppelin recorded so much acoustically based music, Plant used a variety of soft timbres as well, a couple of which I might place in Shepherd's "nurturer" category: "Going to California" and "That's the Way" are two examples of songs sung using a lower register and a warm, undistorted timbre (save for one moment in "Going to California," where Plant breaks into a much higher range and sings much more loudly and intensely). Neither lyric posits the singer as "vulnerable" or a "victim:" "That's the Way" explores a person's realization that his ideological differences with a friend have made it impossible for the friendship to continue. And "Going to California" is about the end of one relationship and the singer's resolve to strike out on a new course. As one male fan put it, "[E]very subtle change in Plant's voice through the years has been exploited by Robert to give the listener the most heartfelt experience. His unique set of pipes makes him an icon of rock vocalists. He can sing soft folk, hard blues, heavy rock, rockabilly, ballads . . . very versatile, original, and passionate."

What is particularly troubling about Shepherd's categories and his explanation of them is how they reproduce essentialist ideas of gender, especially of "correct femininity." This is perhaps clearest in his explanation of women who use the "cock rock" and "woman as sex object" timbres in their singing. Shepherd suggests that this is in the first instance a male way of singing that women appropriate when they "begin to occupy male locations in the social structure."[84] The "woman as sex object" timbre suggests "a shift, psychologically coded, from the 'feminine heart' to the 'masculine head' with its cerebral, intellectual, controlled view of the world."[85] He speaks of black women blues singers whose "hard" vocal timbres suggest that they "frequently needed to develop a 'masculine' assertiveness and independence to survive while, at the same time, remaining 'women.'"[86] About Janis Joplin, Shepherd writes that "this stridency is doomed to failure because it derives from the same notions of 'sexuality' that also give rise to the rasping timbres of 'cock' rock.... [B]y invoking closure of her 'intrinsic' femininity to provide that same objectified form, the woman (singer) as sex object runs the risk of losing touch with her already atrophied self, of being taken over by a masculine image of her 'own' inner nature."[87]

So rigid a concept of gender identity—including the suggestion that aspects of femininity might be "intrinsic"—denies, once again, that as part of the performance of their gender women who sing or listen to hard rock can enjoy a visceral kind of sex or that the men who create those distorted, strained timbres are making themselves emotionally vulnerable and available. And where is the evidence that the use of strain or distortion was, in the first instance, a characteristic of men's singing and not women's? In fact, the moaning, screaming, and "overflowing of channels" characteristic of hard rock singing point very strongly to an emotional landscape that has traditionally (and also essentially) been associated with femininity.

Let me explore these ideas further with respect to "Whole Lotta Love." Murray's reading of the text denies an aspect of it that urgently needs to be addressed, that of the woman's sexuality. While this lyric is certainly partly about male sexual desire and bravado, it is also about a woman's sexual desire, physical desire that is not romantic but carnal. She is portrayed as yearning, as "hot." Plant emphasizes the issue by placing the lyric "You need coolin'" first. If there is an acknowledgment that women, as well as men, crave sexual gratification by a man—not just want it but also *burn* for it, as is suggested in this lyric—then the rest of the lyric can be read differently. This trope of "woman on fire" emerges elsewhere in songs that come out of the blues tradition—Jimi Hendrix's "Fire," for example, which offers the image of a woman made incredibly powerful by her sexual arousal, something the man begs, simply, to "stand next to." It might then be possible that a woman has gotta have love way down inside, that there might be a lot of "good things" she's been missing, that she might yearn to be pleasurably "cooled" by a capable man. Female fans who responded to my questionnaire suggest that this is their reading of Zeppelin's "Whole Lotta Love." And in the January 1990 issue of the Robert Plant fanzine, *Nirvana*, a woman named "Diane" took on Murray's interpretation of "Whole Lotta Love" herself in an editorial, commenting:

Yeah, "Whole Lotta Love" was about pure, unadulterated, "faceless" sex. So What? As a female I was never offended by the "macho" of it. It was one hell of a good song—and women could relate to the "hormonal urges" being expressed as well as the men could. Mr. Murray (and those like him) seems to me to have a very low opinion of men and a very unrealistic view of women.

Much of the meaning(s) of the song not only comes from the lyrics and singing style, of course but also depends upon what is happening in the music. While Shepherd's location of gender and sexuality in singing styles offers a way into understanding the phenomenon, it artificially isolates the voice—and, further, one aspect of it, such as vocal timbre (and even then generalizing that there are a handful of available timbres when, as I have tried to point out with respect to Plant's voice, there are, in fact, many different ones), from melodic range, harmonic motion, instrumental parts, and various other aspects of the music. In other words, it is of limited use in trying to get at the cultural meanings in a song because we do not hear an element such as timbre on its own. The music of Zeppelin's version is much more varied than is Waters's and therefore much more open to interpretation by both men and women listeners. For example, harmonic change in both versions is minimal, which tends to exaggerate the monodimensional message of the lyric (there are no distractions from its intensity in this respect). Harmonic stasis has been coded as an engagement with the present moment, and this interpretation seems workable here, where the music, together with the lyrics, stays fixed on the immediate goal of carnal pleasure.[88] But in Waters's version there is no relief from it at all throughout the song. There is no differentiation, either, between the music of the verse and that of the chorus. In fact, this formal structure is extremely loose: there are clearly three verses, but each of them is marked by a minimal amount of new lyric, slipping back, quickly, into the same line ("Baby way down inside . . .") and then into the refrain, which consists of variations on the line "You need love." There is no musical differentiation between these sections: no harmonic or timbral change and no change in the groove. There is also little interplay between guitar and voice in Waters's version. Guitarist Earl Hooker mostly mirrors what Waters sings, occasionally creating a heterophonic texture by diverging slightly from the singer's line. When Hooker is not mirroring Waters's voice, he is playing the main riff of the piece, or he drops out of the texture altogether. In other words, there is no call and response between voice and guitar as there so often is in the blues, no dialogue, but rather a monologue, the guitar and voice banding together in their common purpose of pursuit. The driving groove set up by the drummer, Casey Jones, is also unchanging throughout the song.

The bass guitar and organ enjoy the most independence from the other instruments and voice, but even this is restricted. There is quite a bit of movement in both instruments (by quarter notes, mostly), but this movement is confined to improvising on the tonic chord. The one big change in timbre comes when the organist gets a solo, but again what he plays is confined to a variation of the melody of the verse.

Musically, Zeppelin's version contrasts this in just about every way imaginable. Perhaps the most defining musical gesture is Page's riff, which in terms of pitch and rhythm is also mostly static, adding to the insistence implied by the restricted harmonic motion. The riff consists of a pickup to the tonic, the implied harmony of which is the flat VII chord (the pitches are b and d♮), which comes to rest on the downbeat on the tonic E—doubling the tonic an octave lower, so that the sense of release that comes with the tonic is magnified by the downward motion of the octave drop. This tonic chord is repeated for nearly two full measures during the introduction (before Plant enters) prior to the pickup being repeated, using a rhythm that emphasizes the beat (beats 1, 2, and 3) and consists of regular eighth notes. (The riff is contracted when Plant enters, one measure of these repeated eighth notes being dropped.) The pickup notes are set in rhythmic and harmonic relief to this regularity. The pickup comes on the second half of beat 3, beginning with a sixteenth note that moves to an eighth note on the last sixteenth note of beat 3, creating syncopation. The sound of Page's guitar playing the riff for the first time is also important to consider here. Not only is there a raw timbre created through the use of distortion, but also the notes sound slightly "out of tune," the pitches bent out of shape, perched precariously on the edge of where they should be, pulling the body with them, coaxing it to come along, to conspire with the transgression. The timbre is further distorted and amplified through the use of backward echo on the guitar.[89] The riff is also played in a low register on the guitar—magnified by the lowness of the bass when it comes in—and I always map the image of Page's low-slung guitar onto the low sound of this riff when I hear it, much as I do when I hear the riffs to "Heartbreaker" and "Moby Dick," which are similarly low in range.

The effect of the pickup—syncopation, its metric placement just before the downbeat, the harmonic change, and the raw timbre—is physical in a very specific way: we experience the pickup as an intense force acting on the body, which is released when the timbre, rhythm, melody, and harmony change to the tonic. The riff might be experienced metaphorically as the body being jolted back during the pickup and released at the tonic. Because the riff is so short and because it repeats throughout the verses and choruses of the song, the body is continually—relentlessly—hit by the intensity of the pickup. In effect, the body is kept in a fairly constant state of intensity or arousal by this riff.

The riff is heard in both the verse and chorus, so, as in Waters's version, there is no letting up of the intensity (in fact, it is occasionally increased when Bonham doubles the syncopated rhythm of the pickup on the drums). But unlike in Waters's version, there are other important musical differences between verse and chorus. Even though it is clearly Plant singing in both, his vocal "personality" is different in each. In the verse, he is singing higher in his range than in the chorus; he uses distortion and strain, as well as rhythmic freedom—stretching out syllables along beats, repeating them, and so forth, all of which suggest emotional overload. In the verse, he repeats the line "Wanna whole lotta love" four times, in a lower register, with no distortion, and with rhythmic precision (the rhythm is the same each time the line is sung, and the sixteenth notes are sung evenly each time). The quickness of the rhythmic pattern, its regularity, and the repeated notes of the melody create an intensity different from that of the verses—much more mechanical, coldly insistent. The other musical difference is the addition of a downward slide on the guitar by Page, which comes after every repetition of the lyric. This powerful wash of sound cuts through the texture like a knife and foreshadows—or is linked to—the free-form section that follows the second chorus.

Waksman argues very effectively that this free-form section is of crucial importance to the gendered meanings of the song. He reads it as an "interruption of the throbbing, single-minded riff" that "enacts a crisis in the representation of phallic potency." He argues further that the guitar solo by Page that follows this section (which Waksman calls an attempt at "resuscitation") is "rigidly constrained," the result of "his virtuosity [being] hemmed in by the wall of sound produced by the band as a whole."[90] (I would argue that it is the particular timbre of his guitar, including the dead sound of the production, and the particular licks he is playing—confined to a very narrow range—that create the effect of containment.) While acknowledging the important step Waksman has taken in recognizing the middle section to be of crucial semiotic importance, my interpretation of this section would move in a different direction from that of "crisis" (and it is important to consider that our different readings may well stem from our different gendered positions with respect to the music). I hear the downward slide/wash of sound and the electronic music of the middle section as fulfilling the role of a partner for Plant (it is precisely Murray's failure to take the music into account that makes him suggest that Plant has no partner), and in an interesting way. Plant's gasps ("ah, ah, ah, ah," steadily rising in pitch) and ecstatic cries ("love me, love me; no, no, no; luuuuuuuuv . . . luauauauav") are made *in response to* the washes of electronically produced sound, which begin to occur and are developed before he enters. These dominate his voice, which, except for his cry of "love" near the end of the section, is kept far back in the mix. In their ebb and flow, their movement in and out of the metric framework maintained by the percussion, they suggest a generally very intense but richly varied experience, a sumptuous sexual encounter, one lingered over, not hurried through; furthermore, the electronic sounds create multiple climactic moments in this section, perhaps suggesting a representation of femininity.

But it is too easy to state emphatically that Plant is the male in this musical/sexual encounter. This is certainly one interpretation, and there are no doubt lines of lyric that suggest he is performing a masculine role here ("every inch of my love" is the strongest but also "way down inside, woman you need love"). But the high register of his voice may be suggestive of femininity (as opposed to the deep sound of Waters's voice)—it could be Joplin singing, for example. And what of the emotional landscape that Plant paints during the verses of the song, during the middle section and at the end, during his a cappella section, and after, during the outro? To me, there is a great deal of gender ambiguity at these points. During the verses, Plant's over-the-top emotional delivery of the lyrics contradicts masculine gender stereotypes of hardness and control: the break in his voice in the first "coolin'" and the taunting/teasing/flirting delivery of the lines "I'm gonna give you my love" in both the first and second verses—in the second verse adding "ahhh" with an upward slide after the first time singing this line—these are the flirtatious sounds a young girl might make. There is also the wonderful incoherence and at times ambivalence of the lyric he delivers:

> I'm gonna send ya
> back to schoolin'

or:

> You been learnin'
> baby I been learnin'
> All the good times baby baby I been yearnin' ah
> Way way down inside, ah honey you need ah

In Plant's performance, thoughts are interrupted or broken off as a sign of his distractedness or inability to focus due to his state of heightened sexual arousal. And the ambivalence is interesting in terms of the gender identity of the singer: who's being sent back to school? Both people are "learnin'"; during the chorus, there is never a pronoun: the line delivered is "wanna whole lotta love," not "*I* want it," not "*you* want it," not "*she* wants it." A woman can yearn for "good times" as well as a man and, in the following verse, can feel as though s/he's misused potentially "good times" in the past. Musically, Plant's performance suggests that he, too, has multiple climaxes: near the end of the middle section, when his voice is foregrounded as he cries, "Luuuuuv"; again at the end of the a cappella section, when he again cries, "Luuuuv"; and just before the song fades away, when he emits an ecstatic scream (the fade coming during the scream quite a brilliant production decision, one that suggests all kinds of readings, including an abrupt end to the encounter—the hand of the engineer reaching in and turning it off—or its ad infinitum continuation, to offer only two possibilities).

Despite the insistence of the riff, with its intense physicality, there are three moments in Zeppelin's version of this song when it is not heard, during which the rhythmic/metric structure of the song collapses into something entirely different: the electronic free-form section, the stop-time guitar solo, and Plant's a cappella singing (punctuated—a bit like recitative—by chords from the band) near the end of the tune. Two of these moments are not dominated by Plant at all—the electronic middle section, as I have described earlier, and Page's guitar solo, the latter of which is like a third party coming into the narrative (we haven't heard Page's solo guitar at all up to this point). The different "speakers" or "players" in this song, with the varied musical languages that they speak, offer a narratively open text, one that encompasses multiple possibilities for a semiotic reading of gender identity and sexual experience.

In live performances, "Whole Lotta Love" generally held the privileged position as the final piece of the concert (prior to the encore) or as the last encore.[91] There were probably several reasons for this: First, it quickly became one of the best-known Zeppelin songs because it was the only one released as a single (against the band's wishes) and so received widespread radio airplay. Waiting until the end of a concert to play a particularly well known song helps bring an already-excited audience to a higher level. Second, and in keeping with this last point, the song is among the band's heaviest, loudest, and most energized tunes and putting it at the end of the show leaves the audience at a high point. The band always made sure to do this: if "Whole Lotta Love" wasn't the last piece, it was "Rock and Roll," "Immigrant Song," or some other fast, heavy song. The idea was to bring the audience to a fevered pitch and then leave them there—to have them depart the stadium in that energized state. On these points, Jones told me:

> [In terms of running order] all four [band] members would arrive at a provisional running order through suggestion, discussion and trial, to be fine tuned during the early shows of the tour. The main consideration was to give a dynamic shape to the whole show in terms of tension and release, a sort of macro version of what we would do when writing and arranging a single song. I feel that this holistic approach to the show gave Zeppelin the edge over a lot of bands at the time who were still subscribing to the "wandering on and playing what they felt like" ethic. After the at times amateurish approach to shows by many other bands, the audiences of 1969–70 simply didn't know what had hit them! "Whole Lotta Love" seemed from the outset a good show closer. I think that encores always followed it but am not entirely sure. A quiet ending was never considered, as you say, leave them electrified, and wanting more!

This contrasts with the aesthetic of other bands, who make sure to bring the audience back down from the ecstatic experience at the end of the show.[92] The placement of the song in the running order is significant: its overtly sexual lyric and the physicality of the music come at the peak of the show. The audience has been taken through a musical experience of peaks and valleys—usually an explosive beginning, which continues for a bit to build up momentum, then a more acoustically based or slow set and a return to high energy. Placing "Whole Lotta Love" at the end of this intensifies its sexual-cathartic effect.

Moreover, beginning fairly early in the song's performance history, it was modified in two significant ways from the studio version. From 1969 onward, Page regularly used the theremin during the song's "middle section." In light of the analysis that I have given earlier, that the electronic sounds in the studio version of this song may be interpreted as Plant's partner, Page's use of the theremin lends a fascinating visual aspect to this. In order to make the instrument produce sounds, Page must coax them out, bringing his hands nearer or farther away from the antenna in order to get lower or higher sounds, respectively. In live performances he liked to begin this section by getting the instrument to emit sounds very gradually, seeming to pull the sounds out, beginning with low sounds and moving to increasingly higher ones. The sounds begin in a halting manner—as if hesitating to come out—and then become increasingly wild. Both the visual and aural iconography is of Page as seducer, of the theremin as his partner (there is also ritualistic or religious, if you will, iconography here, of Page as the sorcerer of sound).

By 1970, the song was modified in another way. At the point near the end of the song where Plant sings "woman" a cappella, the song was opened up for a jam that included a number of songs (which varied from performance to performance), including Elvis Presley's "That's Alright," a number of blues tunes, including "Honey Bee" and "Hoochie Koochie Man," among others, Buffalo Springfield's "For What It's Worth," and so forth. In some shows, Plant continually comes back to "woman" in between the songs as a kind of tease.[93] The medley of songs can be interpreted in a variety of ways with respect to the song's narrative, but certainly one way of viewing it is as an attempt to seduce through the display of a virtuosic knowledge of a diverse musical repertory or as a playful engagement with different musical possibilities—a trying on and then discarding of musics, of possibilities, that tease and delight the listener.

ULTIMATELY, MURRAY'S championing of Waters and vilification of Zeppelin have less to do with gender than with notions about authenticity that are connected to race and the desire of the white male critic to identify with these notions: Black blues musicians are the "real thing," not only the inventors of the genre but also those who lived the stories they were telling. White rockers appropriate the surface but can never match the "depth" of black blues performers. Without invoking race or connecting it to the question of authenticity overtly (and thereby masking the ideology that informs his statements), Murray acknowledges this himself in the preface to his book: "[Hendrix's] music had the wayward adventurousness and sheer sensory overload I loved in the loud, weird rock of those immediately pre-psychedelic times, but it was weighted in the solid humanity and emotional authenticity I'd found only in soul music and the blues. Hendrix was hugely and quixotically *himself*; he was everything which the Townsends and Mayalls and Jaggers and Claptons had only pretended to be."[94] This point of view, which often comes into play in rock criticism and which in itself is in need of more detailed examination, enables Murray to ignore what actually transpires in the music; it allows him to invent narratives about the music that unproblematically valorize the black performer and condemn the white imitators. While this may at times be justifiable, it is troublesome as a blanket modus operandi. As I alluded to in the introduction with respect to the reception of Hendrix, it tends to perpetuate stereotypes and fantasies about the black male body, and also, importantly, it devalues the experience of those who are invested in the music that is being criticized, prescribing the "correct" point of view for listeners; it is an act of power.

Earlier in this essay I cited Sue Wise's question—why has male rock music been so unproblematically interpreted as phallic?—without really offering an answer. In fact, Wise supplies the answer herself, the same one that I would offer here: that interpretations are based on a selective understanding of an artist's career, that it is mostly men doing the interpreting, and, perhaps most important, that it is undoubtedly a prospect threatening to men and many women that male rock stars' power and sexuality could be understood, appropriated, or even controlled by women (as a woman wrote to me concerning my work on this project, "[A] woman ... taking the 'phallic' power for herself ... I think that this is what scares the beejesus out of many people"). It is much easier always to begin from the premise that the music and images are sexist and macho because not only is it a comforting notion that this kind of semiotic stability might exist, but it also locks out the dangerous possibility of woman as sexual and powerful—simultaneously. As Wise puts it, "[T]his is something that we, as feminists, must recognize: that is, we must never take anything on trust, we must ask our own questions, seek out our own knowledge, and always look gift horses, in the form of other people's knowledge, firmly in the mouth."[95]

Furthermore, Wise notes the importance of bringing personal experience into scholarly studies of this kind, for "[i]t is in the examination of personal experience that the disjuncture between subjective and objective realities is most clearly seen."[96] It was my profound involvement with Led Zeppelin that made me want to study the band academically—in order to try to understand my experience more fully—it was the disjuncture that I observed between my experience of the music and the way journalists and academics were writing about it that prompted me to write a book about Led Zeppelin. One of my hopes is that it will suggest to the latter, those generally on the outside of a music culture, that they handle more delicately and with greater subtlety the experiences of those who love a particular music and admit the possibility that an interpretation based on the surface noise of a song or image might need to be probed more deeply. Increasingly, those inside the culture should be given louder voices (one of the reasons I reproduced so many and such lengthy fan comments here was to allow the individuality of these voices to be heard, to allow the "informants," as James Clifford suggests, to "begin to be considered as co-authors"[97]). We should also make sure to check a discourse that slips unproblematically into a particular point of view, examining the ideologies that lie behind such entrenched positions.

Appendix
Fan Questionnaire

The questionnaire was posted on the Internet site zoso.net and sent to the major Led Zeppelin e-mail discussion list, "For Badgeholders Only," in June of 1998 and appeared in the October 1998 issue of the U.S. Led Zeppelin fanzine *Proximity*. Answers were collected between June and November 1998.

Hi Everyone,

I'm a musician and huge fan writing a book on Led Zeppelin's music that will be published by Oxford University Press. I want the book to include the opinions of a wide range of people who listen to Zep, not just mine, so I'd appreciate your taking a moment to answer the questions below. Thanks a lot for your help. If you have more to say, I'd love to hear from you: e-mail or write to me at the address at the end of the questionnaire.

1. Do you listen to Led Zeppelin casually, fanatically, somewhere in between?
2. Which albums do you own?
3. What is it you like about the band's MUSIC (as opposed to the lyrics, image, etc.)?
4. What is it you like about the band's image, lyrics, etc.?
5. How would you categorize Zeppelin: heavy metal, progressive rock, hard rock, something else? Is it important to categorize them?
6. Which is your favorite Zeppelin album?
7. Which is your favorite Zeppelin song?

8. Can you explain why this album and song are your favs (be as detailed as you can be—mention specific parts of the song you like, etc.)?

9a. Which band member(s) do you identify with most closely and why?

9b. Do you think you relate to the music in a specific way because of your sex/gender (I'm especially interested in knowing why women listen to the band and how they listen)? [Question only included on the *Proximity* version of the questionnaire.]

10. If you ever saw the band live, describe your experience.

11. Do you collect Zeppelin bootlegs? If so, why? Do you have a favorite?

12. If you haven't already commented on the following songs, please feel free to do so (again, be as detailed as you can about why you like/don't like them, why you think they work or don't work, what's most important about them, etc.):

> Dazed and Confused   Whole Lotta Love
> Kashmir   Black Dog
> Achilles Last Stand   Tangerine

13. Your comments on:

> riffs
> Jimmy Page's solos
> the acoustic set that was usually part of their shows
> Robert Plant's voice
> the use of "Eastern" elements in Zep's music
> the epic quality of pieces like "Stairway to Heaven" or "Achilles Last Stand"
> the importance and/or place of the blues in Zep's music
> John Bonham's drumming

14. What do you think Zeppelin's influence on rock music has been?

15. Any other comments:

Personal info:

1. Sex: male _____   female _____
2. Age
3. Do you play music? If so, what instrument(s)?
4. Have you had any formal music training?
5. Education completed: some high school _____   high school diploma _____
   some college _____   college degree _____
6. Occupation

Follow-up Question Sent to "For Badgeholders Only" on August 9, 1998:

From: F. Susan Fast
Date: Sunday, August 09, 1998, 8:08 P.M.
To: Zeppelin-1@lists.Stanford.Edu
Subject: Zeppelin/Sexuality/Gender

Hi Badgeholders,

You may remember that I posted a questionnaire to this list a couple of months ago as part of my research for my book on Zep. Thanks again to everyone who responded. I have a follow-up question (it's actually three questions: it's nearly impossible for me to be succinct!), which I hope that you'll answer for me; I'm especially interested in hearing from the women on the list, but men please answer too!

Is Zep's music "sexual" to you (I mean the music, not the guys . . . but maybe it's impossible to distinguish between the two for some of you, which is fine); if so, how? Any tunes in particular? Do you think that you relate/respond to the music in a specific way because of your sex/gender? According to many writers, Zeppelin is supposed to be "guy" music. Why? If this is so, why, Lady Badgeholders, do you listen to it? Any further reflections around this subject welcome.

PERSONAL INFORMATION STATISTICS—LED ZEPPELIN QUESTIONNAIRE

Total mumber of surveys: 323

Male	247 (76%)
Female	76 (24%)

Age:

10–19	118 (37%)	40–49	27 (8%)
20–29	76 (24%)	50–59	2 (.06%)
30–39	99 (30%)	no response	1 (.03%)

Do you play music?

Yes	200 (62%)
No	23 (38%)

If yes, what insturments (some respondents play more than one)?

Guitar	131	Vocalist	18
Piano/Keyboard	38	Woodwind/Brass	37
Drums	34	Strings	7
Bass	29	Harmonica/Banjo/etc.	12

Have you had any formal music training?

Yes	122 (38%)
No	199 (62%)
no response	1

Education completed:

Some High School	70	Some College	97
High School Diploma	38	College Degree	118

Occupation:

Professional	61	Artist/Musician	9
Student	131	Administration	13
Computer Programmer	20	Small Business Owner	7
Consultant	5	Retail	18
Management	13	Disabled	1
Laborer	44	No response	1

Responses received from:

"For Badgeholders Only"	82
zoso.net	189
Proximity	52

Notes

Introduction

1. Robert Palmer, "Led Zeppelin: The Music," in *Led Zeppelin*, vol. 2 (London: Warner Chappell Music, 1991).

2. The band is so characterized in "Led Zeppelin," *The Penguin Encyclopaedia of Popular Music*, ed. Donald Clarke (London: Viking, 1989), pp. 690–691; "Led Zeppelin," in *Encyclopaedia of Pop, Rock, and Soul*, revised edition, ed. Irwin Stambler (New York: St. Martin's Press, 1989), pp. 394–395; and "Led Zeppelin," in *The Oxford Companion to Popular Music*, ed. Peter Gammond (New York: Oxford University Press, 1991), p. 335, as well as in other in encyclopedias and surveys of rock music, and in the more academic studies by Allan F. Moore, in *Rock: The Primary Text* (Milton Keynes, UK: Open University Press, 1993), Edward Macan, *Rocking the Classics: English Progressive Rock and the Counterculture* (New York: Oxford University Press, 1997), and Robert Walser (Walser acknowledges that Robert Plant, at least, rejects the moniker; see Walser's *Running with the Devil: Power, Gender and Madness in Heavy Metal Music* [Middletown: Wesleyan University Press, 1993]).

3. J. D. Considine, interview with Page, Plant, and Jones, *Rolling Stone* (September 20, 1990), p. 58.

4. The incident is chronicled in Merril Shindler, "The Wrong Goodbye: Zeppelin Leaves America," *Rolling Stone* (September 8, 1977), pp. 14–15.

5. Richard Cole, with Richard Trubo, *Stairway to Heaven: Led Zeppelin Uncensored* (Harper Collins, 1992); Stephen Davis, *Hammer of the Gods: The Led Zeppelin Saga* (New York: Ballantine, 1985).

6. Davis, *Hammer of the Gods*, p. 65.

7. John Landau, quoted in Iain Chambers, *Urban Rhythms: Pop Music and Pop Culture* (Basingstoke, Hampshire: Macmillan, 1985), pp. 243–244.

8. Jim Miller, "Led Zeppelin," in *The Rolling Stone Illustrated History of Rock and Roll*, revised and updated edition (New York: Random House, 1992), p. 456.

9. "Concert Reviews: Woody Herman Orchestra, Led Zeppelin, Delaney and Bonnie (Filmore East, N.Y.)," *Variety* (June 4, 1969), p. 57.

10. Keith Richards, quoted in Gene Santoro, "Keith Richards: Stealing from the Best," *Guitar World: Special Jimmy Page Issue* (July 1986), p. 72.

11. Mikhail Bakhtin, *Rabelais and His World*, trans. Helene Iswolsky (Blooming-ton: Indiana University Press, 1984), quoted in Peter Stallybrass and Allon White, *The Politics and Poetics of Transgression* (Ithaca, NY: Cornell University Press, 1986), p. 7.

12. For a fuller discussion of how black music and performers have been essen-tialized in this way by white writers, see David Brackett, "James Brown's 'Superbad' and the Double-Voiced Utterance," in *Interpreting Popular Music* (Cambridge: Cambridge University Press, 1995), pp. 108–231. See also my discussion of sexuality, race, and music criticism at the end of chapter 5.

13. Stallybrass and White, *The Politics and Poetics of Transgression*, p. 8.

14. Moore, *Rock: The Primary Text*, p. 66.

15. Ibid., 72.

16. Ibid., 70.

17. Ibid.

18. Ibid., 71.

19. Ibid., 72.

20. David Hatch and Stephen Millward, *From Blues to Rock: An Analytical History of Pop Music* (Manchester: Manchester University Press, 1987), pp. 106–107.

21. Ed Ward, Geoffrey Stokes, and Ken Tucker, *Rock of Ages: The Rolling Stone History of Rock and Roll* (New York, 1986), pp. 484–485.

22. Neil Nehring, *Popular Music, Gender, and Postmodernism: Anger Is Energy* (London: Sage, 1997), p. 145. Nehring is referring specifically to Willfred Mellers's study of the Beatles' "Hard Day's Night," in which Mellers discusses the "plagal" "flat" feeling at the beginning of the tune, created by the use of a particular harmony, the fact that the tune is predominantly pentatonic, etc. Nehring's criticism seems to stem from a lack of understanding of the technical terms: what, for example "plagal" means or how this might feel "flat" or what "pentatonic" sounds like.

23. Richard Middleton, *Studying Popular Music*, (Buckingham, UK: Open Uni-versity Press, 1990), p. 7.

24. Lawrence Kramer, *Music as Cultural Practice 1800–1900* (Berkeley: Univer-sity of California Press, 1990). The place of musical analysis in popular music stud-ies is hotly contested. For some of the issues involved see Susan McClary and Robert Walser, "Start Making Sense! Musicology Wrestles With Rock," in *On Record: Rock, Pop and the Written Word*, ed. Simon Frith and Andrew Goodwin (New York: Rout-lege, 1990), pp 277–292. See also the introductory chapters in Walser, *Running With the Devil*, and Brackett, *Interpreting Popular Music*, and chapter 4 of Middleton, *Studying Popular Music*.

25. Some of the transcriptions are mine; where I have agreed with the transcrip-tion I have used *Led Zeppelin*, scores to accompany boxed set recordings, 2 vols. (London: Warner Chappell Music, 1990).

26. To name only one outstanding Web site: "Electric Magic" www.led-zeppe-lin.com. Last accessed May 24, 2000.

27. In her review of Robert Walser, *Running with the Devil*, Deborah Wong criti-cizes him for not speaking directly with the metal musicians about whom he was writing and for relying instead on journalistic literature in which these musicians had given interviews. Given how difficult it is to convince popular musicians—espe-cially those who have achieved a certain amount of commercial success—to speak with academics, this seems to me an unfair criticism. See Wong's review in the *Jour-nal of the American Musicological Society* 51/1 (Spring 1998), pp. 148–157.

28. Using record sales as one measure of the band's continued popularity, it can be noted that three of the band's albums—*Led Zeppelin II*, the fourth album, and *Houses of the Holy*—won the Recording Industry Association of America's (RIAA's) Diamond Award (for sales over 10 million per album in the United States alone) in March 1999. The RIAA statistics (which can be found at riaa.com) show that between December 1990 and March 1999 *Houses of the Holy* (released in 1973) sold 5 million copies in the United States, *Led Zeppelin II* (1969) 6 million copies in the same time period, and the fourth album (1971) 7 million copies between December 1990 and November 1997. For the week of May 5, 1999, *Billboard* Magazine Online (billboard-online.com) reports the fourth album with sales of 21 million, up 4 million from the November 1997 statistic given by the RIAA; it also shows *Physical Graffiti* with sales of 14 million.

29. James Clifford and George E. Marcus, eds., *Writing Culture: The Poetics and Politics of Ethnography* (Berkeley: University of California Press, 1986), p. 2. This entire collection of essays is valuable for the ways in which the authors problematize various aspects of ethnographic research.

30. For a quite different approach to fan ethnography, see Daniel Cavicchi, *Tramps Like Us: Music and Meaning Among Springsteen Fans* (New York: Oxford University Press, 1998). Cavicchi's is a landmark study of the ways in which many rock fans (not only Springsteen's) relate to the music they love and should be required reading for anyone researching rock music.

31. Bootlegs have been catalogued in Robert Godwin, *The Illustrated Collector's Guide to Led Zeppelin* (Burlington, Ontario: CG, 1997)

One Dazed and Confused

1. Performances after 1975 consisted of the solo sections of the piece only, without reference to the song itself. See later in this chapter for further discussion.

2. The version on *The Song Remains the Same*, for example, runs twenty-eight minutes.

3. For an excellent exegesis of the counterculture in Britain see Paul E. Willis, *Profane Culture* (London: Routledge, 1978).

4. Sheila Whiteley, *The Space Between the Notes: Rock and the Counterculture* (New York: Routledge, 1992), p. 4.

5. Jim DeRogatis, *Kaleidoscope Eyes: Psychedelic Rock from the '60s to the '90s* (Secaucus, NJ: Carol, 1996), p. 10.

6. Ibid., p. 9.

7. On progressive rock as gnostic see Allan F. Moore, *Rock: The Primary Text* (Milton Keynes, UK: Open University Press, 1993), pp. 100–102.

8. Stephen Davis, *Hammer of the Gods: The Led Zeppelin Saga* (New York: Ballantine, 1985), p. 49.

9. Richard Middleton, *Studying Popular Music* (Buckingham, UK: Open University Press, 1990), pp. 27–32.

10. Biographical details can be found in Ritchie Yorke, *Led Zeppelin: The Definitive Biography*, revised edition (Novato, CA: Underwood-Miller, 1993), and Davis, *Hammer of the Gods*. Neither biography is authorized; the latter is especially sensationalistic and should be read with a healthy dose of skepticism. Wherever possible, I have taken my information from journalistic interviews with members of the band or from my conversations with John Paul Jones.

11. C. Welch, "Jimmy Page: Paganini of the Seventies," *Melody Maker* 45 (February 28, 1970), p. 10.

12. M. M. Bakhtin, "Discourse in the Novel," in *The Dialogic Imagination*, ed. Michael Holquist, trans. Caryl Emerson and Michael Holquist (Austin: University of Texas Press, 1981), p. 367.

13. Theodore Adorno, "On Popular Music," in *On Record: Rock, Pop and the Written Word*, ed. Simon Frith and Andrew Goodwin (New York: Routledge, 1990), pp. 301–314.

14. Holmes's recording of the piece can be found on the bootleg recording *James Patrick Page: Session Man*, vol. 1 (1963–1967). It should be noted that Page may or may not have heard this recorded version and that it may differ from the live version he heard, although the similarities among this version, the Yardbirds' version, and Led Zeppelin's are striking.

15. Ellen Rosand, "The Descending Tetrachord: An Emblem of Lament," *Musical Quarterly* 65/3 (1979), pp. 346–359.

16. Stephen Davis describes the lyrics in these words in *Hammer of the Gods*, p. 34.

17. Yorke, *Led Zeppelin*, pp. 52–53. *Why* the audience sounds bothered Page is interesting to consider: "There was one number ["Dazed and Confused"] where there was supposed to be utter silence and the guy dubbed in the clinking of cocktail glasses and a whole club atmosphere." In Page's view, the song was intended to be consumed in reverential silence, in a formal concert setting, not a "club atmosphere." The piece, in other words, is intended for serious listening, not as background music.

18. For further analysis of these lyrics, including fan commentary, see chapter 5.

19. In fact, although Plant was given no songwriting credit for this tune on the first album, Page has recently said that the singer did write "some of the lyrics" (Matt Resnicoff, "In Through the Out Door: Jimmy Page Goes Back to Led Zeppelin," *Musician* 145 (November 1990), p. 62. Plant was not given credit originally because it would have breached his contract with Columbia Records.

20. Robert Palmer, "Led Zeppelin: The Music," in *Led Zeppelin*, vol. 2 (London: Warner Chappell Music, 1991), n.p.: "It is the custom, in blues music, for a singer to borrow verses from contemporary sources, both oral and recorded, add his own tune and/or arrangement, and call the song his own."

21. Davis, *Hammer of the Gods*, p. 57.

22. See Robert Walser's discussion of power in heavy metal music throughout his *Running with the Devil: Power, Gender and Madness in Heavy Metal Music* (Hanover, NH: Wesleyan University Press, 1993).

23. Welch "Jimmy Page," p. 10: "When I use violin bow on guitar, it's not just a gimmick as people think. It's because some great sounds come out. You can employ legitimate bowing techniques and gain new scope and depth."

24. Ibid.

25. Peter Wicke, *Rock Music: Culture, Aesthetics, and Sociology* (Cambridge: Cambridge University Press, 1990), pp. 95–99. Wicke cites the pioneering article "Welcome to Bohemia," Warwick Working Papers in Sociology (University of Warwick, Coventry, 1984), by Simon Frith and Howard Horne, with respect to this issue.

26. Wicke, *Rock Music*, p. 96.

27. Frith quoted in ibid., p. 97.

28. Willis, *Profane Culture*, p. 8.

29. An extended article on the theremin by Philip Hayward has recently appeared ("Danger! Retro-Affectivity! The Cultural Career of the Theremin," *Convergence: The Journal of Research into New Media Technologies* 3/4 [Winter 1997]), pp. 28–53. Page is given two sentences, saying that he "experimented with the instrument on-stage in 1969 and the early 1970's" (p. 42), without going into further detail. In contrast, Brian Wilson's use of the theremin in the song "Good Vibrations" (which amounts to a fairly simple melody that does not exploit the possibilities of the instrument to any great extent) is given three lengthy paragraphs (pp. 43–44).

30. Charles R. Cross, "The Song Remains the Same," in *Led Zeppelin: Heaven and Hell*, ed. Charles R. Cross and Erik Flannigan (New York: Harmony Books, 1991), p. 132.

31. See chapter 2 for a detailed discussion of these.

32. "Concert Reviews," *Variety*, review of Knebworth concert August 4, 1979 (August 22, 1979), p. 54.

33. This occurred with his making of the album *Now and Zen*, released in 1988. In interviews from this point to the present, Plant has spoken of his conscious retreat from the music of Led Zeppelin after the demise of that group and his return to it with the making of *Now and Zen*. See, for example, interviews with the singer in *Musician*, March 1988, pp. 76–82, and June 1990, pp. 45–51.

34. Stephen Rosen, "Jimmy Page," *Guitar Player* (July 1977), p. 44. For a definition of backward echo, see chapter 5, note 93.

35. Deena Weinstein, "Listener's Guide to Heavy Metal," *Heavy Metal: A Cultural Sociology* (New York: Lexington Books, 1991), p. 278.

36. As told to Charles M. Young by Plant's then-guitarist and keyboard player Phil Johnstone in Charles M. Young, "'I'm Not Such an Old Hippie': Robert Plant Stops Being Polite," *Musician* 140 (June 1990), p. 46.

37. Jancee Dunn, "Rock and Roll: Getting the Led Out," *Rolling Stone* (December 1, 1994), p. 31.

38. J. D. Considine, interview with Page, Plant, and Jones, *Rolling Stone* (September 20, 1990), p. 109.

39. Tricia Rose, *Black Noise: Rap Music and Black Culture in Contemporary America* (Hanover, NH: Wesleyan University Press, 1994), p. 89, quoted in Paul Théberge, *Any Sound You Can Imagine: Making Music Consuming Technology* (Hanover, NH: Wesleyan University Press, 1997), p. 205.

40. DeRogatis, *Kaleidoscope Eyes*, p. 12.

41. Willis, *Profane Culture*, pp. 85–86.

42. DeRogatis, *Kaleidoscope Eyes*, p. 14.

43. Wicke, *Rock Music*, p. 99.

44. Whiteley, *The Space Between the Notes*, pp. 2–3.

45. Middleton, *Studying Popular Music*, pp. 31–32.

46. Moore, *Rock: The Primary Text*, p. 98.

47. Ibid., p. 100.

48. Ibid., p. 98.

49. Ibid., pp. 98–102.

50. This is a pervasive theme in Walser's book *Running with the Devil*.

51. See Steven Rosen's interview with Page ("Jimmy Page: The Interview") in *Guitar World: Special Jimmy Page Issue* (July 1986), p. 55.

52. DeRogatis, *Kaleidoscope Eyes*, p. 13.

53. See for example *Classics off the Air*, vol. 2.

54. William Burroughs's interview with Jimmy Page ("Rock Magic: Jimmy Page, Led Zeppelin, and a Search for the Elusive Stairway to Heaven") was published in *Crawdaddy* 49(June 1975). The quotation is on page 40. The interview is reprinted in *Guitar World: Special Jimmy Page Issue* (July 1986).

55. Ibid.

56. Steve Waksman, "Every Inch of My Love: Led Zeppelin and the Problem of Cock Rock," *Journal of Popular Music Studies* 8 (1996), p. 7.

57. On the album *Live Yardbirds Featuring Jimmy Page*, recorded in 1967 and released by CBS Records in 1971, withdrawn due to an injunction from Page. Waksman connects the use of the bow to Page's "power and mystery" as a guitarist, pointing to the fantasy sequence in the film under which is heard Page's bow solo, but does not theorize the bow itself as a code for this "mystery" (Waksman, "Every Inch of My Love," pp. 7–8).

58. Willis, *Profane Culture*, p. 90.

59. DeRogatis, *Kaleidoscope Eyes*, p. 12.

60. With respect to the 1980 tour, John Paul Jones said, "We felt it the start of a new era. Punk had come along and shaken everybody up and so everybody came back sort of leaner and meaner.... The energy was coming back and we were much more streamlined" (Yorke, *Led Zeppelin*, p. 230).

61. Although the bow solo is "directly analogous to the section in Dead concerts referred to as 'space.'" Thanks to Rob Bowman for this observation.

62. Page has often used this phrase to describe Led Zeppelin's approach to making music. See, for example, Davis, *Hammer of the Gods*, p. 52. The name of the group, in fact, reflects the contrast.

63. Walser, *Running with the Devil*, p. 158.

64. Ibid., p. 157.

65. Willis, *Profane Culture*, p. 159.

66. Ibid.

67. The idea of the rock guitar solo as "transcendent" is Robert Walser's (*Running with the Devil*, p. 54); the way in which "Dazed and Confused" is structured, with its slow buildup of tension that is released in the explosion of the fast guitar solo, seems to me a particularly good example of what Walser theorizes as the transcendent guitar solo breaking out of the boundaries of the song.

68. Wicke, *Rock Music*, p. 99.

69. Televised interview with Robert Plant, November 2, 1976, on the BBC program *Old Grey Whistle Test*.

70. Televised interview with Robert Plant, January 17, 1975, on the BBC program *Old Grey Whistle Test*.

71. Mark J. Petracca, "Ramble On" (interview with Robert Plant), *Creem* 2/9 (1993), p. 39.

72. "Jimmy Page: The Interview," *Guitar World: Special Jimmy Page Issue* (July 1986), p. 52.

73. Charles M. Young, "Jimmy Page's True Will," *Musician* 117 (July 1988), pp. 74–75.

74. Roland Barthes, "The Grain of the Voice," in *Image, Music, Text*, trans. Stephen Heath (New York: Fontana Collins, 1977), pp. 179–189.

75. Ibid., p. 188.

76. Ibid., pp. 181–182.

77. Weinstein, *Heavy Metal*, p. 26.

78. Jim Miller, "Anglo-Graffiti: Hardest-Core Rock," (review of *Physical Graffiti*), *Rolling Stone* 183 (March 3, 1975), pp. 48, 51.

79. Interview with Robert Plant, September 23, 1993, on the radio program *Rockline*.

80. *Old Grey Whistle Test*, January 17, 1975.

81. Susan McClary, *Feminine Endings: Music, Gender and Sexuality* (Minneapolis: University of Minnesota Press, 1991). See especially the essay "Sexual Politics in Classical Music," pp. 53–79.

82. Walser, *Running with the Devil*, p. 108.

83. See Gilbert Rouget, *Music and Trance: A Theory of the Relations Between Music and Possession*, trans. Brunhilde Biebuyck (Chicago: University of Chicago Press, 1985), pp. 223–224.

84. For a historiography of Gregorian and Old Roman chant as masculine and feminine see Leo Treitler, "Gender and Other Dualities of Music History," in *Musicology and Difference: Gender and Sexuality in Music Scholarship*, ed. Ruth A. Solie (Berkeley: University of California Press, 1993), pp. 23–45.

85. Simon Frith and Angela McRobbie, "Rock and Sexuality," in Frith and Goodwin, *On Record*, pp. 272–292. See chapter 5 for extended discussion of this article's contents.

86. Weinstein, *Heavy Metal*, p. 25.

87. Ibid.

88. See chapter 5.

89. *Classics off the Air*, vol 2 (bootleg recording of a BBC live performance from 1971).

90. Waksman, "Every Inch of My Love," p. 15.

91. I thank Philip Todd for making this observation to me.

92. My thanks to Rob Bowman for suggesting this idea to me.

Two Stairway to Heaven

1. For the running time, see Luis Rey, *Led Zeppelin Live: An Illustrated Exploration of the Underground Tapes*, updated edition (Owen Sound, Ontario: Hot Wax Press, 1993), pp. 255–256.

2. My thanks to Michele George and George Paul, professors in the Classics Department at McMaster University, for helping me to locate these specific examples. Professor George commented that when she issued a call for help on this question to her colleagues in classics they "agreed that there are so many examples of fanfares (depending on how you define the term) throughout ancient literature that it would be a large task to find the best one." The examples given here are chosen at random. Sources are: Tacitus, *Annales*, trans. George Gilbert Ramsey (London: John Murray, 1909), p. 187; Homer, *Iliad*, trans. Richmond Lattimore (Chicago: University of Chicago Press, 1951), p. 428; and Caesar, *Commentaries on the Gallic Wars*, trans. H. J. Edwards (Cambridge, MA: Harvard University Press, 1917), p. 547.

3. These images and others that fit the model can be easily accessed in H. W. Jan-

son, *History of Art: A Survey of the Major Visual Arts from the Dawn of History to the Present Day*, 2d edition (Englewood Cliffs, NJ: Prentice-Hall, 1977).

4. Simon Frith, *Sound Effects: Youth, Leisure, and the Politics of Rock 'n' Roll* (New York: Pantheon, 1981), p. 213. Frith actually locates 1967 as the specific year. It should be pointed out that in this context Frith outlines a history of rock and roll and rock music as he perceives it to be often told and that this is not necessarily his own point of view.

5. See Christopher Williams, *The Song Remains the Same* (unpublished Ph.D. dissertation, Department of Sociology, New York University, 1995, UMI microfilm 9609252), for a critique of Frith and others who are dismissive of the powerful experiences that fans have with rock music and Led Zeppelin in particular.

6. Ibid., pp. 58–59.

7. Not everyone brought the issues of myth, mystery, and spirituality into the discussion, of course; some responses were more mundane, focusing, for example, on the poetic value of Plant's lyrics: "Plant has some beautiful imagery in his lyrics. In fact, I have a quote list of favorite lines. He captures so much in a single phrase and has such a way with words. . . . I love the imagery evoked in songs like 'Battle of Evermore,' 'Carouselambra,' 'Stairway,' 'Going to California,' 'Achilles' Last Stand,' 'All My Love,' 'Ten Years Gone,' etc. He really knows how to paint vivid pictures with his words."

8. The "dragon pants" can be seen in the film *The Song Remains the Same*.

9. For a discussion of definitions see Masaki Mori, *Epic Grandeur: Toward a Comparative Poetics of the Epic* (New York: State University of New York Press, 1997), and Alan Dundes, ed., *Sacred Narrative: Readings in the Theory of Myth* (Berkeley: University of California Press, 1984).

10. Catherine Bell, *Ritual: Perspectives and Dimensions* (New York: Oxford University Press, 1997), p. 157.

11. Paul Ricoeur, *The Symbolism of Evil*, trans. Emerson Buchanan (New York: Harper and Row, 1967), p. 5.

12. Ibid, p. 162–163.

13. Ibid., p. 167.

14. Robert Walser has made a similar point concerning the use of mythological and religious symbology in heavy metal in general: "If religion functions both to explain the world—providing models for how to live, tenets of faith, and comfort when they don't work—and to offer a sense of contact with something greater than oneself, then heavy metal surely qualifies as a religious phenomenon" (*Running with the Devil: Power, Gender and Madness in Heavy Metal Music* [Hanover, NH: Wesleyan University Press, 1993], p. 154).

15. Ricoeur, *The Symbolism of Evil*, pp. 167–168.

16. Branislav Malinowski, "The Role of Myth in Life," in Dundes, *Sacred Narrative*, p. 199.

17. Ibid., p. 201.

18. Eric Daredl, "The Mythic," in Dundes, *Sacred Narrative*, p. 231.

19. There is a school of thought that finds myth and ritual to be inextricably linked. The "myth-ritual approach" began as an attempt to locate the origin of myths in rituals, but there are also those who simply believe that myth and ritual are "parallel expressions." (See Dundes, *Sacred Narrative*, especially pp. 110–136, which includes the essay "Myth and Story" by Theodor H. Gaster, a proponent of the fun-

damental connection between myth and ritual.) Linking the two is crucial if one believes in the importance of the performance in mythology.

20. Victor Turner, *From Ritual to Theatre: The Human Seriousness of Play* (New York: Performing Arts Journal Publications, 1982), p. 84. I also use Turner's concept of the subjunctive in chapter 4 to correspond with what John Blacking calls the ability of music to create a "virtual time" distinct from actual time.

21. Ibid.

22. Ibid.

23. Mary Douglas, *Purity and Danger: An Analysis of the Concepts of Pollution and Taboo* (London: Routledge, 1966, 1993), pp. 63–64.

24. Williams, *The Song Remains the Same*, p. 81.

25. Ibid., p. 80.

26. Fred and Judy Vermorel, *Starlust: The Secret Fantasies of Fans* (London: W. H. Allen, 1985); an extract is reprinted in *On Record: Rock, Pop and the Written Word*, ed. Simon Frith and Andrew Goodwin (London: Routledge, 1990), pp. 481–490.

27. Williams, *The Song Remains the Same*, p. 83: "The origin of Led Zeppelin fandom is found in the physiologically isolated experience of listening to the music."

28. I take the point, made by one anonymous reviewer of this book, that "the largeness of the stereo space, the sonic/timbral onslaught and, in the live context, the sheer volume of 'Whole Lotta Love' could seem pretty epic/mythical in some senses." My categorization can certainly be contested here, but I think it is useful to draw a distinction between those songs that are overtly, through their lyrics, tied to epic/myth in some sense and those that are not.

29. Vladimir Propp, *Morphology of a Folk Tale*, trans. Laurence Scott (Austin: University of Texas Press, 1968, 1988), the function of the hero discussed on pp. 36–65; Mori, *Epic Grandeur*, pp. 3–46.

30. M. M. Bakhtin, "Epic and Novel," in *The Dialogic Imagination*, ed. Michael Holquist, trans. Caryl Emerson and Michael Holquist (Austin: University of Texas Press, 1981), p. 31.

31. Walser, *Running with the Devil*, pp. 158–159.

32. Edward Macan, *Rocking the Classics: English Progressive Rock and the Counterculture* (New York: Oxford University Press, 1997), p. 73.

33. From an interview with Page in *Record Mirror*, February 1970, quoted in Robert Godwin, *Led Zeppelin: The Press Reports* (Burlington, Ontario: CG, 1997), p. 96.

34. Susan McClary, *Feminine Endings*, p. 157.

35. Jim Miller, "Led Zeppelin," in *The Rolling Stone Illustrated History of Rock and Roll*, revised and updated edition (New York: Random House, 1992), p. 458.

36. Walser, *Running with the Devil*, p. 158.

37. Eero Tarasti, *Myth and Music: A Semiotic Approach to the Aesthetics of Myth in Music, Especially That of Wagner, Sibelius and Stravinsky* (The Hague: Mouton, 1979), pp. 52–54.

38. And I would argue that hearing traces of Tudor England in this and other "progressive" rock music of the 1970s, where such references are frequent, suggests a certain politics for its producers. Elsewhere I comment that "[t]he young white males making [it] were identifying with the power of a specific monarch [Henry VIII] as well as with that of the ruling class in general," claiming the power of those symbols for themselves. See Susan Fast, "Days of Future Passed: Rock, Pop and the

Yearning for the Middle Ages," in *Mittelalter-Sehnsucht? Texte des interdisziplinären Symposions zur musikalischen Mittelalterrezeption an der Universität Heidelberg, April 1998*, ed. Annette Kreutziger-Herr and Dorothea Redepenning, (Kiel: Wissenschaftsverlag Vauk, 2000), pp. 35–36.

39. Dave Lewis, *Led Zeppelin: A Celebration* (London: Omnibus Press, 1991), p. 52.

40. Ricoeur, *The Symbolism of Evil*, p. 5.

41. Lewis, *Led Zeppelin*, p. 52.

42. Ritchie Yorke, *Led Zeppelin: The Definitive Biography*, revised edition (Novato, CA : Underwood-Miller, 1993), p. 137.

43. Walser, *Running with the Devil*, p. 158.

44. My thanks to Cynthia for allowing me to identify her and quote her words.

45. Douglas, *Purity and Danger*, p. 64.

46. The juxtaposition of the dilapidated wall with the newer high rises may bring to mind the Docklands in East London after World War II, where bombed-out buildings coexisted with buildings that had survived the bombing and the new postwar construction. I thank Maureen Buja for this observation.

47. The jacket cover described here is that for the original LP; CD reissues significantly alter the imagery, many placing the image of the hermit on the back of the jewel case, the four symbols and lyrics to "Stairway" on the inside of the single folded sheet insert. At least one reissue, Atlantic A2-19129, does not include the four symbols. Since CD is the medium through which the majority of listeners who come to Led Zeppelin now will consume the music, the original symbology of the album artwork is perhaps less significant to the understanding of this album, although historically it is crucial.

48. Bell, *Ritual*, p. 157.

49. The entire saying is: "Do what thou wilt shall be the whole of the law." It comes from Crowley's *Liber al vel Legis (the Book of the Law)*, chapter 1, verse 40, reprinted in Scott Michaelsen, ed., *Portable Darkness: An Aleister Crowley Reader* (New York: Harmony Books, 1989), p. 209.

50. Robert Godwin makes a similar observation in the preface to his book *Led Zeppelin: The Press Reports*, for which he combed through the majority of journalistic writings on the band: "In many histories written about Led Zeppelin and indeed in many interviews with the band there are an abundance of references to how cruelly they were treated by the media. There are in fact so many references to this unjust bias that it has become a truism. However, when you start to actually examine the evidence, as presented in this book, you will find that for the most part the press were quite generous" (p. 10).

51. *Rolling Stone*'s reviews of Led Zeppelin albums are as follows: John Mendelssohn, review of *Led Zeppelin* (March 15, 1969), p. 28, and review of *Led Zeppelin II* (December 13, 1969), p. 48; review of *Led Zeppelin III* (November 26, 1970), p. 34; Lenny Kaye, review of the fourth album (December 23, 1971), pp. 62–63; Gordon Fletcher, "Today's 'Safe' Led Zeppelin, sans Blues: A Limp Blimp," review of *Houses of the Holy* (June 7, 1973), p. 54; Jim Miller, "Anglo-Graffiti: Hardest-Core Rock," review of *Physical Graffiti* (March 3, 1975), pp. 48, 51; Stephen Davis, review of *Presence* (May 20, 1976), p. 64; Charles M. Young, "Sad Zep," review of *In Through the Out Door* (October 18, 1979), pp. 72, 79; and Kurt Loder, "Led Zep Goes Out with Class," review of *Coda* (January 20, 1983), pp. 47–48.

52. C. Crowe, "The Durable Led Zeppelin: A Conversation with Jimmy Page and Robert Plant," *Rolling Stone* (March 13, 1975), p. 32.

53. Ibid.

54. Interview with Dave Schulps given in *Trouser Press*, 1977, reprinted as "The Crunge: Jimmy Page Gives a History Lesson," in *Led Zeppelin: Heaven and Hell*, ed. Charles R. Cross and Erik Flannigan (New York: Harmony Books, 1991), p. 62.

55. Paul Green, "Led Zep: No. 1 Album but Delays Touring," *Billboard* (September 15, 1979), p. 30.

56. J. D. Considine, interview with Page, Plant, and Jones, *Rolling Stone* (September 20, 1990), p. 59.

57. The idea of linking McLuhan's theory of hot and cold media to Led Zeppelin belongs to Simon Wood (see later). For McLuhan's ideas on hot and cold media see Marshall McLuhan, *Understanding Media* (New York: McGraw-Hill, 1964).

58. Simon Wood, "Are They Going to Turn That Down? Led Zeppelin, *Rolling Stone*, and the Thoughts of Marshall McLuhan," unpublished paper, 1997.

59. It is, obviously, a fairly common occurrence for a singer or someone else in a band to point attention to a soloist in this way. I would argue that in the context of a rock concert, in which the performers are clearly known to the audience, the point of this exercise is the same as I have indicated earlier for Led Zeppelin, i.e., to point to the wonder or "genius" of the musician.

60. For one such picture from an interview in 1969 see Cross and Flannigan, *Led Zeppelin: Heaven and Hell*, p. 52.

61. Crowe, "The Durable Led Zeppelin," p. 34.

62. Stephen Davis, *Hammer of the Gods: The Led Zeppelin Saga* (New York: Ballantine, 1985), p. 10.

63. Crowe, "The Durable Led Zeppelin," p. 37.

64. I can confirm this since I own bootleg recordings of these shows; Rey reports that Page also introduced "Black Dog" at several other shows from 1980 and mentions how rare this is twice: "Page ... even speaks on stage!" and, of the Dortmund, Germany, concert: "Page salutes the audience in German introducing 'Black Dog.' Probably the first time he has ever spoken 'seriously' in a concert!" (Rey, *Led Zeppelin Live*, pp. 258–259).

65. Steve Gett, "Led Zeppelin über Alles," *Melody Maker* (July 12, 1980), p. 48.

66. Davis, *Hammer of the Gods*, p. 300.

67. Schulps, "The Crunge," p. 66.

68. Jim DeRogatis makes a similar comment about Hendrix: "These songs didn't exist just so Hendrix could solo over them. On all of these tracks, Hendrix is more interested in creating moods with the sound of his guitar than impressing people with the notes that he's playing." (*Kaleidoscope Eyes: Psychedelic Rock from the '60s to the '90s* [Secaucus, NJ: Carol, 1996], p. 95).

69. Crowe, "The Durable Led Zeppelin," p. 35.

70. Lewis, *Led Zeppelin: A Celebration*, p. 46.

71. Charles R. Cross, "Shadows Taller than Our Souls," in Cross and Flannigan, *Led Zeppelin: Heaven and Hell*, p. 27.

72. Chris Welch, "Led Zeppelin at Carnegie Hall," *Melody Maker* 44 (October 26, 1969), p. 20.

73. *Led Zeppelin: Remasters*, interview disk (Atlantic 82371-2, October 1990):

"The early Boston Tea Party concerts . . . the longest concert we ever did, we played 4 and a quarter hours, I think."

74. "Concert Reviews," *Variety* (August 1, 1973), p. 271.

75. Douglas, *Purity and Danger*, p. 54.

76. Ibid.

77. Ibid., p. 96.

78. Ibid. The flexibility of the improvisations in Led Zeppelin has been somewhat exaggerated: listening to bootleg recordings, one can hear how certain improvisations crystallized into a set form—the bow solo in "Dazed and Confused" is a good example (see chapter 1), the medley in "Whole Lotta Love" another (see chapter 5). Further, pieces such as "Achilles Last Stand," "Stairway," and "Kashmir" did not change that much in performance but followed the studio versions, including guitar solos, quite closely. I asked Jones about this and he concurred: "You are right, songs that were composed and arranged 'through' were not opened up [to improvisation]. Blues-based songs were considered more Robert's domain, and wherever they actually stopped he could go into whatever he felt like. When this worked well it would give us the chance to stretch a bit." The integrity of a musical text such as "Stairway" is important because, as I have tried to demonstrate through the preceding analysis, the power and effectiveness of this song lie partly in its "order" or structure, which would have been compromised had it been opened up to improvisation.

79. Neil V. Rosenberg, "Introduction," in *Transforming Tradition: Folk Music Revivals Examined*, ed. Neil V. Rosenberg (Urbana: University of Illinois Press, 1993), p. 5.

80. See Rosenberg, "Introduction," for further explications of these characteristics of "authenticity" in the folk music revivals of the twentieth century.

81. See Rey, *Led Zeppelin Live*, p. 63, for a complete track listing for this concert.

82. The most extensive acoustic sets occurred during the 1972 and 1977 tours (an acoustic set was also played at the Earl's Court gigs in 1975 but not on the U.S. tour of that same year). A good representative bootleg of the acoustic set from 1972 is Koseinenkin Kaikan (festival hall), Osaka, Japan, September 29, 1972 ("That's the Way," "Going to California," "Tangerine," "Friends," "What Is and What Should Never Be") and *Listen to This Eddie*, Los Angeles Forum, June 21, 1977 ("Battle of Evermore," "Going to California," "Black Country Woman," "Bron-Yr-Aur Stomp," "White Summer").

Three Over the Hills and Far Away

1. *Led Zeppelin: Remasters*, interview disk (Atlantic 82371-2, October 1990).

2. Quoted in Robert Palmer, "Led Zeppelin: The Music," liner notes to *Led Zeppelin*, Four-CD boxed set (Atlantic 82144-2, October 1990).

3. Ibid.

4. The term "cultural capital" belongs to Pierre Bourdieu. See Pierre Bourdieu, *The Field of Cultural Production*, ed. Randal Johnson (New York: Columbia University Press, 1993).

5. Edward W. Said, *Orientalism* (London: Routledge, 1979), p. 121.

6. Alan DiPerna, "Steady Rolling Man" (interview with John Paul Jones), *Guitar World: Special Led Zeppelin Issue* (January 1991), p. 38.

7. Comments made on ABC TV's *Good Morning America*, October 12, 1994.

8. Cited in Robert Walser, *Running with the Devil: Power, Gender and Madness in Heavy Metal Music* (Hanover, NH: Wesleyan University Press, 1993), p. 153.

9. Ibid., p. 154.

10. For an overview of the use of Indian music in rock of the British Invasion groups see Jonathan Bellman, "Indian Resonances in the British Invasion, 1965–1968," in *The Exotic in Western Music*, ed. Jonathan Bellman (Boston: Northeastern University Press, 1998), pp. 292–306.

11. Timothy D. Taylor, *Global Pop: World Musics, World Markets* (New York: Routledge, 1997), p. 71.

12. Chris Welch, "The Zeppelin Remains," *Melody Maker* (November 5, 1977), p. 9.

13. David Fricke, "Robert Plant" (the *Rolling Stone* interview), *Rolling Stone* (March 24, 1988), p. 64. See also J. D. Considine, "Robert Plant: Life in a Lighter Zeppelin," *Musician* (December 1983), p. 50.

14. The *taqsim* is a slow introductory section to a piece used in some forms of Arabic music. The objective is to explore the mode that will be used in the piece. Page's introduction is much shorter than these sections normally are, but he is clearly following the same principle.

15. J. D. Considine, interview with Page, Plant, and Jones, *Rolling Stone* 587 (September 20, 1990), p. 60. However, John Paul Jones told me that "there were no plans discussed during Led Zeppelin to record with anyone else or tour the Far East," making it clear that Page's desire to do so did not move much beyond these musings.

16. Cameron Crowe, "The Durable Led Zeppelin: A Conversation with Jimmy Page and Robert Plant," *Rolling Stone* (March 13, 1975), p. 35.

17. Palmer, "Led Zeppelin: The Music," n.p.

18. Robert Plant interview in *Circus* magazine, 1976; quoted in Robert Godwin, *Led Zeppelin: The Press Reports* (Burlington, Ontario: CG, 1997), p. 333.

19. Palmer, "Led Zeppelin: The Music," n.p.

20. Paul E. Willis, *Profane Culture* (London: Routledge, 1978), p. 93.

21. Ibid.

22. Ray Coleman, "Zeppelin over America," *Melody Maker* (June 25, 1977), p. 35.

23. Reported by Stephen Davis in Stephen Davis, *Hammer of the Gods: The Led Zeppelin Saga (New York: Ballantine, 1985)*, p. 214.

24. He has made this comment often; one interview in which it appears in on *Led Zeppelin: Remasters*, interview disk.

25. Interestingly, Plant's mythic idea of Kashmir as remote, exotic, and spiritual is shattered for me as I write this chapter in mid-1999, with images of the Indian and Pakistani armies fighting over the territory coming across the television on a daily basis.

26. Page makes these comments in Matt Resnicoff, "In Through the Out Door: Jimmy Page Goes Back to Led Zeppelin," *Musician* (November 1990), p. 50.

27. See Habib Hassan Touma, *The Music of the Arabs*, trans. Laurie Schwartz (Portland, OR: Amadeus, 1996), p. 34.

28. Ralph P. Locke, "Constructing the Oriental 'Other': Saint-Saëns's *Samson et Dalila*," *Cambridge Opera Journal* 3/3 (1991), p. 268.

29. Allan F. Moore comments that Bonham "frequently leaves the third downbeat [*sic*] of every four empty" in this song, but this is not the case. I assume Moore is referring to the empty third beat in the B section. See Allan F. Moore, *Rock: The Primary Text* (Milton Keynes, UK: Open University Press, 1993), p. 71.

30. Palmer, "Led Zeppelin: The Music," n.p.

31. Gerry Farrell, *Indian Music and the West* (Oxford: Oxford Clarendon Press, 1997), p. 173.

32. Ibid., pp. 180–188.

33. Ibid., p. 188.

34. Ellie M. Hisama, "Post-colonialism on the Make: The Music of John Mellencamp, David Bowie and John Zorn," *Popular Music* 12/2 (1993), p. 94.

35. Palmer, "Led Zeppelin: The Music," n.p.

36. Taylor, *Global Pop*, pp. 41–52.

37. Farrell, *Indian Music and the West*, p. 184.

38. Said, *Orientalism*, p. 71.

39. Jonathan Bellman, "Introduction," in *The Exotic in Western Music*, ed. Johnathan Bellman (Boston: Northeastern University Press, 1998), pp. xii–xiii.

40. Walser, *Running with the Devil*, p. 154.

41. Willis, *Profane Culture*, p. 143.

42. Interview on ABC TV's *Good Morning America*, October 12, 1994.

43. For comments on Simon's *Graceland* see Louise Meintjes, "Paul Simon's *Graceland*, South Africa, and the Mediation of Musical Meaning," *Ethnomusicology* (Winter 1990), pp. 37–73, as well as Steven Feld, "Notes on 'World Beat,'" in Music *Grooves*, ed. Charles Keil and Steven Feld (Chicago: University of Chicago Press, 1994), pp. 238–246, and Charles Hamm, "Graceland Revisited," in *Putting Popular Music in Its Place* (Cambridge: Cambridge University Press, 1995), pp. 336–343. For Peter Gabriel, see Taylor, *Global Pop*, pp. 41–52. All these authors explore the politics of the collaborations.

44. George Lipsitz, *Dangerous Crossroads: Popular Music, Postmodernism and the Poetics of Place* (London: Verso, 1994), pp. 4–5.

45. Taylor, *Global Pop*, pp. 41–52.

46. Said, *Orientalism*, p. 158.

47. David Cavanagh, "The Rovers Return," *Q Magazine* (August 1995), p. 86.

48. My thanks to Ellen Koskoff for pointing this out to me.

49. Feld, "Notes on 'World Beat,'" p. 238.

50. Baz Kershaw, *The Radical in Performance: Between Brecht and Baudrillard* (New York: Routledge, 1999). Thanks to Catherine Graham for pointing me to this source.

51. Ibid, pp. 145–146.

52. The collection of essays entitled *Western Music and Its Others: Difference, Representation, and Appropriation in Music*, ed. Georgina Brown and David Hesmondhalgh (Berkeley: University of California Press, 2000), continues this kind of work, pioneered by such musicologists as Ralph Locke. Unfortunately the book was published too late for me to take into account here.

Four The Wanton Song

1. In the studio version this line of text is "let my love come running in."

2. "Fictional Body" is theater anthropologist Eugenio Barba's term, which he uses in conjunction with his notion of the extradaily use of the body in theater performance. These terms will be further discussed later.

3. Neil Nehring, *Popular Music, Gender, and Postmodernism: Anger Is Energy* (London: Sage, 1997), pp. 128–149.

4. John Blacking, ed., *How Musical Is Man?* (London: Faber and Faber, 1976), p. 111.

5. David Lidov, "Mind and Body in Music," *Semiotica* 66 (1987), p. 82.

6. Richard Middleton, *Studying Popular Music* (Buckingham, UK: Open University Press, 1990), p. 177.

7. Ibid.

8. In Roy Shuker's *Key Concepts in Popular Music* (London: Routledge, 1998), for example, riff is defined as "a short melodic or rhythmic pattern repeated over and over while changes take place in the music along with it" (pp. 24–25). This is a less than accurate definition of riff itself, which at least consists of both rhythmic and melodic shape, and it is a very narrow definition of how riffs work within songs.

9. See the detailed analyses of how various riffs work in Zeppelin's songs later.

10. The octave leap plays a significant role in many songs, among them "Whole Lotta Love," "Dazed and Confused" "Ramble On," "Over the Hills and Far Away," "Trampled Underfoot" (in clavinet, left hand), "Moby Dick," "The Crunge," and "Bring It On Home." In "The Ocean" there is a fall of a sixth, but the guitar continues to slide downward to an undifferentiated pitch and so the feel of a larger leap downward exists. In "Communication Breakdown" there is an upward leap of a seventh and in "Heartbreaker" there is the repeated large leap downward of a sixth. These riffs can be contrasted with the much more limited use of stepwise motion, such as in "Custard Pie," which is particularly confined in its melodic movement, or even "Kashmir," which is defined by the rising chromatic movement through a fourth (but which then still includes a fall of a fourth back down).

11. There is another pattern used with some frequency that does not include the octave leap but rather a descending gesture: the descending minor tetrachord of "Babe I'm Gonna Leave You" the standard harmonic pattern I–vi–V–IV used in "D'yer Maker" and the pattern that includes the descent of a step followed by a larger drop of either a third (as in "Misty Mountain Hop") or a fourth (as in "Your Time Is Gonna Come" and "All My Love"). In these last three examples there is also an important harmonic element to take into consideration. In "Your Time Is Gonna Come," for example, the riff descends to the tonic, while in "Misty Mountain Hop" it descends from the tonic to the dominant. In the former case, then, the descent moves toward harmonic stability; in the latter, away from it.

12. I have used the notated version of the riff from the Warner scores but checked with Jones to make sure that the way in which it had been notated was reasonably accurate. He agreed that it was.

13. Middleton, *Studying Popular Music*, p. 172.

14. For a succinct explanation of some of the basic principles of Lacanian psychoanalysis and a very interesting application to popular music see David Schwarz, *Listening Subjects: Music, Psychoanalysis, Culture* (Durham: Duke University Press, 1997), especially the chapter "Scatting, the Acoustic Mirror, and the Real in the Beatles' 'I Want You (She's So Heavy).'"

15. For further discussion of this point see Susan McClary and Robert Walser, "Theorizing the Body in African-American Music," *Black Music Research Journal* 14/1 (Spring 1994), pp. 75–84.

16. Jacques Attali, *Noise: The Political Economy of Music* (Minneapolis: University of Minnesota Press, 1985), p. 9.

17. John Shepherd and Peter Wicke, *Music and Cultural Theory* (Cambridge: Polity Press, 1997), p. 126.

18. For a fascinating case study of how the envelopment of the body in the volume and distortion of the MC5's music was political (indeed, revolutionary) in its intent, see Steve Waksman, "Kick Out the Jams: The MC5 and the Politics of Noise," in *Mapping the Beat: Popular Music and Contemporary Theory*, ed. Thomas Swiss, John Sloop, and Andrew Harman (Oxford: Blackwell, 1998), pp. 47–75.

19. Blacking, *How Musical Is Man?* p. 51.

20. Claude Lévi-Strauss, *The Raw and the Cooked*, trans. John and Doreen Weightman (New York: Harper and Row, 1969), pp. 15–16.

21. Victor Turner, *From Ritual to Theatre: The Human Seriousness of Play* (New York: Performing Arts Journal Publications, 1982), pp. 82–83.

22. Blacking, *How Musical Is Man?* pp. 51–52.

23. John Blacking, ed., *The Anthropology of the Body* (London: Academic Press, 1977), p. 6.

24. Ibid. Merleau-Ponty (see later) posits that a similar phenomenon occurs in spoken language (thus agreeing with some of what Lévi-Strauss says concerning hearing myth):

There is thus, either in the man who listens or reads, or in the one who speaks or writes, a thought in speech, the existence of which is unsuspected by intellectualism. To realize this, we must turn back to the phenomenon of speech and reconsider ordinary descriptions which immobilize thought and speech. . . . We must recognize first of all that thought, in the speaking subject, is not a representation, that is, that it does not expressly posit objects or relations. The orator does not think before speaking, nor even while speaking; his speech is his thought. In the same way the listener does not form concepts on the basis of signs. . . . [W]hen a text is read to us, provided it is read with expression, we have no thought marginal to the text itself, for the words fully occupy our mind . . . we are possessed by it. The end of the speech or text will be the lifting of a spell. (Maurice Merleau-Ponty, "The Body as Expression and Speech," chapter 4 of *The Phenomenology of Perception*, reprinted in *The Essential Writings of Merleau-Ponty*, ed. Aiden L. Fisher [New York: Harcourt, Brace and World, 1969], pp. 191–192).

But while I find much about what Merleau-Ponty has to say about speech and the body very useful and important, I cannot follow him on this last point: we very often do let our thoughts wander during the course of a conversation; we think about how we might respond to what the speaker is saying or, as the speaker, think about what we will say next or how we might turn the conversation in a new direction. It is possible to be transfixed by someone's speech and therefore put under a spell–or taken out of everyday time–by it, but how often does this occur?

25. Michel Serres, as quotes in Attali, *Noise*, p. 9.

26. Ibid.

27. Lévi-Strauss, *The Raw and the Cooked*, p. 16.

28. Attali, *Noise*, p. 9.

29. Merleau-Ponty, "The Body as Expression and Speech," p. 194.

30. Ibid., p. 196.

31. Ibid., p. 197.

32. Ibid., p. 196.

33. Ibid., p. 198.

34. Ibid., p. 211.

35. M. M. Bakhtin, "Discourse and the Novel," in *The Dialogic Imagination*, ed. Michael Holquist, trans. Caryl Emerson and Michael Holquist (Austin: University of Texas Press, 1981), pp. 259–422.

36. This is Eugenio Barba's term, used by him to describe the creation of a "fictional body" in theater; I use it in this way later, but think it is also useful to employ it here as a way of thinking about how music takes us out of everyday time.

37. Tricia Rose, *Black Noise: Rap Music and Black Culture in Contemporary America* (Hanover, NH: Wesleyan University Press, 1994), p. 65.

38. Middleton, *Studying Popular Music*, p. 212.

39. Ibid., p. 205.

40. Ibid., p. 200.

41. Ibid., p. 201.

42. Mark Johnson, *The Body in the Mind: The Bodily Basis of Meaning, Imagination, and Reason* (Chicago: University of Chicago Press, 1987), p. 29.

43. Ibid., p. 34.

44. Ibid.

45. Ibid., p. 82.

46. Ibid., p. 83.

47. Merleau-Ponty, "The Body as Expression and Speech," p. 200.

48. Robert Walser, "The Body in the Music: Epistemology and Musical Semiotics," *College Music Symposium* 31 (1991), pp. 117–126.

49. Ibid., p. 123.

50. Johnson, *The Body in the Mind*, p. 74.

51. Ibid., p. 75.

52. Ibid., p. 83.

53. Ibid., p. 80.

54. Ibid., p. 124.

55. On the concepts of over- and undercoding in popular music see Middleton, *Studying Popular Music*, p. 173.

56. Johnson, *The Body in the Mind*, p. 120.

57. Ibid., p. 119.

58. Ibid., p. 120.

59. Ibid., p. 119.

60. Ibid., p. 117.

61. Ibid.

62. Lidov, "Mind and Body in Music," p. 85.

63. I had initially thought of composing a chart of riff-based songs that indicated how the riff was used in each, but the use of riffs proved to be much too complex and subtle for this exercise to be of much value.

64. In the case of "Immigrant Song" most of the rhythmic quality of the riff is maintained at the beginning of each verse through the drums; the riff is only, therefore, suspended by guitar and bass.

65. Robert Walser comments that many metal songs combine acoustic and electric sections, which he calls the sensitive and the aggressive, without reconciling these elements, but "Babe I'm Gonna Leave You" is one instance in which these sections are musically reconciled. In this song, the acoustic and electric sections both use the same riff (*Running with the Devil: Power, Gender and Madness in Heavy Metal Music* [Middletown: Wesleyan University Press, 1993]), p. 158.

66. Interview with Dave Schulps, given in *Trouser Press*, 1977, reprinted as "The Crunge: Jimmy Page Gives a History Lesson," in *Led Zeppelin: Heaven and Hell*, ed. Charles R. Cross and Erik Flannigan (New York: Harmony Books, 1991), p. 67. For details on Plant's car accident and how it impacted the recording of *Presence*, see Ritchie York, *Led Zeppelin: The Definitive Biography*, revised edition (Novato, CA: Underwood-Miller, 1993), pp. 185–190.

67. Richard Leppert, *The Sight of Sound: Music, Representation and the History of the Body* (Berkeley: University of California Press, 1993), p. xxii.

68. Ibid., p. xxi.

69. Ibid.

70. David McNeil, *Hand and Mind: What Gestures Reveal About Thought* (Chicago: University of Chicago Press, 1992), p. 1.

71. Blacking, *How Musical Is Man?* p. 111. For a fascinating account of the physicality of musical production from the point of view of a performer, in this case a cellist engaged in performing a sonata by the eighteenth-century composer Luigi Boccherini, see Elizabeth Le Guin, "Cello and Bow Thinking: Boccherini's Cello Sonata in E♭ Major, 'Fuori Catalogo,'" *Echo: A Music-Centered Journal* 1/1 (Fall 1999), Http://www.humnet.ucla.edu/echo/Volume1-Issue1/leguin/leguin-article.html. Leguin discusses the physical gestures required in order to produce particular passages in the sonata and the social implications of these gestures in much the same way in which I discuss some of Page's physical gestures in performance later.

72. Merleau-Ponty, "The Body as Expression and Speech," p. 191.

73. This idea is developed in Richard Leppert's conference paper "Desiring Difference: Virtuosic Display and Audience Subjectivity." The paper was read at the 1997 meeting of the North American Society for the Study of Romanticism, held at McMaster University. A much-revised published version appears as "Cultural Contradiction, Idolatry, and the Piano Virtuoso: Franz Liszt" in *Piano Roles*, ed. James Parakilas (New Haven: Yale University Press, 1999), pp. 252–281. My thanks to Professor Leppert for sharing a copy of the unpublished paper with me.

74. Personal conversation with Catherine Graham.

75. Eugenio Barba, *The Paper Canoe: A Guide to Theatre Anthropology*, trans. Richard Fowler (New York: Routledge, 1995), p. 9.

76. Ibid., p. 16.

77. Ibid., p. 9.

78. Ray Coleman, "Zeppelin over America," *Melody Maker* (June 25, 1977), p. 35.

79. Ibid.

80. I thank Catherine Graham for making this point to me.

81. Leppert, "Desiring Difference," p. 9.

82. Ray L. Birdwhistell, *Kinesics in Context: Essays on Body Motion Communication* (Philadelphia: University of Pennsylvania Press, 1970), p. 80.

83. The quotation comes from Robert Schumann, who is referring to watching Franz Liszt in performance (quoted in Leppert, "Desiring Difference," p. 6).

84. Leppert, "Desiring Difference," p. 11.

85. McNeil, *Hand and Mind*, p. 76.

86. Ibid., p. 2.

87. Ibid., p. 183.

88. Ibid., pp. 183–217.

89. Ibid., p. 184.

90. Leppert, "Desiring Difference," p. 9.

91. Ibid., p. 14.

92. Ibid., p. 12. Emphasis mine.

93. Ibid., p. 4.

94. Ibid., p. 8.

95. Ibid.

96. These questions were posed to me by Catherine Graham.

Five Whole Lotta Love

1. Robert Walser, *Running with the Devil: Power, Gender and Madness in Heavy Metal Music* (Hanover, NH: Wesleyan University Press, 1993), p. 23.

2. Elspeth Probyn, *Sexing the Self: Gendered Positions in Cultural Studies* (New York: Routledge, 1993), p. 2.

3. Barbara Ehrenreich, Elizabeth Hess, and Gloria Jacobs, *Re-making Love: The Feminization of Sex* (New York: Anchor/Doubleday, 1986).

4. Ibid., p. 33.

5. Ibid., p. 32.

6. Ibid., p. 34.

7. Ibid., p. 27.

8. Simon Frith and Angela McRobbie, "Rock and Sexuality," in *On Record: Rock, Pop and the Written Word*, ed. Simon Frith and Andrew Goodwin (New York: Routledge, 1990), p. 376.

9. Ibid., p. 375.

10. Ibid., p. 372.

11. Simon Frith, *Sound Effects: Youth, Leisure, and the Politics of Rock 'n' Roll* (New York: Pantheon, 1981), p. 227.

12. Frith and McRobbie, "Rock and Sexuality," p. 372.

13. Ibid., p. 375.

14. See Jennifer Taylor and Dave Laing, "Disco-Pleasure-Discourse," *Screen Education* 31 (1979), pp. 43–48; Keith Negus, *Popular Music in Theory: An Introduction* (Middletown: Wesleyan University Press, 1996), pp. 124–125; Richard Middleton, *Studying Popular Music* (Buckingham, UK: Open University Press, 1990), pp. 259–260; and Simon Frith, "Afterthoughts," in Frith and Goodwin, *On Record*, pp. 419–424 (originally published in *New Statesman*, August 23, 1985).

15. Taylor and Laing, "Disco-Pleasures-Discourse," p. 45.

16. Frith, "Afterthoughts," p. 420.

17. Ibid., p. 422.

18. Deena Weinstein, *Heavy Metal: A Cultural Sociology* (New York: Lexington, 1991), p. 102.

19. Ibid., p. 36.

20. John Shepherd, "Music and Male Hegemony," in *Music as Social Text* (Cam-

bridge: Polity Press, 1991), pp. 152–173, first published in *Music and Society: The Politics of Composition, Performance and Reception*, ed. Susan McClary and Richard Leppert (Cambridge: Cambridge University Press, 1987), pp. 157–172.

21. John Savage, "The Enemy Within: Sex, Rock and Identity," in *Facing the Music: A Pantheon Guide to Popular Culture*, ed. Simon Frith (New York: Pantheon, 1988), p. 143.

22. Will Straw, "Sizing Up Record Collections: Gender and Connoisseurship in Rock Music Culture," in *Sexing the Groove: Popular Music and Gender*, ed. Sheila Whiteley (London: Routledge, 1997), pp. 3–16.

23. Norma Coates, "(R)evolution Now: Rock and the Political Potential of Gender," in Whiteley, *Sexing the Groove*, p. 50.

24. Ibid., pp. 52–53. I have recently been in conversation with Norma Coates and, to be fair, wish to report that her views on this issue have mellowed since her article was published.

25. In the mid-1980s, Iain Chambers described "progressive music," under which category he placed Led Zeppelin, as participating in a "particular mode of male romanticism," which "acknowledged women (chicks) as so many signposts towards a barely disguised misogyny" *Urban Rhythms: Pop Music and Pop Culture* [Basingstoke, Hampshire: Macmillan, 1985], pp. 122–123). Theodore Gracyk in his book *Rhythm and Noise* reflects that "[r]ock is often celebrated as a vehicle of sexual liberation. A closer look reveals an infestation of sexism. Most rock reinforces the most repressive gender roles" (Durham: Duke University Press, 1996, p. 210). Rock journalist Charles M. Young has characterized Led Zeppelin's music as having "a heavy metal macho style" and further discusses the band's "celebration of male sexuality" in terms of its effect on those who are struggling under the oppression of the dominant culture: "They made men feel proud of being men, a subversive and wondrous discovery for high school students who have been castrated by the educational process." In an interesting, if unusual, connection, Young relates the "sexism" of Zeppelin's music to their wealth (and by extension class): "Rich people can easily isolate themselves, don't have to deal with any idea they choose to avoid, and attract certain personality types to which it is easy to feel superior" ("Jimmy Page's True Will," *Musician* [July 1988], p. 77). Or, as one journalist neatly wrapped it up in 1995, "Led Zeppelin's music is young men's music—and forever will be" (David Cavanagh, "The Rovers Return," *Q Magazine* [August 1995], p. 85).

26. Simon Reynolds and Joy Press, *The Sex Revolts: Gender, Rebellion and Rock 'n' Roll* (Cambridge, MA: Harvard University Press, 1995).

27. Robert Walser, review of *The Sex Revolts: Gender, Rebellion and Rock 'n' Roll*, *Music Library Association Notes* 53/3 (March 1997), p. 776. As of early 1999, *Notes* is the only academic music journal to have published a review of the book. Walser acknowledges that the authors' treatment of masculinity in rock music often falls short of the mark, calling it reductive and essentialist (p. 777).

28. Reynolds and Press, *The Sex Revolts*, p. 24.

29. Ibid., p. 96.

30. Ibid., pp. 117, 267.

31. Ibid., p. 96.

32. Stephen Davis, *Hammer of the Gods: The Led Zeppelin Saga* (New York: Ballantine, 1985), pp. 3–9.

33. Reynolds and Press, *The Sex Revolts*, p. 96.

34. Ibid., p. 24.

35. Ibid., p. 19.

36. Walser also points to the misplaced emphasis given to Cave in his review of *The Sex Revolts*, p. 777.

37. Sue Wise, "Sexing Elvis," in Frith and Goodwin, *On Record*, pp. 390–398.

38. Steve Waksman, "Every Inch of My Love: Led Zeppelin and the Problem of Cock Rock," *Journal of Popular Music Studies* 8 (1996), p. 18.

39. Ibid.

40. Ibid., pp. 18–19.

41. Waksman cites the well-known incident that involved *Life* magazine journalist Ellen Sander, who was allegedly attacked by members of the band and their entourage while she was traveling with them in 1969. She mentions John Bonham in her account but names no one else; her clothes were torn, but she was not otherwise physically harmed. This kind of behavior is unspeakable, of course, but Waksman's allegations that "such behavior was effectively normalized in the context of 1970s rock" and "[r]ock stars of Zeppelin's stature were expected to play dirty . . . even when the stakes involved something on the order of rape" (p. 17) are not supported by further evidence, which is surely required if one is going to level such serious charges. As I mentioned in the introduction to this book, since the publication of Stephen Davis's biography, which was largely compiled from accounts offered by Zeppelin's road manager, Richard Cole (band members did not cooperate with Davis), and Cole's own account in Richard Cole, with Richard Trubo, *Stairway to Heaven: Led Zeppelin Uncensored* (New York: Harper Collins, 1992), the question of who was responsible for the antics that took place during Zeppelin tours is no longer very clear. Cole himself claims responsibility for instigating and participating in many of them.

42. Ibid., p. 19.

43. Walser, *Running with the Devil*, p. 115.

44. Ibid., pp. 115–116.

45. Ibid., pp. 128–129.

46. Ibid., pp. 130–131.

47. Judith Butler, *Gender Trouble: Feminism and the Subversion of Identity* (London: Routledge, 1990), p. 116.

48. Ehrenreich, Hess, and Jacobs, *Re-making Love*, p. 36.

49. Davis, *Hammer of the Gods*, p. 70.

50. The issue of comprehensibility of rock music lyrics and the tendency of listeners to hear some but ignore others has been broached by Greil Marcus; his point of view is discussed by Neil Nehring, together with that author's own wonderfully humorous and informative account of his experiences, in Neil Nehring, *Popular Music, Gender, and Postmodernism: Anger Is Energy* (London: Sage, 1997), pp. 141–143.

51. Butler, *Gender Trouble*, p. 136.

52. Guitarist Vivian Campbell said of Page, "[A]nyone who's serious about playing guitar doesn't play as low as Page does" Joe Lalaina, "Vivian Campbell: The Quintessential Guitar Hero" (*Guitar World: Special Jimmy Page Issue* [July 1986], p. 72).

53. Weinstein, *Heavy Metal*, p. 102.

54. Suzanne Moore, "Here's Looking at You, Kid," in *The Female Gaze: Women as Viewers of Popular Culture*, ed. Lorraine Gamman and Margaret Marshment (London: Women's Press, 1988), p. 45.

55. See, for example, Frith and McRobbie, "Rock and Sexuality," p. 375; and Walser, *Running with the Devil*, p. 132.

56. Laura Mulvey, "Visual Pleasure and Narrative Cinema," in *Visual and Other Pleasures* (Bloomington: Indiana University Press, 1989), pp. 14–26.

57. Gamman and Marshment, *The Female Gaze*.

58. Moritz Gottlieb Saphir, writing about the nineteenth-century virtuoso pianist Franz Liszt in performance, quoted in Richard Leppert, "Desiring Difference: Virtuosic Display and Audience Subjectivity," paper read at the 1997 meeting of the North American Society for the Study of Romanticism held at McMaster University, published as "Cultural Contradiction, Idolatry, and the Piano Virtuoso: Franz Liszt," in *Piano Roles*, ed. James Parakilas (New Haven: Yale University Press, 1999), pp. 252–281. My thanks to Professor Leppert for providing me with a copy of his paper.

59. Butler, *Gender Trouble*, p. 123.

60. Mulvey, "Visual Pleasure," p. 19.

61. Ibid.

62. Savage, "The Enemy Within," pp. 150, 156.

63. Mulvey, "Visual Pleasure," p. 20.

64. Laura Mulvey, "Afterthoughts on 'Visual Pleasure and Narrative Cinema' Inspired by King Vidor's *Duet in the Sun*," in *Visual and Other Pleasures*, p. 37.

65. Robert L. Doerschuk, "Tori Amos: Dancing with the Vampire & the Nightingale," *Keyboard* (November 1994), p. 36.

66. My thanks to Melissa West for allowing me to share her insight.

67. Page's "delicacy" is inscribed in that part of his early biography as a musician that deals with the glandular fever he contracted while out on the road with a band. He claims that his inability physically to cope with the rigors of touring at this time drove him to quit for a while, first enrolling in art school and then becoming a session player instead. See Ritchie Yorke, *Led Zeppelin: The Definitive Biography*, revised edition (Novato, CA: Underwood-Miller, 1993), p. 25; also Davis, *Hammer of the Gods*, p. 13.

68. Chris Welch, "Zeppelin over America," *Melody Maker* (June 25, 1977), p. 30.

69. Butler, *Gender Trouble*, p. 123.

70. Wise, "Sexing Elvis," p. 395.

71. Ibid.

72. It would seem to be fairly commonplace for rock fans, both male and female, to create a sense of familiarity with their heroes by referring to them as "the boys." My die-hard Led Zeppelin fan friends refer to them this way regularly; it is common on the "For Badgeholders Only" Internet discussion list, and I have also noticed how regularly it occurs on the U2 Internet discussion list, "Wire," as well.

73. The song is the first cut on the album *Led Zeppelin II* (Atlantic, October 1969).

74. For a detailed musical analysis of what Zeppelin's version borrows from Waters see Dave Headlam, "Does the Song Remain the Same? Questions of Authorship and Identification in the Music of Led Zeppelin," in *Concert Music, Rock and Jazz Since 1945: Essays and Analytical Studies*, ed. Elizabeth West Marvin and

Richard Hermann (Rochester: University of Rochester Press, 1996), pp. 313–363. Muddy Waters's version of the song can be found on *Muddy Waters: His Best, 1956 to 1964* (Chess Records/MCA CHSD 9380, 1997).

75. Charles Shaar Murray, *Crosstown Traffic: Jimi Hendrix and Post-War Pop* (London: Faber and Faber,1989), p. 60.

76. Shepherd, "Music and Male Hegemony," p. 170.

77. Walser, *Running with the Devil*, p. 42, emphasis mine.

78. Mark Johnson, *The Body in the Mind: The Bodily Basis of Meaning, Imagination, and Reason* (Chicago: University of Chicago Press, 1987), as cited in Robert Walser, "The Body in the Music: Epistemology and Musical Semiotics," *College Music Symposium* 31 (1991), p. 120.

79. Johnson, *The Body in the Mind*, p. 88.

80. Simon Frith, *Performing Rites: On the Value of Popular Music* (Cambridge, MA: Harvard University Press, 1996), p. 195.

81. A recent posting on "Wire," points to a similar phenomenon with other bands. A male fan wrote: "At the San Antonio concert [lead singer] Bono jumped into the crowd, well he was really leaning over the rail, but I caught him. I've held Bono. The man actually sweat on me. It was the most sexually arousing experience of my life, and I'm heterosexual. Go figure. Rock-n-Roll. Stop the traffic."

82. Shepherd, "Music and Male Hegemony," p. 169.

83. Ibid., p. 168.

84. Ibid., p. 170.

85. Ibid., p. 168.

86. Ibid., p. 170.

87. Ibid., p. 171.

88. See Tricia Rose, *Black Noise: Rap Music and Black Culture in Contemporary America* (Hanover, NH: Wesleyan University Press, 1994), pp. 66-67. Rose is actually quoting Christopher Small on this issue.

89. Backward echo is a production technique invented by Page. As he explains it, it involves "reversing the tape, recording the echo and then putting [the tape] round the right way again, so that [when it is played] the echo would precede the signal" ("Led Zeppelin Profiled," *Led Zeppelin: Remasters*, interview disk (Atlantic 82371-2, October 1990).

90. Waksman, "Every Inch of My Love," p. 14.

91. Bootlegs are not a very reliable source for this information, since they may not replicate an entire show; still one can glance through the set lists of the shows that Luis Rey lists in his book *Led Zeppelin Live: An Illustrated Exploration of the Underground Tapes*, updated edition (Owen Sound, Ontario: Hot Wax Press, 1993) or Robert Godwin's *The Illustrated Collector's Guide to Led Zeppelin* (Burlington, Ontario: CG, 1997) and see that in most cases after its release the song appears at the end or near the end of the show. The song ends the band's concert film *The Song Remains the Same*; this is also a good performance in which to see Page using the theremin and the song opened up for a blues medley, both of which I discuss later.

92. For example, Robert Walser notes that at the end of an Iron Maiden concert he attended soothing ("mindless," he called it) music was played over the public-address system as people exited, which was "intended to disperse the energy of the concert" (*Running with the Devil*, p. 56).

93. Rey notes this in particular for the August 21, 1970, show in Tulsa, Oklahoma (*Led Zeppelin Live*, p. 67).

94. Murray, *Crosstown Traffic*, pp. 6–7.

95. Wise, "Sexing Elvis," p. 397.

96. Ibid., p. 198.

97. James Clifford and George E. Marcus, eds., *Writing Culture: The Poetics and Politics of Ethnography* (Berkeley: University of California Press, 1986), p. 17.

Bibliography

Adorno, Theodore. "On Popular Music," in Frith and Goodwin, *On Record*, pp. 301–314.

Attali, Jacques. *Noise: The Political Economy of Music*. Minneapolis: University of Minnesota Press, 1985.

Bakhtin, M. M. *The Dialogic Imagination*, ed. Michael Holquist, trans. Caryl Emerson and Michael Holquist. Austin: University of Texas Press, 1981.

Bakhtin, Mikhail. *Rabelais and His World*, trans. Helene Iswolsky. Bloomington: Indiana University Press, 1984.

Barba, Eugenio. *The Paper Canoe: A Guide to Theatre Anthropology*, trans. Richard Fowler. New York: Routledge, 1995.

Barthes, Roland. "The Grain of the Voice," in *Image, Music, Text*, trans. Stephen Heath. New York: Fontana Collins, 1977, pp. 179–189.

Bell, Catherine. *Ritual: Perspectives and Dimensions*. New York: Oxford University Press, 1997.

Bellman, Jonathan, ed. *The Exotic in Western Music*. Boston: Northeastern University Press, 1998.

Birdwhistell, Ray L. *Kinesics and Context: Essays on Body Motion Communication*. Philadelphia: University of Pennsylvania Press, 1970.

Blacking, John. *How Musical Is Man?* London: Faber and Faber, 1976.

Blacking, John, ed. *The Anthropology of the Body*. London: Academic Press, 1977.

Bourdieu, Pierre. *The Field of Cultural Production*, ed. Randal Johnson. New York: Columbia University Press, 1993.

Brackett, David. *Interpreting Popular Music*. Cambridge: Cambridge University Press, 1995.

Burroughs, W. "Rock Magic: Jimmy Page, Led Zeppelin and a Search for the Elusive Stairway to Heaven," *Crawdaddy* 49 (June 1975), pp. 34–40. Reprinted in *Guitar World: Special Jimmy Page Issue* (July 1986), pp. 38–46.

Butler, Judith. *Gender Trouble: Feminism and the Subversion of Identity*. London: Routledge, 1990.

Carlsson, Jon, "Warming Up in Denmark: Duck-Walks and Lasers," *Melody Maker* (August 4, 1979), 27–29.

Cavanagh, David. "The Rovers Return," *Q Magazine* (August 1995), pp. 82–91.

Cavicchi, Daniel. *Tramps Like Us: Music and Meaning Among Springsteen Fans*. New York: Oxford University Press, 1998.

Chambers, Iain. *Urban Rhythms: Pop Music and Pop Culture*. Basingstoke, Hampshire: Macmillan, 1985.

Clifford, James, and George E. Marcus, eds. *Writing Culture: The Poetics and Politics of Ethnography*. Berkeley: University of California Press, 1986.

Cole, Richard, with Richard Trubo. *Stairway to Heaven: Led Zeppelin Uncensored*. New York: Harper Collins, 1992.

Coleman, Ray. "Zeppelin over America," *Melody Maker* (June 25, 1977), pp. 29–36.

"Concert Reviews: Woody Herman Orchestra, Led Zeppelin, Delaney and Bonnie (Filmore East, N.Y.)," *Variety* (June 4, 1969), p. 57.

"Concert Reviews," *Variety* (August 1, 1973), p. 271.

"Concert Reviews," *Variety* (August 22, 1979), p. 54.

Considine, J. D. Interview with Page, Plant, and Jones, *Rolling Stone* (September 20, 1990), pp. 56–60.

Considine, J. D. "Robert Plant: Life in a Lighter Zeppelin," *Musician* (December 1983), pp. 45–50.

Cross, Charles R., and Erik Flannigan, eds. *Led Zeppelin: Heaven and Hell*. New York: Harmony Books, 1991.

Crowe, C. "The Durable Led Zeppelin: A Conversation with Jimmy Page and Robert Plant," *Rolling Stone* (March 13, 1975), pp. 32–37.

Davis, Stephen. *Hammer of the Gods: The Led Zeppelin Saga*. New York: Ballantine, 1985.

Davis, Stephen. Review of *Presence*, *Rolling Stone* (May 20, 1976), p. 64.

DeRogatis, Jim. *Kaleidoscope Eyes: Psychedelic Rock from the '60s to the '90s*. Secaucus, NJ: Carol, 1996.

DiPerna, Alan. "Steady Rolling Man" (interview with John Paul Jones), *Guitar World: Special Led Zeppelin Issue* (January 1991), pp. 32–39.

Doerschuk, Robert L. "Tori Amos: Dancing with the Vampire & the Nightingale," *Keyboard* (November 1994), pp. 34–39.

Douglas, Mary. *Purity and Danger: An Analysis of the Concepts of Pollution and Taboo*. London: Routledge, 1966, 1993.

Dundes, Alan, ed. *Sacred Narrative: Readings in the Theory of Myth*. Berkeley: University of California Press, 1984.

Dunn, Jancee. "Rock and Roll: Getting the Led Out," *Rolling Stone* (December 1, 1994), pp. 29–31.

Ehrenreich, Barbara, Elizabeth Hess, and Gloria Jacobs. *Re-making Love: The Feminization of Sex*. New York: Anchor/Doubleday, 1986.

"Electric Magic" Web site: www.led-zeppelin.com.

Farrell, Gerry. *Indian Music and the West*. Oxford: Oxford Clarendon Press, 1997.

Fast, Susan. "Days of Future Passed: Rock, Pop and the Yearning for the Middle Ages," in *Mittelalter-Sehnsucht? Texte des interdisziplinären Symposions zur musikalischen Mittelalterrezeption an der Universität Heidelberg, April 1998*, ed.

Annette Kreutziger-Herr and Dorothea Redepenning. Kiel: Wissenschaftsverlag Vauk, 2000, pp. 35–56.

Fletcher, Gordon. "Today's 'Safe' Led Zeppelin, sans Blues: A Limp Blimp" (review of *Houses of the Holy*), *Rolling Stone* (June 7, 1973), p. 54.

Fricke, David. "Robert Plant" (the *Rolling Stone* interview), *Rolling Stone* (March 24, 1988), pp. 56–64, 170–171.

Frith, Simon. "Afterthoughts," in Frith and Goodwin, *On Record*, pp. 419–424 (originally published in *New Statesman*, August 23, 1985).

Frith, Simon. *Performing Rites: On the Value of Popular Music*. Cambridge, MA: Harvard University Press, 1996.

Frith, Simon. *Sound Effects: Youth, Leisure, and the Politics of Rock 'n' Roll*. New York: Pantheon, 1981.

Frith, Simon, and Andrew Goodwin, eds. *On Record: Rock, Pop, and the Written Word*. New York: Routledge, 1990.

Frith, Simon, and Angela McRobbie. "Rock and Sexuality," in Frith and Goodwin, *On Record*, pp. 371–389.

Gamman, Lorraine, and Margaret Marshment, eds. *The Female Gaze: Women as Viewers of Popular Culture*. London: Women's Press, 1988.

Gett, Steve. "Led Zeppelin über Alles," *Melody Maker* (July 12, 1980), p. 48.

Godwin, Robert. *The Illustrated Collector's Guide to Led Zeppelin*, compact disc edition. Burlington, Ontario: CG, 1995.

Godwin, Robert. *Led Zeppelin: The Press Reports*. Burlington, Ontario: CG, 1997.

Gracyk, Theodore. *Rhythm and Noise*. Durham: Duke University Press, 1996.

Green, Paul. "Led Zep: No. 1 Album but Delays Touring," *Billboard* (September 15, 1979), p. 30.

Guitar World: Special Jimmy Page Issue (July 1986).

Guitar World: Special Led Zeppelin Issue (January 1991).

Hamm, Charles. "Graceland Revisited," in *Putting Popular Music In Its Place*. Cambridge: Cambridge University Press, 1995.

Hatch, David, and Stephen Millward. *From Blues to Rock: An Analytical History of Pop Music*. Manchester: Manchester University Press, 1987.

Hayward, Philip. "Danger! Retro-Affectivity! The Cultural Career of the Theremin," *Convergence: The Journal of Research into New Media Technologies* 3/4 (Winter 1997), pp. 28–53.

Headlam, Dave. "Does the Song Remain the Same? Questions of Authorship and Identification in the Music of Led Zeppelin," in *Concert Music, Rock and Jazz Since 1945: Essays and Analytical Studies*, ed. Elizabeth West Marvin and Richard Hermann. Rochester: University of Rochester Press, 1996, pp . 313–363.

Hisama, Ellie M. "Post-colonialism on the Make: The Music of John Mellencamp, David Bowie and John Zorn," *Popular Music* 12/2 (1993), pp. 91–104.

Janson, H. W. *History of Art: A Survey of the Major Visual Arts from the Dawn of History to the Present Day*, 2d edition. Englewood Cliffs, NJ: Prentice-Hall, 1977.

Johnson, Mark. *The Body in the Mind: The Bodily Basis of Meaning, Imagination, and Reason*. Chicago: University of Chicago Press, 1987.

Kaye, Lenny. Review of the fourth album, *Rolling Stone* (December 23, 1971), pp. 62–63.

Keil, Charles, and Steven Feld. *Music Grooves*. Chicago: University of Chicago Press, 1994.

Kershaw, Baz. *The Radical in Performance: Between Brecht and Baudrillard.* New York: Routledge, 1999.

Kramer, Lawrence. *Music as Cultural Practice, 1880–1900.* Berkeley: University of California Press, 1990.

Le Guin, Elizabeth. "Cello and Bow Thinking: Boccherini's Cello Sonata in E♭ Major, 'Fuori Catalogo,' *Echo: A Music-Centered Journal* 1/1 (Fall 1999). Online at Http://www.humnet.ucla.edu/echo/Volume1-Issue1/leguin/leguin-article.html.

"Led Zeppelin," in *Encyclopaedia of Pop, Rock and Soul*, revised edition, ed. Irwin Stambler. New York: St. Martin's Press, 1989, pp. 394–395.

"Led Zeppelin," in *The Oxford Companion to Popular Music*, ed. Peter Gammond. New York: Oxford University Press, 1991, p. 335.

"Led Zeppelin," in *The Penguin Encyclopaedia of Popular Music*, ed. Donald Clarke. London: Viking, 1989, pp. 690–691.

Led Zeppelin. Scores to accompany boxed set recordings. 2 vols. London: Warner Chappell Music, 1990.

Leppert, Richard. "Desiring Difference: Virtuosic Display and Audience Subjectivity." Paper read at the 1997 meeting of the North American Society for the Study of Romanticism, held at McMaster University, published as "Cultural Contradiction, Idolatry, and the Piano Virtuoso: Franz Liszt," in *Piano Roles*, ed. James Parakilas. New Haven: Yale University Press, 1999, pp. 252–281.

Leppert, Richard. *The Sight of Sound: Music, Representation and the History of the Body.* Berkeley: University of California Press, 1993.

Lévi-Strauss, Claude. *The Raw and the Cooked*, trans. John and Doreen Weightman. New York: Harper and Row, 1969.

Lewis, Dave. *Led Zeppelin: A Celebration.* London: Omnibus Press, 1991.

Lidov, David. "Mind and Body in Music," *Semiotica* 66 (1987), pp. 69–97.

Lipsitz, George. *Dangerous Crossroads: Popular Music, Postmodernism and the Poetics of Place.* London: Verso, 1994.

Locke, Ralph P. "Constructing the Oriental 'Other': Saint-Saëns's Samson et Dalila," *Cambridge Opera Journal* 3/3 (1991), pp. 261–302.

Loder, Kurt. "Led Zep Goes Out with Class" (review of *Coda*), *Rolling Stone* (January 20, 1983), pp. 47–48.

Macan, Edward. *Rocking the Classics: English Progressive Rock and the Counterculture.* New York: Oxford University Press, 1997.

McClary, Susan. *Conventional Wisdom: The Content of Musical Form.* Berkeley: University of California Press, 2000.

McClary, Susan. *Feminine Endings: Music, Gender and Sexuality.* Minneapolis: University of Minnesota Press, 1991.

McClary, Susan, and Robert Walser. "Start Making Sense! Musicology Wrestles with Rock," in Frith and Goodwin, *On Record*, pp. 277–292.

McClary, Susan, and Robert Walser. "Theorizing the Body in African-American Music," *Black Music Research Journal* 14/1 (Spring 1994), pp. 75–84.

McLuhan, Marshall. *Understanding Media.* New York: McGraw-Hill, 1964.

McNeil, David. *Hand and Mind: What Gestures Reveal About Thought.* Chicago: University of Chicago Press, 1992.

Meintjes, Louise. "Paul Simon's *Graceland,* South Africa, and the Mediation of Musical Meaning," *Ethonomusicology* (Winter 1990), pp. 37–73.

Mendelsohn, John. Review of *Led Zeppelin, Rolling Stone* (March 15, 1969), p. 28.

Mendelsohn, J. Review of *Led Zeppelin II*, *Rolling Stone* (December 13, 1969), p. 48.

Merleau-Ponty, Maurice. "The Body as Expression and Speech," chapter 4 of *The Phenomenology of Perception*, reprinted in *The Essential Writings of Merleau-Ponty*, ed. Alden L. Fisher. New York: Harcourt, Brace and World, 1969, pp. 185–213.

Michaelsen, Scott, ed. *Portable Darkness: An Aleister Crowley Reader*. New York: Harmony Books, 1989.

Middleton, Richard. *Studying Popular Music*. Buckingham, UK: Open University Press, 1990.

Miller, Jim. "Anglo-Graffiti: Hardest-Core Rock" (review of *Physical Graffiti*), *Rolling Stone* (March 3, 1975), pp. 48, 51.

Miller, Jim. "Led Zeppelin," in *The Rolling Stone Illustrated History of Rock and Roll*, revised and updated edition (New York: Random House, 1992), pp. 455–458.

Moore, Alan F. *Rock: The Primary Text*. Milton Keynes, UK: Open University Press, 1993.

Mori, Masaki. *Epic Grandeur: Toward a Comparative Poetics of the Epic*. New York: State University of New York Press, 1997.

Mulvey, Laura. "Visual Pleasure and Narrative Cinema," in *Visual and Other Pleasures*. Bloomington: Indiana University Press, 1989, pp. 27–77.

Mulvey, Laura, "Afterthoughts on 'Visual Pleasure and Narrative Cinema' Inspired by King Vidor's *Duel in the Sun*," in *Visual and Other Pleasures*. Bloomington: Indiana University Press, 1989, pp. 79–107.

Murray, Charles Shaar. *Crosstown Traffic: Jimi Hendrix and Post-War Pop*. London: Faber and Faber, 1989.

Negus, Keith. *Popular Music in Theory: An Introduction*. Hanover, NH: Wesleyan University Press, 1996.

Nehring, Neil. *Popular Music, Gender, and Postmodernism: Anger Is Energy*. London: Sage, 1997.

Palmer, Robert. "Led Zeppelin: The Music," in *Led Zeppelin*, vol. 2. London: Warner Chappell Music, 1991.

Petracca, Mark J. "Ramble On" (interview with Robert Plant), *Creem* 2/9 (1993), pp. 37–41.

Probyn, Elspeth. *Sexing the Self: Gendered Positions in Cultural Studies*. New York: Routledge, 1993.

Propp, Vladimir. *Morphology of a Folk Tale*, trans. Laurence Scott. Austin: University of Texas Press, 1968, 1988.

Resnicoff, Matt. "In Through the Out Door: Jimmy Page Goes Back to Led Zeppelin," *Musician* (November 1990), pp. 48–64.

Review of *Led Zeppelin III*, *Rolling Stone* (November 26, 1970), p. 34.

Rey, Luis. *Led Zeppelin Live: An Illustrated Exploration of the Underground Tapes*, updated edition. Owen Sound, Ontario: Hot Wax Press, 1993.

Reynolds, Simon, and Joy Press. *The Sex Revolts: Gender, Rebellion and Rock 'n' Roll*. Cambridge, MA: Harvard University Press, 1995.

Ricoeur, Paul. *The Symbolism of Evil*, trans. Emerson Buchanan. New York: Harper and Row, 1967.

Rosand, Ellen. "The Descending Tetrachord: An Emblem of Lament," *Musical Quarterly* 65/3 (1979), pp. 346–359.

Rose, Tricia. *Black Noise: Rap Music and Black Culture in Contemporary America.* Hanover, NH: Wesleyan University Press, 1994.

Rosen, Stephen. "Jimmy Page," *Guitar Player* (July 1977), pp. 32–58.

Rosenberg, Neil V., ed. *Transforming Tradition: Folk Music Revivals Revisited.* Urbana: University of Illinois Press, 1993.

Rouget, Gilbert. *Music and Trance: A Theory of the Relations Between Music and Possession,* trans. Brunhilde Biebuyck. Chicago: University of Chicago Press, 1985.

Said, Edward W. *Orientalism.* London: Routledge, 1979.

Savage, Jon. "The Enemy Within: Sex, Rock and Identity,"in *Facing the Music: A Pantheon Guide to Popular Culture,* ed Simon Frith. New York: Pantheon, 1988, pp. 131–172.

Schwarz, David. *Listening Subjects: Music, Psychoanalysis, Culture.* Durham: Duke University Press, 1997.

Shepherd, John. *Music as Social Text.* Cambridge: Polity Press, 1991.

Shepherd, John, and Peter Wicke. *Music and Cultural Theory.* Cambridge: Polity Press, 1997.

Shindler, Merril. "The Wrong Goodbye: Zeppelin Leaves America," *Rolling Stone* (September 8, 1977), pp.14–15.

Shuker, Roy. *Key Concepts in Popular Music.* London: Routledge, 1998

Stallybrass, Peter, and Allon White. *The Politics and Poetics of Transgression.* Ithaca, NY: Cornell University Press, 1986.

Tarasti, Eero. *Myth and Music: A Semiotic Approach to the Aesthetics of Myth in Music, Especially That of Wagner, Sibelius and Stravinsky.* The Hague: Mouton, 1979.

Taylor, Jennifer, and Dave Laing. "Disco-Pleasure-Discourse," *Screen Education* 31 (1979), pp. 43–48.

Taylor, Timothy D. *Global Pop: World Music, World Markets.* New York: Routledge, 1997.

Théberge, Paul. *Any Sound You Can Imagine: Making Music Consuming Technology.* Hanover, NH: Wesleyan University Press, 1997.

Touma, Habib Hassan. *The Music of the Arabs,* trans. Laurie Schwartz. Portland, OR: Amadeus, 1996.

Treitler, Leo. "Gender and Other Dualities of Music History," in *Musicology and Difference: Gender and Sexuality in Music Scholarship,* ed. Ruth A. Solie. Berkeley: University of California Press, 1994, pp. 23–45.

Turner, Victor. *From Ritual to Theatre: The Human Seriousness of Play.* New York: Performing Arts Journal Publications, 1982.

Vermorel, Fred and Judy, excerpt from *Starlust: The Secret Fantasies of Fans* (London: W. H. Allen, 1985) in Frith and Goodwin, *On Record*; pp. 481–490.

Waksman, Steve. "Every Inch of My Love: Led Zeppelin and the Problem of Cock Rock," *Journal of Popular Music Studies* 8 (1996), pp. 5–25.

Waksman, Steve. "Kick Out the Jams: The MC5 and the Politics of Noise," in *Mapping the Beat: Popular Music and Contemporary Theory,* ed. Thomas Swiss, John Sloop, and Andrew Herman. Oxford: Blackwell, 1998, pp. 47–75.

Walser, Robert. "The Body in the Music: Epistemology and Musical Semiotics," *College Music Symposium* 31 (1991), pp. 117–126.

Walser, Robert. *Running with The Devil: Power, Gender and Madness in Heavy Metal Music.* Hanover, NH: Wesleyan University Press, 1993.

Walser, Robert. Review of *The Sex Revolts: Gender, Rebellion and Rock 'n' Roll*, *Music Library Association Notes* 53/3 (March 1977), pp. 776–778.

Ward, Ed, Geoffrey Stokes, and Ken Tucker. *Rock of Ages: The Rolling Stone History of Rock and Roll*. New York: Rolling Stone Press/Summit, 1986.

Weinstein, Deena. *Heavy Metal: A Cultural Sociology*. New York: Lexington, 1991.

Welch, C. "Jimmy Page: Paganini of the Seventies," *Melody Maker* (February 14, 21, 28, 1970), pp. 17–18; 12; 10.

Welch, Chris. "Led Zeppelin at Carnegie Hall," *Melody Maker* (October 25, 1969), p. 20.

Welch, Chris. "Zeppelin over America," *Melody Maker* (June 25, 1977), p. 30.

Welch, Chris. "The Zeppelin Remains," *Melody Maker* (November 5, 1977), pp. 8–9.

Whiteley, Sheila. *The Space Between the Notes: Rock and the Counterculture*. New York: Routledge, 1992.

Whiteley, Sheila, ed. *Sexing the Groove: Popular Music and Gender*. London: Routledge, 1997.

Wicke, Peter. *Rock Music: Culture, Aesthetics, and Sociology*. Cambridge: Cambridge University Press, 1990.

Williams, Christopher. *The Song Remains the Same*. Unpublished Ph.D. dissertation, Department of Sociology, New York University, 1995. UMI microfilm 9609252.

Willis, Paul E. *Profane Culture*. London: Routledge, 1978.

Wise, Sue. "Sexing Elvis," in Frith and Goodwin, *On Record*; pp. 390–398.

Wong, Deborah. Review of Robert Walser, *Running with the Devil: Power, Gender and Madness in Heavy Metal Music* (Hanover, NH: Wesleyan University Press, 1993), *Journal of the American Musicological Society* 51/1 (Spring 1998), pp. 148–157.

Wood, Simon. "Are They Going to Turn That Down? Led Zeppelin, *Rolling Stone*, and the Thoughts of Marshall McLuhan." Unpublished paper, 1997.

Yorke, Ritchie. *Led Zeppelin: The Definitive Biography*, revised edition. Novato, CA: Underwood-Miller, 1993.

Young, Charles M. "'I'm Not Such an Old Hippie': Robert Plant Stops Being Polite," *Musician* 140 (June 1990), pp. 45–51.

Young, Charles M. "Jimmy Page's True Will," *Musician* 117 (July 1988), pp. 74–80.

Young, Charles M. "Sad Zep" (review of *In Through the Out Door*), *Rolling Stone* (October 18, 1979), pp. 72, 79.

Young, Charles M. "Zeppelin to Zen: Robert Plant Digs Through His Past to Uncover His Future," *Musician* (March 1988), pp. 76–82.

Discography/Videography

Led Zeppelin (Atlantic, UK: 588 171, March 1969; US: SD 8216, January 1969)

Led Zeppelin II (Atlantic, UK: 588 198, US: SD 8236, October 1969)

Led Zeppelin III (Atlantic, UK: 2401 002, US: SD 7201, October 1970)

Untitled (known as *Zoso*, Four Symbols, or the fourth album) (Atlantic, UK: 2401 002, US: SD 7208, November 1971)

Houses of the Holy (Atlantic, UK: K50014, US SD 7255, March 1973)

Physical Graffiti (Swansong, UK: SSK89400, US SS2 200, February 1975)

Presence (Swansong, UK: SSK59402, US: SS8416, April 1976)

Soundtrack from the film *The Song Remains the Same* (Swansong, UK: SSK89402, US: SS2 201, October 1976)

In Through the Out Door (Swansong, UK: SSK59410, US: SS16002, August 1979)

Coda (Swansong, UK: A0051; US: 79 00511, November 1982)

The Song Remains the Same, footage shot 1973; released on film 1976 (Warner Home Video, 11389, 1984)

Supershow, footage shot March 25, 1969; premiered at the London Lyceum, November 1969 (Virgin Vision VVD 167, September 1986)

Led Zeppelin, four-CD boxed set (Atlantic 82144-2, October 1990)

Led Zeppelin: Remasters, with interview disk (Atlantic 82371-2, October 1990)

Led Zeppelin, Boxed Set 2 (Atlantic 82477-2, 1993)

Led Zeppelin: BBC Sessions (Atlantic 83061, 1997), includes recordings found on the bootlegs *Classics off the Air* (see "Bootleg Recordings")

Jimmy Page and Robert Plant, *No Quarter* (Atlantic, 82706, 1994)

Jimmy Page and Robert Plant, *Unledded* (Warner Home Video, 1994)

Puff Daddy featuring Jimmy Page, "Come with Me" performance on *Saturday Night Live*, May 9, 1998, *Soundtrack to the Motion Picture Godzilla* (Epic/Sony, 1998)

Anthologie de la musique arabe, Oum Kaltsoum (1931–1932), vol. 5 (Les Artistes Arabes Accocies, AAA 027; distributed by Club du disque Arabe, Paris, 1990)

Robert Plant, "Our Song/Laughing, Crying, Laughing" (CBS 202656, March 1967)

Robert Plant, "Long Time Coming/I've Got a Secret" (CBS 2858, September 1967)
Robert Plant, *Now and Zen* (Es Paranza/Atlantic 90863, 1988)
Robert Plant, *Manic Nirvana* (Es Paranza/Atlantic 91336, 1990)
Robert Plant, *Fate of Nations* (Es Paranza/Atlantic 92264, 1993)
The Yardbirds, "Happenings Ten Years Time Ago," available on Jeff Beck, *Beckology* (Epic/Legacy 48661, 1991)

Bootleg Recordings (For further information on these consult Robert Godwin, *The Illustrated Collector's Guide to Led Zeppelin*)

Aeolian Hall, London, April 26,1969
Brussels, June 20, 1980
Classics off the Air, vol. 1 (BBC live recording, 1969)
Classics off the Air, vol. 2 (BBC live recording, 1969 and 1971)
Dallas, August 31,1969
Dallas, March 4, 1975
Danish television special, March 19, 1969 (video)
Destroyer, Cleveland, April 27,1977
Earl's Court, London, May 24, 1975
Filmore West, San Francisco, January 9, 1969
Filmore West, San Francisco, January 10, 1969
Filmore West, San Francisco, April 27, 1969
Hiawatha Express (rehearsals and studio sessions from 1967, 1970, 1973, and 1974)
James Patrick Page: Session Man, vol. 1 (1963–1967), issued under license from Jimmy Page International Fan Club, 1990
Knebworth, August 11, 1979 (video)
Listen to This Eddie, Los Angeles Forum, June 21, 1977
Live on Blueberry Hill Part 1, Los Angeles, September 4, 1970
Live Yardbirds Featuring Jimmy Page (1967)
London, March 25, 1971
Moonlight, Frankfurt, June 30, 1980
Olympic Gold (studio outtakes from 1968–1969)
Osaka, Japan, September 29,1971 (Koseinenkin Kaika [Festival Hall])
Osaka, Japan, October 4,1972 (Koseinenkin Kaika [Festival Hall])
Songs from the Vaults (studio and live performances from 1969–1977)
"Stairway to Heaven," outtakes
Stockholm, March 14, 1969
Studio Daze (studio and live performances from 1970, 1972, and 1978)
Tampa, April 9, 1970
Third album rehearsals, et cetera.
Totally Tangible (studio outtakes, rehearsals for *Physical Graffiti*)
Winterland, San Francisco, April 26, 1969
Zeppelin Express, San Francisco, April 27, 1969

Index

9746876R0

Made in the USA
Lexington, KY
24 May 2011